Teaching on Days After

Teaching on Days After

Educating for Equity in the Wake of Injustice

Alyssa Hadley Dunn

TEACHERS COLLEGE PRESS

TEACHERS COLLEGE | COLUMBIA UNIVERSITY
NEW YORK AND LONDON

Published by Teachers College Press, ® 1234 Amsterdam Avenue, New York, NY 10027

Front cover art and design by Allyssa Harris.

Library of Congress Cataloging-in-Publication Data

Names: Dunn, Alyssa Hadley, author.
Title: Teaching on days after : educating for equity in the wake of injustice / Alyssa Hadley Dunn.
Description: New York, NY : Teachers College Press, [2022] | Includes bibliographical references and index. | Summary: "What should teachers do on the days after major events, tragedies, and traumas, especially when injustice is involved? This beautifully written book features teacher narratives and youth-authored student spotlights that reveal what classrooms do and can look like in the wake of these critical moments. Dunn incisively argues for the importance of equitable commitments, humanizing dialogue, sociopolitical awareness, and a rejection of so-called pedagogical neutrality across all grade levels and content areas. By highlighting the voices of teachers who are pushing beyond their concerns and fears about teaching for equity and justice, readers see how these educators address negative reactions from parents and administrators, welcome all student viewpoints, and negotiate their own feelings. These inspiring stories come from diverse areas such as urban New York, rural Georgia, and suburban Michigan, from both public and private schools, and from classrooms with both novice and veteran teachers. Teaching on Days After can be used to support current classroom teachers and to better structure teacher education to help preservice teachers think ahead to their future classrooms"— Provided by author.
Identifiers: LCCN 2021037067 (print) | LCCN 2021037068 (ebook) | ISBN 9780807766224 (hardcover) | ISBN 9780807766217 (paperback) | ISBN 9780807780664 (ebook)
Subjects: LCSH: Social justice and education—United States. | Educational equalization—United States. | Classroom environment—United States. | Teacher-student relationships—United States. | Culturally relevant pedagogy—United States.
Classification: LCC LC192.2 .D86 2022 (print) | LCC LC192.2 (ebook) | DDC 370.11/5—dc23/eng/20211006
LC record available at https://lccn.loc.gov/2021037067
LC ebook record available at https://lccn.loc.gov/2021037068

ISBN 978-0-8077-6621-7 (paper)
ISBN 978-0-8077-6622-4 (hardcover)
ISBN 978-0-8077-8066-4 (ebook)

Printed on acid-free paper
Manufactured in the United States of America

To Owen and Oliver,
for being the best part of all my days

Let's begin by saying that we are living through a very dangerous time. To any citizen of this country who figures himself as responsible and particularly those of you who deal with the minds and hearts of young people must be prepared to go for broke. Or to put it another way, you must understand that in the attempt to correct so many generations of bad faith and cruelty, when it is operating not only in the classroom but in society, you will meet the most fantastic, the most brutal, and the most determined resistance. There is no point in pretending that this won't happen.

—James Baldwin, "A Talk to Teachers," 1963

In order to do this work, you will need to visualize what you are fighting for. When it comes to the work of social justice, we often become so consumed by what we are fighting against that we hardly take the time to truly envision the kinds of schools, communities, and societies that we are fighting for.

—Jamila Lyiscott (2019, p. xiii)

Contents

Acknowledgments

The teachers whose stories are in this book gave so generously of their time and energy. This book is only possible because of their belief in the power of stories and their willingness to share them. Thank you to these wonderful educators for trusting me with their stories of vulnerability, pain, healing, commitment, and love.

The youth who wrote for the Student Spotlight sections in this book are talented, thoughtful, and just generally badass young people who inspire me. Thank you for sharing your powerful words in this book: Ava, Camille, Corabella, Deirdre, Marjorie, Marlena, Maya, Paige, Roxy, Sue, and Taliyah. To Terry Yuncker, whose story appears in Chapter 4, thank you for sharing Travis's memory with me and allowing me to share it with others.

I am honored to have a second book published with Teachers College Press and delighted that I could work with Brian Ellerbeck as editor again. I am also thankful for the support of the entire editorial staff throughout the publication process. Allyssa Harris designed this beautiful cover for the text. She took great care in representing the stories in visual form, and I am so impressed with her talent and vision!

Thank you to the graduate research assistants who cared about this project as if it were their own and who helped with interviews, transcription, literature reviews, and editing. I am so grateful for your thoughtful work: Effat Id-Deen, Amieris Lavender, Briana Markoff, Ashley Moore, Romina Peña-Pincheira, and Renée Wilmot. Thank you to undergraduate student and future teaching extraordinaire, Ellie Friedman, for compiling the list of social media resources.

This project was supported by two small seed grants from the College of Education at Michigan State University. I am truly lucky to work in a department and college of supportive colleagues and friends. This section would go on for pages if I were to name everyone who has encouraged me in this work. Thanks especially for the leadership and support of Ann Austin and Dorinda Carter Andrews. Among the incredible academic colleagues and friends are those who generously read this book proposal or versions of this work along the way: Alex Allweiss, Lucia Cárdenas-Curiel, Erica Dotson, Kara Kavanagh, Joanne Marciano, Lauren McKenzie, Vera Stenhouse, Laura Tortorelli, and Bethany Wilinksi. To Beth Sondel and

Hannah Carson Baggett, thank you for giving this project its grounding in our postelection studies. Your support at a time when it felt like things were falling apart is something I will never forget. To Erica Dotson, for all of the late-night talks, encouragement, and laughter-into-tears, merci mille fois.

I am also indebted to a special group of teachers in my personal life: the amazing educators at Spartan Child Development Center who cared for and taught my children while I was doing this research and writing this book. It is not lost on me that other people are teaching my children so that I can be a teacher educator and write about teaching. As a fellow educator, I am daily impressed by their creativity, patience, love, and dedication. As a mother, I am forever grateful for how these brilliant teachers see—really, truly see—my children for all that they are and all that they can be. I wish that all children had a chance to learn in such spaces of joy and wonder. Danielle, Katie, Brooke, Britanie, Khursheed, Kaitlin, Katie, Emily, Sue, Britney, Lea, Madison, and Jackie: Thank you for making my life as a working mom possible and for loving Owen and Oliver.

To my family, for their support and encouragement in my pursuit not just of this research but of this career that takes us far away from where they are, especially my parents, Helen Hadley and the late Dave Hadley. One of the last moments that my father and I shared before he died was sitting together in the living room in my childhood home, as I read him the introduction to my earlier book. I thought about that moment often as I was writing this book, and I desperately wish I could do the same now. That book was also written before I was a mother, hence why this one took a lot longer! In my own mother, I had a powerful example of what it meant to be a working mom. I am grateful every day for that example.

To my husband, John Dunn, who makes everything in life better and more filled with happiness and laughter. John is a gifted and caring professor, father, and partner. I know this book is better because of your tireless support, including reading through drafts at 1:00 in the morning. I truly could not have done it without you.

To my children, Owen and Oliver, for giving this book and this life more meaning than I could ever have imagined. Thank you for reminding me to slow down, wonder at the world, and notice all of its beauty. In the year of writing this book, when that world seemed to crumble around us, thank you for fingerpainting, stargazing, cookie-making, fort-building, blueberry-picking turned to apple-picking turned to pumpkin-picking, and snow-sledding turned to bike-riding turned to leaf-peeping turned to snow-sledding again. Thank you for loving each other fiercely and for sharing your love and magic with those around you.

CHAPTER 1

Introduction

We didn't know what 9/12 was going to be like, because we didn't understand 9/11 was 9/11 as it was happening. It was all so confusing, and I didn't
know what I was going to do the next day.

—Teacher participant reflecting on teaching in September 2001

It's weird to say, but they end up being the best teaching days of my career.
Because I am exactly where I need to be: in my classroom, with my kids. And
I think they are where they need to be, too: with each other.

—Teacher participant reflecting on teaching on days after mass shootings

On January 7, 2021, Kendra and Carrie's classes were still meeting virtually. It was the middle of the COVID-19 pandemic and shortly after the
end of winter break, and while some districts around the country had
returned to hybrid or in-person learning, theirs had not. That morning,
as they prepared to meet their students—seniors in IB History and IB
Literature at an urban public school in Atlanta—they were still comb-
ing through news articles and trying to figure out what to do. Headlines
ranged from "Trouble on Capitol Hill" (CNN.com, 2021) to "After Pro-
Trump mob storms Capitol, Congress confirms Biden's win" (*New York
Times*, 2021). Kendra, a Black woman, and Carrie, a white woman, were
veteran educators, each with more than 10 years of experience, so this
was not their first time teaching on the day after a major event. They had
already been discussing "power, language, discrimination, and justice"
in Kendra's literature class, and Carrie's history class had been focusing
on authoritarian states. They talked the night before about if they should
connect the events surrounding the attack on the U.S. Capitol with their
class themes and topics. (A longer description of the Capitol attack can be
found in Chapter 7.) "Throughout the day," Kendra recalled, "I thought
of poetry that would connect, [but] I felt it would have been forced. I
didn't want it to be school-y. I wanted it to be more real." Carrie agreed
and instead "suggested that this time we ask students what they would
want rather than try to pull together a 'lesson,' as well as create a space
for them to discuss and process."

As they planned, their district was also formulating "guidance," which didn't arrive as an email until after they had already taught:

> We would like to take a moment to acknowledge recent, disturbing events and support you as you continue to guide our students amidst challenging topics and real-time historical events. As history unfolds, our students will fervently be in search of answers. It is mandatory that we continue instruction based on a professional approach. Please remind your teachers to refrain from modeling and encouraging discussions involving personal opinions. While it is important to be respectful of one's opinion, should they occur, students must be promptly steered back to discussing the facts. We must continue to be models of effective and appropriate civic discourse. If you need more direction for speaking with your students, please use the following talking points to guide your conversation: How can we have civil conversations about topics when we don't agree? Protesting peacefully is every American's right, but the actions that took place yesterday were not peaceful and escalated beyond protesting to illegal activity. No matter what your political opinions are, we all have a right to feel heard and safe.

Later came the "guidance" from the state department of education that echoed the district's missives.

Although the school had shifted to an asynchronous format that week, Kendra and Carrie invited their combined classes to a synchronous virtual session. Just under half of the students attended. The guiding question was, "How should teachers respond during/the day after a major societal (political/tragic) event?" A robust discussion followed, and two students' comments stuck out because they directly contradicted the guidance from the district. First, one student challenged the myth of teachers being neutral: "Neutrality is an illusion and is intellectually dishonest." Another student did not like the idea of connecting to standards and forcing an academic lesson: "If you come in with it being so academically focused, it doesn't feel as genuine. It feels like learning versus understanding." For Kendra and Carrie, these comments meant "that this wasn't a time to learn more about the event or even events like it, and they needed to discuss, process, and participate in some way with others, especially in a virtual learning environment."

What Kendra and Carrie took away from the days after discussion on January 7 is just how little the district and state education officials know about what students want in these critical moments. "It's important for students to see that we have feelings and opinions and there's a level of passion and interest that is behind what we do in the classroom. I think that's part of our role. That's what we have to do as educators. We have to be intellectually honest in every way," Kendra remarked. Indeed, it's hard to read those guidelines and not immediately want to take a characteristic red pen to them, crossing out the suggestions that run counter to decades of research and teachers' experiences.

Carrie feels similarly about these directives. "I think instructions such as these are really anathema to what I am trying to accomplish in my classroom and what I think is the responsibility of school districts nationwide," she argued. "The idea of 'discussing facts versus opinions' is a pipe dream. How do we determine facts? How do I teach my students *Hard Question* facts versus opinions in history? I don't. We can agree on the dates of particular events. 'Columbus sailed the ocean blue in 1492,' but beyond that, historians branch in many directions. Why did he sail? What did he do when he arrived? What were the outcomes of his arrival? Were any of those beneficial? How do we judge? Who has written the history? Who's rewritten it? Who is reading it? Facts? Pft. No way. It's a messy, challenging process, and it's ridiculous at best and brutally harmful at worst to pretend we are opinion-less in our teaching of 'facts.'"

"This is not a curriculum. This is not something you can script," Kendra adds, as if talking to the administrators who dictate such things, especially in urban public schools and especially on days after when there is heightened awareness and attention to supposedly controversial issues. "Let us do what we are trained and knowledgeable to do. Don't worry that we're trying to steer kids in a certain direction. Don't mess it up and make [us do a] worksheet. We make magic happen every day with little," including on days after.

It's clear why Kendra and Carrie are award-winning educators. They exemplify the spirit of teaching for equity and justice, and they engage in critical discussions with and for students, even and especially in moments when it feels like they are "teaching when the world is on fire" (Delpit, 2018). In what they do and who they are, Kendra and Carrie demonstrate what teaching on days after is all about.

Perhaps Kendra and Carrie's story sounds familiar. Teachers know what it is like to "bring work home." To grade late into the evening, to think about students during dinner and while trying to fall asleep. To get back up out of bed to plan or replan a lesson, to write an email, to check on something for tomorrow. The most important of these nights is when the replanning and the late checks are because *something* has happened. You might hear about it on the radio on the drive home, see it on the news, read about it on social media. You might get calls or text messages from family or colleagues. Whatever this *something* is, you know that you need to address it tomorrow. But how? When? There are so many other things that need to be covered, and you are already behind. You look at the stack of papers to be graded and they are already towering on the verge of tipping over. You have progress reports to fill out, parent–teacher conferences to schedule. There is *no* time, it seems. There is *never* time, it seems. And yet, you know it's time to make time.

So, you get out of bed, exhausted. You go back to your laptop and you open up a news site, and you start reading. You take notes; you try to digest the information, even as it's not clear if the information you're reading is complete or even if it's accurate. You learn all you can learn in the few hours before you sleep or in the few hours before children arrive in your classroom and ask, Did you hear? Can we talk about it? What do we do?

DAYS AFTER THAT I REMEMBER, AS STUDENT AND TEACHER

2001

"Beauty is truth, truth beauty,—that is all Ye know on earth, and all ye need to know."

—John Keats

It is the second week of my first year of college. Everything is new. I don't even know my way around campus yet. But I do know how to get to my poetry class, even though I don't like going. I am the only freshman amid older students, and the way the professor speaks is at once beautiful and brilliant and entirely confusing. I do not understand the theories she talks about, the words she uses, or the things she wants us to do. That day, we were to have read John Keats's "Ode on a Grecian Urn." I remember this because the following week, I was supposed to make a class presentation about it and the various poetic elements and allusions in it. I've read it over and over, and I don't understand it well. So that morning, I go in, thinking that I am prepared for "the worst."

But I am not. Because the worst is yet to happen. Because when I get there, there are other students already there and they are saying something about planes, airplanes from Logan Airport, in Boston, where we are. I don't know anyone well yet, and I don't ask questions. Then the professor comes in. It is just before our class is to begin at 9:30. She is flustered and flushed and rushing. "We're not going to have class today," she tells us, "Go back to your dorms. I'm not sure what they're going to have us do." I am so confused. Others are, too. And this is when those who saw the news before they came in speak. They talk about the World Trade Center and a big fire. This is before anyone knew the severity of what had just happened, before anyone was using the word "attack."

So we pack up our bags and leave. "We'll talk about Keats next time," the professor says. I walk to one of the student centers on campus, and it is hard to get through the doors. There are large TVs mounted high up on the walls in the lobby, and there are hundreds of people standing there, staring up at them, blocking the entrances and walkways. No one is moving. My professor comes in another door. She stands and stares, too. This is how we all are—standing, staring—when the first tower falls.

There is a vigil that night, because it is a Catholic college. I hand out candles because I am in a freshmen mentorship program for the student government. I stand with my roommate and the other girls from our hall. Even though many would later become my best friends, we barely know each other at this point.

Two days later, I go back to my poetry class. I had prepared my presentation because I didn't know if we were going to push back the discussion or change the syllabus. My professor comes over to me when she gets to class. "Are you ready to give your presentation today?" "Yes," I say hesitantly. I do not know if this is the right answer, or if there even is a right answer. "Good," she says, "Let's do that." She does not seem to know the right answer either.

And this is the first time I think about what it means to be a teacher on days after.

2007

It is the day after a shooting on the campus of Virginia Tech, and I am teaching an undergraduate class on diversity in education at Emory University. It is almost the end of the semester. I have to see them before I can get any guidance from my department about what to do. There has been no university statement yet. I am a doctoral student, and this is the first undergraduate course I'm teaching. I'm supposed to be a "professor"; I'm supposed to know how to do this. I'm the "adult" in the room. School shootings, at this point, are nothing new, but on a university campus—that is a rarity. And we are on a college campus this morning. It feels very close.

I arrive 15 minutes early for class, and they are already there. All of them. This is . . . rare. And they are in a circle, the desks pushed closely together. This is not so rare, because this is how we always sit. But what is different this time is that I didn't have to tell them to put their desks that way. For the past 12 weeks, every time I asked them to put their desks in a circle for our discussion, it was almost as if I was saying it for the first time. But today they are all there, and they are in a circle. And then they are looking at me, and it is silent and at least four are crying. And then someone says, so quietly that I almost don't hear him, "Are we going to talk about it?"

Yes.

2007

It is the first time I am being observed as a new English teacher. The evaluator is an assistant principal, and he has a checklist on a clipboard and a walkie talkie on his belt. He walks in and stands at the back of the classroom. There is an extra desk for him there (only possible because multiple students are absent today—usually there are not enough desks for all the students if everyone is present)—but it seems he wants to stand instead. He is leaning up against a bulletin board that my students—juniors in a high school English class—have decorated with "issues we care about." It is early in the school year, about 2 months in, so there is still some open space on the bulletin board. He looks at it and writes something on the checklist. I also see him looking at the board at the front of the room, checking to make sure the state standard is written there, in the appropriate place. He is white, and I am white. All but two of my students are people of color.

Today's lesson is on persuasive writing techniques. The students have to prepare for a graduation test where they write a persuasive essay to a prompt that is, undoubtedly, narrowly or not at all related to issues they care about. Today's lesson happens to be on the Jena 6, a group of Black youth in Jena, Louisiana, who were arrested and charged with the beating of a white student. Yesterday, there had been massive protests about the trial, tens of thousands in Louisiana and around the country, arguing that the charges were racially motivated.

Of course, he would pick today to come in. I am nervous about what he will think. This is not in the textbook and it's not part of the curriculum. I also don't know my students very well yet, and this is the first time we are tackling something so explicitly about racial justice.

Most of the students know what has happened in Jena, as we've been talking about the case. Indeed, it is listed on the bulletin board as one of their issues they care about. Today, after we review what happened with the protests, they are eager to develop arguments that they'd make to get the charges dropped, anticipating what the counterarguments might be and how to argue against those, as well. Eventually, they will turn their thoughts into an essay, but today, they are brainstorming and gathering resources from those I have printed out and put into stations around the room.

When they circulate through the stations, he doesn't move from the back of the room. "Feel free to move around if you want," I say to him as I walk past him on the way from one group to another. This is the kindest way I can think of to wonder aloud why on earth he is not moving. "That's okay," he replies, "I don't know anything about what's happening there." "They can teach you!" I say, likely too eagerly because he doesn't reply, just gives me a "look." He stays standing at the back for 40 minutes and then leaves in the middle of the lesson. My students sigh, take a deep breath when he leaves. I do, too, for different reasons. "I felt like he was watching me the whole time," someone says, and another replies, "That's 'cause he was. You think he was here to watch the teacher or watch us?"

I get a copy of my evaluation a month later. It is the checklist, with most of the things checked off except for "follows benchmark guidelines," which of course I did not because the benchmark guidelines had me teaching something entirely unrelated to the Jena 6 that week. There is one comment on the bottom: "It is very loud, but students seem interested. Does not align with district pacing guidelines." We never have a meeting to talk about the evaluation.

2008

My students are crying. I am crying. It is a different kind of "day after" today. It is November 2008, the day after Barack Obama was elected president for the first time. We are all exhausted, especially in my first period class where students rub the sleep out of their eyes and emerge with sheer joy on their faces. "I couldn't go to bed without knowing," someone says. "I just had to see it for myself." My 32 students that morning all identify as people of color. Just days earlier, they had presented a project on one element of one candidate's campaign plans. We had a policy panel in the cafeteria, and they invited other students to attend and learn about the candidates' proposals. They chose the candidate and the issue they cared most about. "Even when we were doing the project," a student says the next day, "And I saw that everyone was choosing Obama, and we all said we would vote for him if we could, I still didn't think it would happen." "My grandma said it would never happen in her lifetime," another commented, "And I'm so glad she was wrong."

Amazingly, the Internet works on my computer that day, so we are able to project onto the screen stories and images from CNN and the *New York Times*. Giant headlines, photos of the smiling new First Family, waving as they take the stage in Grant Park in Chicago, surrounded by thousands and thousands of cheering fans. We look at graphs of voter turnout and stories about potential voter suppression and long lines at polls in urban communities around the country. But it is still a day of, yes, hope . . . as much a day after as a new beginning.

2009/2019

It is 10 years later, and I am sitting in a coffee shop in Paris. I am meeting a student who I taught 10 years earlier, on another day after . . . another "good" day after. She was in high school when Obama was elected, and we watched the inauguration in her class. She lives in Paris now, and we talk about what this is like for her as a Black woman. I am here with a group of students in a study abroad program, and it is the highlight of my trip to be able to see her. She is so "grown up" that it takes my breath away. She is as brilliant as I remember her being, but also more confident and self-assured. She tells me that she remembers coming to me for SAT tutoring after school and thanks me for this. "Are you sure that was me?" I ask, laughing. "Yes," she laughs back, "and I sometimes didn't come and I should have." Sure, I stayed after school to work with students all the time, but this I do not remember. What I remember is her on Inauguration Day, sitting at a desk next to her classmates, chin resting on her hands, elbows on her desk, hunched forward, leaning as close to the giant TV on a cart as she could get. There was more crying that day.

2015

It is the first week of a summer program for youth of color from surrounding urban communities who come to the predominantly white university where I work to live on campus and take classes in education, writing, leadership, math, and more. It is, by far, the best thing I have the privilege to do every summer: to teach a class on social justice and urban education for these bright and thoughtful high school students. When they ask to watch the video in class, I'm honestly not sure how to respond. They have all already seen it, of this I am certain. But they want to watch it "as a group," they tell me, "so we can talk about it together." The video is of Sandra Bland's last moments in a jail cell, after she was pulled over by a white police officer in Texas. They also want to look at the mugshot, because there are stories online that say she had already died when the photo was taken. They tell me these things with a mix of such anger and resignation that it devastates me.

Of course, I have other "plans" for our class, a syllabus outlined for each of our days together; there is Baldwin to read and testing policies to analyze. But how can I pretend that Sandra Bland doesn't matter for a class about social justice? Indeed, it seems like this is all that matters at the moment. How can I, as a white person, tell my students of color what they can and can't talk about or process together in a program that is intentionally designed to support them?

In the end, a student makes the decision for me. She is the same age as everyone else, but they look up to her. "I don't think we should watch it again because we all know what it is," she says to the group, "I'd rather spend that time talking. Okay?"

Okay.

In the end, what I have come to realize is that, on days after, there is often no place I'd rather be than in a classroom. I hope this book helps other teachers—and, more important, their students—feel the same.

TEACHABLE MOMENTS IN SERVICE OF JUSTICE

One day, my then 3-year-old son puts his hands above his head and makes two circles with his hands. He links the circles together and says, "I have a connection!" He is so excited to tell us this. But it comes out of nowhere.

And I don't know what he's doing with his hands above his head. Later, he explains to us that this is what his teachers have them do in his classroom when they have a "connection" to make to something they're discussing during their large-group circle time. If you've ever been in an early childhood classroom, you can imagine how many of these connections are brought up every day. Sometimes they relate directly to what is happening, and other times, they're a little more off-topic. But whatever these connections are, the teachers inevitably take moments away from whatever they had planned because they know that the unplanned is just as important.

Indeed, no matter what age their students are, when teachers recall their favorite lessons or the moments in their classroom that mattered the most, many times they are a result of so-called teachable moments. These teachable moments are the unplanned opportunities for teaching and learning that arise as part of everyday classroom life, or when "circumstances accidentally cross paths" (Rethinking Schools, 2008). They may start with a student question that seems slightly off-topic, but the teacher knows that it is wise to divert from the lesson plan because, as "teachable moments" go, now is the time to seize the opportunity to harness students' interest about something. They may start with a teacher observing an interaction between children in the classroom or the hallway and finding a way to integrate it in the lesson plan that day or the following. They are the magic moments, the "aha!" moments, the moments of memories.

Reflecting on the curricular silence about issues of racism, imperialism, and colonialism, as well as the opportunity that current events offer to bring these topics into the classroom, the editors of *Rethinking Schools* (2008) wrote, "We need an extended teachable moment in our schools—collective efforts on the part of educators, parents, and social justice activists to expose and eliminate these silences in our curriculum and teaching." Teaching on days after is the ultimate "teachable moment," the ultimate "connection." But it requires more skill and facilitation than a simple answering of a student question. It requires a refusal to be silent in the face of injustice.

ON SILENCE

Your silence will not save you.

—Audre Lorde

When I tell people that I am researching or writing about what happens in classrooms on the days after "big" events, they all react the same way: by remembering what it was for them, as students, to be in their classrooms on these days. Even for teachers, often what they first reminisce about is what it was like to be a *student*. When Margaret, now an English professor, recalls the days after that stand out, she remembers "teachers talking about the '94 L.A. earthquakes," oddly through thematic word scrambles. But the L.A. riots in 1992? There, Margaret remembers "the lack of conversation." Days after memories are powerful. Amid the many mundane days of schooling from 12 or more years of sitting in a classroom, the stories people tell about *these* days are often very evocative. They remember what the classroom was like, who their classmates were, and, most of all, what their teachers did (or didn't do) in these potentially life-altering moments. If I am talking with a small group of people about the topic, inevitably one story leads into another. The stories build on each other until the group has created a timeline of events, a time capsule of days after elections, deaths, historic moments, tragedies, traumas, and sometimes (but rarely) positive events, too. But far too often, what stands out in their stories is silence. I saw this also in many of the interviews I conducted with teachers about the days after. Many teachers expressed a deep desire to do something, but they didn't know *what* and they didn't know *how*. And, as a result, they stayed silent. Others believed that teaching for justice on days after was "not their job." Their stories, by and large, are not the ones presented here. Their stories are important because they reveal the complexity and multiple perspectives about days after teaching. But this is not a book about the dangers of teaching on days after but the possibilities of it. That is, while every educator teaches on days after, only some do so in an intentional justice-oriented way.

Throughout each chapter, there are examples of when teachers find particular elements of Days After Pedagogy challenging and when they are faced with struggles that make Days After Pedagogy more complicated, such as being an ideological outsider in a community where (they perceive) parents and administrators to disagree with their stance on justice and equity. What I wish to highlight in this text, however, is the educators who push against silence in thoughtful, meaningful ways, as a model for teachers who already know how to do this and wish to learn more, and for those who are searching for models of how to take on this stance in their own practice.

Like many English teachers and many academics, I am a collector of quotations. Many of the quotations that speak to me the most and that I often use in my teaching and research are about silence. Or rather, about the dangers of silence and how silence reinforces and perpetuates injustice. Teachers themselves even have some of these quotations on posters on their wall; people proudly post them on social media updates on MLK Day: "In the end, we will remember not the words of our enemies, but the silence of our friends." "Our lives begin to end the day we become silent about things that matter." Yet the move from *quoting* things about silence to *doing* things about silence is a big one. This book offers one way to combat the silence that too often permeates our classrooms. Teaching on days after necessitates a refusal to be silent.

WHAT THIS BOOK IS ABOUT

In the wake of the killing of Michael Brown in Ferguson, Missouri, Professor Marcia Chatelain took to Twitter and created #FergusonSyllabus, a hashtag that quickly collected readings and activities for classrooms across the United States. Later, other hashtagged syllabi followed for a range of social, cultural, and political events, with lessons for elementary through higher education. Yet even before this social media movement, teachers have been finding ways to address critical issues in the days after world-changing events. From the murder of Trayvon Martin to "natural" disasters like Hurricane Katrina, to Supreme Court rulings, elections, and international tragedies, classrooms have been and always will be sites to make sense of what is happening in the world. Even as I write, world-changing events are happening every day: school shootings, immigration bans and mass deportations, health care debates, and movements against sexual violence and assault. There is no shortage of events for which a Days After Pedagogy is necessary, yet there is a shortage of research on just what that pedagogy might look like. The purpose of *Teaching on Days After* is to explore what classrooms do and can look like in these critical moments. This book highlights how teachers engage in a justice-oriented pedagogy on the days after events that shake communities, be they local, national, or international. It also addresses contextual factors that inhibit or support teachers in implementing their lessons on days after. Finally, through Student Spotlights written by current adolescents and young adults, this book shares stories of students' experiences on days after.

There is a critical need to understand how, in the immediate aftermath of major events and injustices, teachers and students respond in the classroom. Through an investigation of teachers across the country, this book explores several central questions: In the days after a major event or injustice, how do educators respond and modify their pedagogy and curricula? What contextual factors support or inhibit teachers' abilities to enact these responses and modifications? What does Days After Pedagogy look like in various contexts? This text can provide insight into how to make a classroom a responsive place to be on days after.

Importantly, the book is grounded in the theories and literature of social justice and liberatory education. Teaching on days after is not a "neutral" endeavor; it is one that demands a commitment to equity and action. As Freire (1984) writes, "Washing one's hands of the conflict between the powerful and the powerless means to side with the powerful, not to be neutral" (p. 524). Teaching on days after is about telling stories and highlighting the humanity of those inside and outside one's classroom. To acquaint readers with the theoretical underpinnings of justice and equity as pedagogical necessities and moral imperatives—especially on days after injustice—I draw on concepts of sociopolitical teaching, culturally relevant and sustaining pedagogy for social justice, critical consciousness and criticality, and abolitionist and antiracist teaching. Ayers (2005) charges us to remember that "the allure of teaching, that ineffable magic drawing me back to the classroom again and again, issues from an ideal that lies directly at its heart: Teaching, at its best, is an enterprise that helps human beings reach the full measure of their humanity" (p. 1). Here, I argue that teaching on days after helps our students "reach the full measure of their humanity."

The stories in this text are from interviews with teachers from 2018 to 2020, from areas as diverse as New York City to rural Georgia to suburban Michigan. The teachers worked in public schools and private schools, were novice teachers and veteran teachers, identified as teachers of color and white teachers, and taught all grade levels and content areas. We hear teachers' stories about doing this work as an ideological insider and a political outsider, and about doing this work in collaboration with colleagues and students. And finally, we see what it means to do this work in defiance of school rules or policies as an act of revolution and disruption.

WHY TEACHING ON DAYS AFTER MATTERS—AND WHY NOW

While we don't know what will happen or when, what we do know about days after is that they will keep happening. Despite this certainty, little empirical research exists on these unique pedagogical moments. Colleagues and I wrote about these moments in response to the 2016 U.S. presidential election (Dunn, Sondel, & Baggett, 2018; Sondel, Baggett, & Dunn, 2017), moments when there were news reports of children chanting "Build that wall" at their classmates from immigrant families. Similarly, what happened the day after teachers held a noose in a photo during professional development and it went viral? When a young boy was bullied into suicide at only age 11? After an 11-day teachers' strike in Chicago? What is happening in those classrooms, when the world keeps moving at the same time that benchmarks are due and tests are scheduled and curriculum is mandated? Because the world doesn't stop for children to go to school. The world is children going to school.

Yet the election and these examples are just some of many events that teachers must navigate, and this book offers readers a chance to move beyond one incident to see how teachers develop sustained Days After Pedagogy. Furthermore, while there is a large body of literature about teaching "controversial issues" or "current events," this scholarship is largely confined to social studies. Here, as in previous work, I argue that teaching on days after extends beyond social studies and is possible—and necessary—across all grade levels and content areas.

This book may be useful in supporting current teachers through professional development and in better structuring teacher education to help preservice teachers think ahead to their future classrooms. Indeed, many educators say they *want* to teach for justice on days after, but many express concerns and fears about doing this: How do I know what to do? What if parents or administrators are not happy with me addressing issues of injustice? What if my students are upset? What if some of my students feel one way and others feel differently; should I welcome all viewpoints? What do I do if I have mandated or scripted curriculum? How do I negotiate my own feelings in the process? Do I tell them what I believe; aren't teachers supposed to be "neutral"?

Figure 1.1. Days After Pedagogy: Components, Purposes, and Outcomes

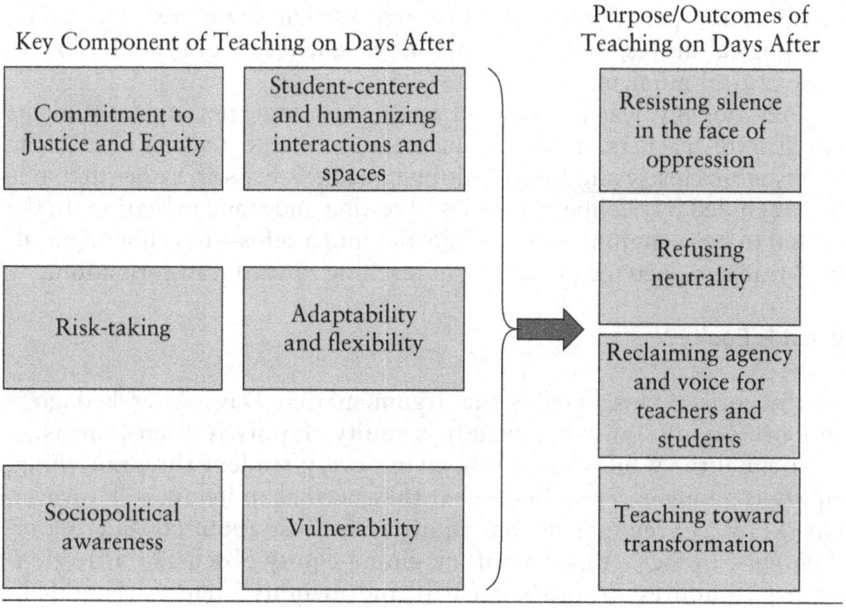

Key Component of Teaching on Days After

Commitment to Justice and Equity	Student-centered and humanizing interactions and spaces
Risk-taking	Adaptability and flexibility
Sociopolitical awareness	Vulnerability

Purpose/Outcomes of Teaching on Days After

- Resisting silence in the face of oppression
- Refusing neutrality
- Reclaiming agency and voice for teachers and students
- Teaching toward transformation

WHAT IS "DAYS AFTER PEDAGOGY"?

Here, I provide a brief summary of a pedagogy of days after, expanded on in later chapters. Teaching on days after is a pedagogy in pursuit of justice and equity. It is something that I argue teachers can and must do if they want to support all children, especially our most vulnerable. Yet it's also a pedagogy that cannot exist in isolation: Teaching on days after only works if you've been teaching for justice on days before and days during. In many ways, what teachers articulated about Days After

Pedagogy (DAP) is similar to existing frameworks of strong teaching, like culturally relevant/sustaining pedagogy, teaching for social justice, and abolitionist teaching. What makes it unique is the confluence of the need for these student-centered and humanizing pedagogical skills with the immediacy and the uncertainty of time-sensitive unfolding events; it requires a willingness to take risks and change your curriculum at the last minute. It requires teachers to be consistent and critical consumers of the news and advocates for critical literacies in students' consumption of the news. It requires teachers to be vulnerable about their own emotions, confusions, and struggles with controversial and sensitive topics, often as new information is still emerging and teachers themselves do not always know how to feel, let alone how to help students. While I do believe that all teaching contexts are different and that some contextual factors may (seem to) limit or promote certain types of days after teaching, my participants' practice evinces that there are overlapping pedagogical moves and stances that all teachers can and should take in these critical moments.

Additionally, teaching on days after is sustaining not just for students but also for teachers. It allows educators to execute a vision of teaching that is more closely aligned to their imagined teacher self, rather than one that is guided by neoliberal policies of testing and standardization. In the refusal to be silent in the face of injustice and a refusal to claim "neutrality," teachers open the possibility of teaching toward transformation.

What Is Equity?

At the core of this book is the argument that Days After Pedagogy supports equity. But what exactly is equity? Equity is often contrasted with equality. While equality is giving every student the same thing, equity is giving every student what they need as individuals. However, Gorski (2020) reminds us that equity is not just about considering *individuals*. In fact, "this way of imagining equity obscures our responsibility to address *institutional* bias and inequity" (emphasis added). Gorski continues,

> Equity is a process through which we ensure that policies, practices, institutional cultures, and ideologies are actively equitable, purposefully attending to the interests of the students and families to whose interests we have attended inequitably. By *recognizing* and deeply understanding these sorts of disparities, we prepare ourselves to respond effectively to inequity in the immediate term. We also strengthen our abilities to foster long-term change by *redressing* institutional and societal conditions that create everyday manifestations of inequity.

When thinking about DAP, then, its goal of advancing equity means committing to institutional change as much as individual student support.

LEARN MORE

Just starting out on your equity and justice journey? Check out these organizations that provide excellent resources and support for educators.

- Abolitionist Teaching Network
- Black Lives Matter at School
- Education for Liberation Network
- Equity Literacy Institute
- Facing History and Ourselves
- Learning for Justice
- National Association for Multicultural Education
- Rethinking Schools
- Teachers 4 Social Justice
- The 1619 Project
- Woke Kindergarten
- Zinn Education Project

HOW THIS BOOK IS ORGANIZED

The book is organized into eight main chapters and several shorter sections called Student Spotlights. After this introduction that frames the scope and significance of the project, Chapter 2 presents the frameworks that guide the project. Chapters 3 through 5 will each tackle one overarching question and component of teaching on days after, including *why* we need it, *who* is taught, and *who* is doing the teaching. In each of these chapters, I highlight the voices and stories of teachers around the country. The stories include both how teachers felt and how they acted in relation to these events, as well as a short historical and contextual overview of the events at the time in case readers are not familiar with them. Throughout, I interweave theoretical and empirical literature. In Chapters 6 and 7, I focus on specific examples of days after: first, those related to politics (such as elections, gun violence, environmental crises, and Supreme Court nominations) and second, those related to racial justice (such as global terrorism, racial violence and white supremacy, immigration, and local racial injustice). In the Conclusion section, I first offer an extended example of how Days After Pedagogy can be supported at a schoolwide level, then summarize the research and consider final tips for how teachers can effectively teach for justice and equity on days after.

In between main chapters, there are shorter sections (Student Spotlights) that feature student reflections on what their teachers did (or did not do) on days after and what that meant to them. Finally, I conclude the text with an Epilogue about the significant national trauma and days after in 2020 and 2021, as well as an appendix with a letter to the youth who lived through 2020 and 2021. Additional appendices include Methods, Participant Descriptions, and Social Media Resources.

Student Spotlight: Days After Sandy Hook

When I walked into my 6th-grade classroom on Friday, December 14, 2012, I had the biggest grin on my face. I always loved going to school, especially on Fridays! Friday was my favorite day of the week because my school always served nachos on Fridays and nachos are my all-time favorite food. I knew that it would also be a fun day because my teachers always created fun lesson plans on Fridays. The day was going very smoothly. I had just gotten to my first class of the day, P.E., when all of a sudden my principal came over the loudspeaker to announce that our school would be going into lockdown. When my principal announced this, I thought nothing of it because we did random practice drills throughout the years, so I figured it was just another drill.

After I had been playing charades, telephone, and rock, paper, scissors with my friends for over an hour, I began to realize that something had to be wrong. The drills had never lasted more than 10 minutes before, so I knew that it wasn't a practice drill. In this very moment, I began to freak out, but I tried my best to not think about it. I did live in Newtown, Connecticut, after all, and nothing big ever happened in our little quiet town. The most extreme thing that ever happened at my school was the one time we went into lockdown because a wolf was spotted near the school's front entrance; maybe the same thing happened again. I continued to play games with my friends, but I still couldn't help wondering what was going on outside the school and why no one was telling us anything. The P.E. teachers seemed just as confused as the rest of us.

When the principal finally came onto the loudspeaker hours after her first announcement, I hoped that what she had to say would disprove all of my concerns. Unfortunately, that was not the case at all. I don't remember her exact words, but essentially, all she said was that an incident had taken place at Sandy Hook Elementary School.

A wave of panic came crashing down on me when I heard the words "Sandy Hook Elementary School." This was the school that my 7-year-old sister Lauren attended, and all I could think about was whether or not she was all right. What did my principal even mean by the word "incident"? Did someone get hurt? Was there a fire? A series of questions danced around in my mind as I carried on with the rest of my school day. I figured that the incident couldn't have been all that bad if they were still having us attend class, yet I still was very worried about my little sister. Not even the delicious plate of nachos I bought at lunch could bring me the slightest bit of joy. My mind was somewhere else. As stories were being spread throughout the school about the "incident," I wanted nothing more than to be at home with my little sister, so I could be reassured that she was safe and alright. Throughout the day, my classmates were being called out of class because their parents had come to pick them up. Every time the phone rang in my classroom, I hoped that the teacher would say my name and tell me that my mom was here to get me. When there were only about five other students in my class, my teacher finally called my name and told me to pack up my stuff.

As I made my way down the hall to the main office, I didn't really know how to feel. My heartbeat started to pick up as I saw my mom turn, waiting for me in the office. Her facial expression and puffy eyes had confirmed all of my fears, and I could tell she was really upset. An awkward silence weighed between us until we got into the car and I finally asked, "What happened at Sandy Hook?" My mom let out a shallow breath and struggled to catch her breath. She attempted to form words, but with every word, she let out a heavy sob. We sat in the parking lot for several minutes until she finally caught her breath long enough to tell me that a shooting had taken place. It was after hearing these words that I felt a knot form in the pit of my stomach and struggled to swallow. I didn't know how to respond to this statement because too many thoughts were racing through my mind. The first question I wanted answered was "Did something happen to Lauren?" My mom immediately responded, "No she's okay, but a lot of first graders and staff members died." I was again at a loss for words after hearing this.

As we drove to my neighbor's house to meet my older and younger sister, I couldn't stop thinking about my little sister and what she had to be going through. As I followed closely behind my mom into my neighbor's house, I could feel the knot in my stomach growing in size. I knew that as soon as I turned the corner into the kitchen there would be a bunch of parents standing around the island with fresh tears and puffy eyes. I didn't want to deal with the hugs and all the sympathy, so I pushed my way past the adults and made a beeline to the living room where I knew I would find my sisters. Sure enough, I found my sisters and close family friends sprawled across the couches watching the news on the TV. I made my way next to my younger sister Lauren and threw my arms across her body, giving her a big hug. As she rested her head on my chest, I felt a single teardrop fall from my right eye. I wiped it away quickly before she could notice because I wanted to be strong for her. Her head remained buried in my chest until she turned her head toward the TV as the news reporter began to list out the names of the confirmed victims of the shooting. As I saw a photo of a little blonde girl in pink clothing flash across the screen, I knew that Lauren would be crying. The girl in the photo was one of our neighbors and was also one of Lauren's best friends from preschool. More photos of children were being displayed on the TV. I didn't know all of them personally, but with each photo, my heart ached more and more. My heart completely shattered when my third-grade teacher's photo appeared on the screen. I had been sitting in her classroom just 3 years ago. How could she be gone? Guilt started to build up inside of me as I recalled the fact that I didn't end on good terms with Ms. Soto. My immature third-grade self was very sassy to Ms. Soto because she was the long-term sub for my teacher when she went on maternity leave, so I wasn't always on my best behavior. Knowing that I never got to make things right with her and apologize to her fills me with a lot of regret.

As all these thoughts rushed through my mind, I was brought back to reality when my mom came into the living room and called my name. As I turned my head away from the screen to look at her, I could tell that she was going to tell me bad news. She told me that my best friend Erin's brother had yet to be found in the school. I was in absolute disbelief. I quickly pulled out my phone to text Erin: "I heard that you haven't been reunited with your brother yet, but you have nothing to worry about, they are going to find him." She never responded to me. After sitting in front of the TV for a few more hours, I discovered why she never texted me back. Her brother had now been identified as one of the victims killed in the shooting.

Everything after that is all a blur. All I really remember is repeating to myself, "This cannot be happening, this isn't real, things like this don't happen in Newtown." I didn't want it to be real. I was convinced that it was all just a really bad nightmare and that I would wake up soon to find that it was all just a dream. I was forced to face the truth, that it had, in fact, happened when I returned to school the following Tuesday. Going back to school that day was really hard for me. I used to love going to school. It was a place I once felt safe, but I now associated it with danger.

When I returned to school, my teachers didn't say much about the shooting. All I really remember was my teachers telling us that if we needed to leave class to talk to the guidance counselor, we could just sign out, no questions asked. My teachers tried to carry out class like it had been before the shooting, but with less of a workload. We were still learning content in class, but we also did fun Christmas-related activities like word puzzles and color-by-code worksheets. My teachers weren't that relaxed compared to the other 6th-grade teachers. However, I noticed that they seemed less strict after the shooting. It wasn't until we returned from winter break that my teacher slowly increased the workload to how it originally was. One thing that really helped me with the transition back to school was the supportive staff. A lot of my friends would start to cry during class, so I would walk with them to the counselor's office. During these walks, at least one staff member would always stop to check on us and make sure everything was all right. Another aspect that helped with the return back to school were the therapy dogs that came to visit my school. My teachers always let us stop to pet the dogs, even when we didn't really have the time to. Petting the dogs was a nice way to take a break from school and to feel at ease.

I was 11 at the time of the shooting, and it was extremely difficult for me, so I can't even begin to imagine the impact it had on my 7-year-old sister, Lauren. Lauren didn't go back to school until after Christmas break, partly because she didn't have a school to return to. When Lauren and her classmates returned to school, they went to a former elementary school in the town next to ours. The teachers continued on with teaching their normal subjects, but they were more sensitive and empathetic to their students. The teachers also told their students that if they ever needed someone to talk to, they could either go to their teacher or go see a guidance counselor. Lauren and her classmates also had a chance to FaceTime with astronauts in space, meet Bill Nye the Science Guy, and visit with different authors. Lauren shared with me that each class kind of created their own community after experiencing such a traumatic event together. Lauren's favorite component of the new school was the art therapy room with blankets, yogibos (beanbag chairs), therapy dogs, and more. She spent a lot of her time in this room because it helped her relax.

After the shooting, I developed a really strong relationship with Lauren. Even though I am not Lauren's oldest sister, I have always felt responsible for her growing up and I felt like I needed to be there for her even more after what happened on 12/14. Since I wasn't there for her at the time that such a traumatic event took place, I always try my best to be there for her regardless of the obstacles that might be in the way. It is also because of my need to feel responsible that I started to develop a lot of guilt because I was playing games with my friends while innocent people were dying in a school minutes away from me.

On the 1-year anniversary of the shooting, all the churches in my town held religious services and vigils for those who died. There have also been several proposed memorials to honor the victims of the shootings, but nothing has been finalized yet. After that, in school on the anniversary of the shooting each year, we would hold a moment of silence after the pledge to honor those who had died. Students would also put green flowers with kind messages on them throughout the school. One thing my mom started to do to honor the victims was put out 26 white bags with angel cutouts in them on my front yard and arrange them into the shape of a heart. We kept this out during the entire month of December and put LED candles in each bag on the anniversary of the shooting.

Over time, I have come to learn that I can't live in the past or blame myself for the events that took place on the day of the shooting. I know that I can't pretend that it never happened and that I instead have to get through life without letting it hold me back forever, while also acknowledging that it took place. I always saw the shooting as something that would hold me back for the rest of my life, but now I recognize how it has shaped me into the strong person I am today.

I first met Marlena as a freshman in my undergraduate social foundations of education class. It is rare to meet students from outside Michigan at our large state school, so I was surprised when, on the first day, Marlena introduced herself as being from Connecticut. Not only surprised, but also excited, since I had also been born and raised there. "Where in Connecticut?" I asked excitedly. "Newtown," Marlena replied, and, as soon as she said it, I gasped. I could not do the math quickly enough in my head to figure out how old she had been at the time of the Sandy Hook shooting, but I knew she would have been in elementary school. I looked at her, and she looked at me. We knew that each other knew what Newtown meant. "I'm glad you're here" was all I ended up being able to say. After that day, I thought about Marlena often, especially since I was working on this book at the time, interviewing teachers around the country about these days after. Even after I learned of Marlena and Lauren's story, there was still one question that lingered. And so, after Marlena wrote this reflection, I finally had a chance to ask her: Despite all of this happening, you still want to be a teacher. Why is that?

The shooting has definitely furthered my interest in becoming a teacher even more. Going through such a traumatic event at the age of 11 caused me to learn responsibility and to reevaluate my outlook on life. A lot of teachers risked their lives on the day of shooting to protect their students and some even lost their lives as a result of their actions, including my former third-grade teacher, Victoria Soto. Several stories have been shared in regards to the brave actions of the teachers on the day of the shooting, but the story that always hits me the hardest is the story about my 1st-grade teacher, Kaitlin Roig-DeBellis. On December 14, 2012, Ms. Roig packed all of her 15 students into the tiny classroom bathroom in order to save their lives. After hearing this story, I have gained even more appreciation for her as a teacher. Most people consider a teacher's job to be to teach their students, but they do so much beyond just teaching. Teachers offer their students emotional support and make their students' safety a priority. When I become a teacher, I want to make my students feel safe at school. There hasn't been a single teacher in my life that I thought wouldn't do everything in their power to protect me and my classmates. Knowing that my teachers cared about me made me want to go to school because I knew that I was safe and being looked after. I hope to become a role model for my students just like my teachers had been for me and maybe even possibly be looked up to as a hero by my students.

Author Bio: Marlena Young is a junior at Michigan State University, majoring in elementary education. She has lived in Sandy Hook, Connecticut, since she was 7 years old. As a young white woman, Marlena believes that it is important to talk about traumatic experiences and how these experiences can impact everyday life regardless of how much time has passed. Some things she likes to do in her free time include spending time with her friends and family, baking, cooking, listening to music, traveling, and enjoying nature.

CHAPTER 2

Guiding Frameworks

There is a great discovery. Education is politics! When a teacher discovers that [they are] a politician, too, the teacher has to ask: What kind of politics am I doing in the classroom? That is, in favor of whom am I being a teacher? The teacher works in favor of something and against something. Because of that, [they] will have another great question: how to be consistent in my teaching practice with my political choice?

—Paulo Freire, *A Pedagogy for Liberation* (Shor & Freire, 1987)

1989: She is a professor now, and it's been decades, but Kara still remembers one "days after" that stands out. "When the Berlin Wall fell in 1989, I was in middle school and my orchestra conductor took time to talk about it in orchestra. I remember it very clearly. It was emotional. He was emotional. He talked about his visits to Berlin and the checkpoints and the freedom this important event represented. I remember when he started the conversation, he asked us about what important event had just happened. I was like, 'the high school football team took state!' (which they had and my brother was on the team). I felt so silly because I did know about the wall coming down, but taking state was a bigger deal to me at the time. I've since spent a lot of time in Germany and been to Berlin many times. There is a lot of personal significance there for me. It means a lot that he took the time to do it. In orchestra. I don't remember any of my other teachers talking about it."

1993: Scott, now an architect, also remembers a particular day after that shook his community, a small town in Michigan where, one day during an after-school meeting, a science teacher shot and killed the district superintendent and wounded two other school employees: "After the shooting, I ironically remember the school feeling like the safest place. The national media descended onto our campus and our school walls and faculty protected us from the shock and trauma of it all. Moreover, during his tenure as superintendent, the deceased had implemented a response team for major traumatic events. Community counselors, clergy, and social workers packed the halls. Being a small town, we knew them all. Even my dad [a Methodist minister] was there. I recall my physics teacher broke from secular protocol and confessed his personal reliance on faith and prayer in times like this. Eventually I believe a prayer circle materialized around the school flagpole. This was before Sandy Hook, before 9/11, before Columbine, before it was routine. 'Thoughts and prayers' wasn't a tagline. We didn't know how to react, but we were somehow prepared."

2001: When Dominique, now a teacher herself, was 9 years old, she was sitting in her 4th-grade classroom in a New York City public school on the morning of 9/11. She remembers another teacher coming into her classroom and saying, "Someone hijacked a plane and crashed into the World Trade Center." This confused Dominique and her classmates. Even though she had grown up in the city, "I didn't even know what the Twin Towers were. I remember they were in movies and seeing them growing up in New York City, but they didn't mean anything specific to me." Until after 9/11, that is. Then they became a symbol of national trauma and tragedy. It was personal for Dominique, too. "My mom was working in that area. She was very affected, like she had to run from the area that day. So there's a lot of trauma for me." Even though "it was such a hazy period, really dark days in New York City," Dominique doesn't remember her teachers talking about it with her and her classmates when they returned to school. Looking back, Dominique is not necessarily surprised by this because "teachers wanting to talk about these things or feeling empowered to talk about these things is newer. I don't think it's always been this way."

The stories above illustrate a variety of responses to decades-passed days after. These now-adults have recalled when individual teachers addressed a significant moment, when there was a whole-school response, and when there was no response at all. The events themselves and their teachers' responses (or lack thereof) made an indelible impact on Kara, Scott, and Dominique. Since these events occurred, as Dominique points to in her comments, much research has been done on how to support students' needs in schools more broadly. The fields of multicultural education, critical pedagogy, and social justice education have grown substantially since the 1980s. These asset-based and justice-oriented pedagogies are the foundational work upon which Days After Pedagogy (DAP) is based. Because DAP is rooted in a commitment to justice and equity, it is another form of asset-based pedagogy that relies on existing theories and practices that center students' lived experiences and make learning relevant and meaningful. Furthermore, when talking with teachers, their own theories of justice and equity were deeply informed by the work of the scholars cited here.

This chapter introduces other related frameworks and literature that readers should recognize to fully understand and enact DAP. In particular, I draw upon theories of asset-based pedagogies, including culturally relevant/sustaining pedagogy for social justice, critical consciousness, and abolitionist/antiracist teaching. I also offer a review of empirical literature on sociopolitical teaching, including pedagogy about current events and controversial social issues. Finally, I consider schools' recent attention to trauma-informed pedagogy and socioemotional learning and what that means for days after.

GUIDING FRAMEWORKS IN CONTEXT: TODAY'S CLASSROOMS AS SPACES FOR DAYS AFTER PEDAGOGY

Delpit (2018) writes that today's educators are "teaching when the world is on fire" and children have fewer and fewer examples of how "the nation has a moral high ground" (p. 3). Instead, they are often surrounded by "the putrid waters of racism, misogyny, homophobia, xenophobia, irrationality, and despotic bluster" (p. 3). This means that, in classrooms, teachers must counter these oppressive forces and, instead, engage in pedagogy that shows that politics, safety, race, gender, climate, and culture matter. On days after, it is usually very clear that the world is on fire. Even if the fire has been burning for a while, as in cases of racism and white supremacy, on the day after another instance of racial violence or police brutality, the fire gets even hotter. This is where DAP comes in.

Not every teacher will approach DAP the same way, and this is a good thing! As mentioned in Chapter 1, there are no templates or standardized lessons because all contexts are different, all teachers are different, and all students are different. That means that what DAP looks like in one school may look very different than another school, and it may also vary among teachers. The teaching force is still overwhelmingly white: "In 2020, while students of Color in U.S. public schools make up over 50 percent of the population, teachers of Color constitute just over 20 percent of educators" (Kohli, 2021, p. 3). A key reason for this flexible and varying approach is that there are structural and institutional factors that will either challenge or support DAP, depending on the school and community. Undoubtedly, some of these factors make it difficult to engage in DAP and other asset-based pedagogies within contexts that often limit teachers' agency. We are teaching at a time of ongoing (and often increasing) surveillance of teachers, standardization of curriculum, and high-stakes testing and assessment-driven teaching (Au, 2020). Much research has demonstrated that teachers may feel a lack of agency and empowerment amid these neoliberal reforms (e.g., Dunn, 2018, 2020) that value "profit over people" (Chomsky, 1999). When competition among schools and students is more valued than humanization and criticality, it may be difficult for teachers to imagine how they are to fit *one more thing* into their school days. It may be even harder to imagine how to resist implicit and explicit messages that make teachers believe they shouldn't even try to do justice and equity-oriented work. As a result, research continues to demonstrate that neoliberal policies have "a track record of undermining equity and democracy" (Sleeter, 2008, p. 1947).

Many educators, especially novice teachers, are fearful of teaching for justice and equity. Among the many teachers I spoke with for this research, I heard the phrase "I don't want to lose my job" dozens and dozens of times. And even if they don't know teachers personally for whom this has happened (indeed, no one could identify this happening at their school or in a surrounding school), we know there are often cases that make national news when teachers are punished for engaging in this difficult work. It may be tempting for teachers to use these news stories as evidence that this work can't be done without repercussions. Yet these cases are the exception, and they rightfully make national news for a reason, because they are an injustice. However, there are thousands of teachers around the country every day who are not fired for doing justice-oriented work. It doesn't mean this work is easy, and it doesn't mean that there are not cases where the worst does, indeed, happen. Yet Love (2019) challenges us, especially white teachers, to be willing to put our jobs on the line when it comes to being co-conspirators in the struggle for educational and racial justice. If we aren't willing to do this on days after, then when will we?

ASSET-BASED AND JUSTICE-ORIENTED PEDAGOGIES

For a particular pedagogy to be "asset based," it must be one that supports teachers' understandings of their students as having assets—or skills, experiences, and knowledges—that they bring with them to the classroom. Rather than viewing students through a deficit lens or seeing their challenges first, teachers who adopt an asset lens find ways to celebrate the joy, brilliance, and strength of the children in their classrooms. When teachers welcome and build on these assets, with the aim of offering their students opportunities to contribute to their own learning and with the goal of nurturing change agents, they are engaging in a form of "justice-oriented" pedagogy. Asset-based and justice-oriented pedagogies disrupt notions of "damage-centered" education (Tuck, 2009).

Days After Pedagogy is a *form* of justice-oriented pedagogy and the asset-based theories discussed here. Justice-oriented pedagogy cannot be truly enacted if you are not doing DAP, and DAP cannot be enacted without consideration to justice more broadly. Days After Pedagogy is unique in that it offers teachers a way "in" to broader understandings of justice and equity. For many teachers (especially those from dominant identity groups), their first time engaging in justice-oriented pedagogy is on a day after. If you are one of those teachers, I want this book to support you in seeing that it does not have to be that way; you do not have to *wait* for an event to talk about social justice issues, and neither should you *ignore* events when they happen. Furthermore, for those educators already committed to justice-oriented pedagogy, days after can still be particularly challenging times where they are questioning their commitments, wondering how to balance their beliefs with contextual factors that might limit their feelings of agency and voice, and responding to students' immediate needs in ways that don't happen on a "normal" day.

Culturally Relevant, Responsive, and Sustaining Pedagogies

Ladson-Billings (1995) first theorized culturally relevant pedagogy (CRP) in response to existing deficit frameworks that framed African American youth as "at risk" or "disadvantaged." Instead, she "dared to ask what was right with these students and what happened in the classrooms of teachers who seemed to experience pedagogical success" (Ladson-Billings, 2014, p. 74). In this foundational work, Ladson-Billings argued that successful teachers showed evidence of supporting students' academic achievement (defined as more than just test scores, importantly), cultural competence, and sociopolitical consciousness. Cultural relevance, however, is not the simplistic inclusion of "multiple cultures" into the classroom or school; this "additive" approach (Banks & Banks, 2001) turns students' identities into mere celebrations of "food and festivals" and ignores the deeper sociopolitical commitments of critical pedagogues. Teachers practicing CRP are "not reluctant to identify political underpinnings of the students' community and social world" (Ladson-Billings, 1995, p. 477).

Gay's (2002) work on culturally responsive teaching aligns with Ladson-Billings's conceptions and pushes teachers to learn as much as possible about their students' identities. As Gay defines it, culturally responsive teaching is as much about strategies as it is about curriculum. Culturally responsive teachers know how to adapt curriculum to include issues of race, ethnicity, gender, class, and power, as well as include multiple ways of knowing beyond factual information. Gay concurs that using students' cultures and experiences offers an important way to expand their academic achievement and emphasizes the necessity of combining care with high expectations for all students.

More recently, Paris and Alim (2014) have extended earlier work on cultural relevance and responsiveness to theorize culturally sustaining pedagogy. They argue that "culturally sustaining pedagogy seeks to perpetuate and foster—to sustain—linguistic, literate, and cultural pluralism as part of the democratic project of schooling and as a needed response to demographic and social change" (p. 88). They see culturally sustaining pedagogy as being flexible and ever-changing, given the intersectional identities of students of color in today's schools.

Each of the theories above emphasizes—rightfully so—the experiences of youth of color, yet teachers of all students would do well to adopt these practices in their classrooms. It is deeply important for white students to also learn and experience, for example, that academic achievement is about more than standardized tests and grade point averages (GPAs). Furthermore, white students need to be explicitly and continuously taught about race and racism so that they can understand their own positionality and complicity in a white supremacist system—and then move to change it.

Critical Consciousness and Criticality

In the pedagogical suggestions above, we see the word "critical" often, as we do in most justice- and equity-focused work. Muhammad (2020) offers a clear definition, drawing a distinction between terms like "critical thinking" and "critical lens" or "critical approach." She argues that that the first critical "means to think deeply about something," while the other terms, such as critical lens, critical consciousness, and criticality, "are connected to an understanding of power, entitlement, oppression, and equity" (p. 120). I argue that DAP offers students an opportunity to develop all of these "critical" skills.

For Freire (1972), likely one of the most well-known but certainly not the only scholar to advance the idea of critical consciousness, or *conscientization*, this means being able to recognize oppression in the world around you (being *conscious* of it) and then taking action against it (being *critical* of it). He sees developing critical consciousness as a form of *praxis*, or "reflection and action on the world in order to transform it" (p. 5). In addition to these reflection and action components, other scholars have highlighted the importance of political efficacy or agency for students who are developing their critical consciousness. That is, not only do youth need the opportunity to critically reflect on the world and an opportunity to engage in critical action, but they also need to feel efficacious and agentic to do so (Watts, Diemer, & Voight, 2011). They need to be supported and encouraged in knowing that, if and when they are ready to engage in social action, they will be able to do it (Seider & Graves, 2020).

Students benefit from teachers who encourage critical consciousness in that it gives them language for explaining the world around them and tools to act as change agents for themselves and others. Part of developing critical consciousness means attending to *criticality*, or "the ability to read texts (including print texts and social con-*texts*) to understand power, authority, and anti-oppression" (Muhammad, 2020, p. 12). This "capacity to read, write, and think in the context of understanding power, privilege, and oppression" is especially vital on days after, when major events intersect with power, privilege, and oppression. Muhammad's argument for criticality also highlights the importance of days after dialogue about what is happening in the world:

> Criticality is also related to seeing, naming, and interrogating the world to not only make sense of injustice, but also work toward social transformation. Thus, students need spaces to name and critique injustice to help them ultimately develop the agency to build a better world. As long as oppression is present in the world, young people need pedagogy that nurtures criticality. (p. 12)

Days After Pedagogy is one such pedagogy. Especially relevant for DAP is that "criticality helps students read the world with a critical eye, refusing to accept unexamined information as factual or true. . . . Criticality pushes questioning of information and the source of the information—and this source may include the teachers" (Muhammad, 2020, p. 122). Importantly, criticality is not just something to teach students; it is something educators must embody and practice, as well. As the teachers in this book demonstrate, "if teachers engage in the teaching of criticality, it is necessary that they assume an active and critical stance in their own lives. It is impossible to teach students to have a Critical lens if teachers don't have one themselves" (Muhammad, 2020, p. 131).

[handwritten margin note: must be true of teacher before they can teach]

Abolitionist and Antiracist Teaching

Tatum (1997/2017) encourages readers of her well-known book, *Why Are All the Black Kids Sitting Together in the Cafeteria?*, to think of racism as a moving walkway in an airport. If you are white, you are born benefiting from racism whether you want to or not, and the walkway moves you along your whole life. It is not enough to stand on the walkway and say you disagree with it or that you did not mean to end up on the walkway. Still, it propels you forward. This is what white privilege looks like. All white people—regardless of other identity markers such as class, sex, and gender—benefit from racism, although not all white people benefit equally. That means that, at some point, if white people do not want to be propelled uncritically forward on this moving walkway, they need to turn around and walk the other way.

To extend Tatum's metaphor, then, think about what would happen if someone turned and walked the other way on a moving walkway in a busy airport. Imagine the looks and comments from other passengers who are actively walking or even just resting with their baggage. Imagine having to move their bags out of the way to make room, and imagine how committed and determined you'd have to be to keep pushing against the grain. It's possible you would never get there, to the end, to solid ground, and you'd just keep walking in the opposite direction, pushing baggage aside, dragging yours with you, being pulled back a few inches each time you got tired. But (hopefully) you know you can't stop walking the other way because, otherwise, you're headed in the same place as those who are actively walking. You have to keep pushing and keep going, even if you see only small progress at first. This, then, is what it means to be antiracist. Kendi (2019) reminds us that "the opposite of racist isn't 'not racist.' It is 'anti-racist.' . . . One either allows racial inequities to persevere, as a racist, or confronts racial inequities, as an anti-racist. There is no in-between safe space of 'not racist'" (p. 9). For white teachers, claiming to be "not racist" means you are still on the moving walkway and not actively walking the other way. To be antiracist means that, in and out of your classroom, you are working to *actively* fight racism and white supremacy. This does not mean that antiracist work has to or should wait for white people to either figure out they're on the walkway in the first place, that they need to walk the other way, or how to walk the other way. Antiracism and racial equity are urgent, as Gorski (2019) explains:

> The hard truth is, racial equity cannot be achieved with an obsessive commitment to "meeting people where they are" when "where they are" is fraught with racial bias and privilege. Students, families, and educators experiencing racism cannot afford to wait for us to saunter toward a more serious racial equity vision. They cannot afford to wait, in particular, for all white educators to ease into racial equity commitments at a pace of our choosing while they suffer the consequences of our casualness. In schools committed to equity, the time is *now*. We must prioritize equity over the comfort of equity-reluctant educators. We move on racial justice first by honestly identifying and addressing all the ways racism operates in our schools, and then we bridge the equity hesitaters to our equity vision. We refuse to equivocate on racial justice. We find the will to implement, and hold one another accountable to, policy and practice changes *today*, rather than waiting for an elusive consensus. (p. 58)

Simmons (2019a) offers five key practices for antiracist educators: "Engage in vigilant self-awareness . . . acknowledge racism and the ideology of white supremacy . . . study and teach representative history . . . talk about race with students . . . when you see racism, do something." These practices support the larger goal of antiracist education: "dismantle the structures, policies, institutions, and systems that create barriers and perpetuate race-based inequities for people of color." Sealy-Ruiz (2021) argues that antiracist teachers need to develop racial literacy, or "a skill and practice by which individuals can probe the existence of racism and examine the effects of race and institutionalized systems on their experiences and representation in US society. . . . Embedded in the concept of racial literacy is the significance of opening and sustaining dialogue about race and the racist acts we witness in schools, home communities, and society writ large" (pp. 2–3).

One way to advance antiracist efforts in schools is to engage in abolitionist teaching (Love, 2019). Love (2019), drawing on the work of historic and contemporary abolitionists, calls for educators to engage in abolitionist teaching that challenges what she calls the "educational survival complex," where systems are built on and continue to perpetuate suffering of children of color. Instead of supporting children of color to thrive, schools are set up for, at minimum, surviving. Teachers, then, can use the methods of abolition—such as centering love and Black joy, protesting, boycotting, and actively naming and fighting racism, to name a few—to restore humanity for children of color.

On days after, it is especially important for teachers to live up to commitments to antiracist and abolitionist teaching that center the voices and experiences of children of color.

A SOCIOPOLITICAL EDUCATION

"Education cannot be neutral. It is always directive in its attempt to teach students to inhabit a particular mode of agency, enable them to understand the larger world and one's role in it in a specific way, define their relationship, if not their responsibility, to diverse others, and experience in the classroom some sort of understanding of a more just, imaginative, and democratic life."

—Giroux (2010, p. 718)

The teachers and students whose stories are shared here operate, as we all do, within a particular sociopolitical context. Drawing on Nieto and Bode (1998), sociopolitical context here means "the larger societal and political forces in a particular society and the impact they may have on student learning. A sociopolitical context considers issues of power and includes discussions of structural inequality based on stratification due to race, social class, gender, ethnicity, and other differences" (p. 142). These societal and political forces shape how teachers operate within their contexts, and in turn, teachers shape how students understand and engage with these societal and political forces. When we consider what sociopolitical contexts mean for teachers' work, Gutiérrez (2013) challenges us to "foreground the political and engage in the tensions that surround that work" (p. 40). It is important for educators to "see knowledge, power, and identity as interwoven and arising from (and constituted within) social discourses . . . uncovering the taken-for-granted rules and ways of operating that privilege some individuals and exclude others" (p. 40). This might feel like a lot of pressure for teachers because understanding school as a sociopolitical site means acknowledging that "even seemingly innocent decisions carry an enormous amount of ideological and philosophical weight" (Nieto & Bode, 1998, p. 142). On days after, then, these decisions may feel even more challenging.

One way to think about these potentially challenging choices is to consider how DAP can support students' sociopolitical development, or the process that "recognize[s] young people's agency in naming and contending with oppressive forces, and position[s] youths as agents and active participants in creating a more equitable world" (Zion et al., 2015, p. 825). Supporting this development means giving students opportunities to understand what oppression looks like across identity markers. It also means supporting their resistance of oppression and their "capacity for action in political and social systems necessary to interpret and resist oppression" (Watts et al., 2003, p. 186). Importantly, we know that students' sociopolitical development does not just happen in schools; from an ecological perspective, many social contexts and life experiences allow students to develop knowledge of and dispositions toward actions and change (Watts et al., 2003). Zion et al. (2015) call this *sociopolitical wisdom* and note that youth from marginalized groups bring this insight to their spaces.

The New York State Education Department (2020) describes sociopolitically conscious educators and students as "inclusive minded, asset-focused [people who] critically examine historical and contemporary structures of power; honor, value, and center various identity perspectives as assets; and recognize how discrimination creates inequality." As in the previous section about asset-based pedagogies, the ultimate goals of a sociopolitical education are "dialogue, solidarity, and action" (Zion et al., 2015, p. 840). Dialogue offers opportunities to support each other's social analysis skills or sociopolitical consciousness. This solidarity is necessary for mobilizing and supporting direct action to change structural and systemic problems (Watts & Hipolito-Delago, 2015; Zion et al., 2015).

Just as sociopolitical development can happen inside and outside of school, the way it looks in schools will necessarily be different depending on the school context and students' identities. For the purposes of this text, we will focus on what it means for teachers to aid in this development on days after. This means getting a clear understanding of what research says about the importance of teaching about current events and controversial issues.

Teaching About Current Events and "Controversial" Issues

Defining what is "current" is generally an easier task than defining what is "controversial." While what is "current" is about what is happening in a particular moment, who gets to decide what is and is not controversial? And, just because something is controversial, does that mean all viewpoints on it should be recognized? What some might consider controversial—or something that can and should be debated—is what others might consider decidedly *un*controversial. Hess (2004) explains that some issues are "open" and "closed," or which ones are up for debate and which ones are not. For the purposes of this book, however, it is important to remember just because some people consider an issue "open" for debate does not mean that it *should* be debated. For example, Black Lives Matter (BLM) should not be an "open" social issue, and while I recognize that this is a reality for many educators, it should not be controversial for teachers to take a stance in support of BLM. Many of the days after events in this book focus on issues that teachers consider closed, or not up for debate, in part because they are issues that relate to people's identities.

Much of the research on teaching about current and "controversial" events has been confined to social studies scholarship, but the rationales and outcomes of teaching these topics extend to all content areas and grade levels. Decades of scholarship (Haas & Laughlin, 2000; Hess, 2002; LeCompte, Blevins, & Ray, 2017; Tiedt & Tiedt, 1967) have shown that teaching about current events offers opportunities for culturally relevant teaching and helps students to

Teaching soc. studies events builds skills

- develop an understanding of the diversity of people, places, and opinions in the world and empathy for others;
- learn academic and social skills, such as critical thinking, problem solving, effective communication, reading comprehension, media literacy, recognizing propaganda, and reading maps;
- enhance commitments to active citizenship; and
- wrestle with conflicting beliefs by learning how to engage in self-expression, challenge others' ideas, and revise their own understandings.

The challenge, then, is not how students will necessarily "receive" the discussions of current events and controversial issues but how teachers make sense of these concepts, how comfortable they feel teaching about them, and what their contexts will (or won't) support. For example, one study shows that, while many social studies teachers say they teach current events at least once a week, high school teachers were twice as likely to teach about current events they considered "controversial" as middle school teachers (two-thirds vs. one-third). Only 20% of elementary school teachers did so, although some with the caveat that they would discuss them if students brought them up (Haas & Laughlin, 2000).

Behind this reticence, teachers may be concerned about high-stakes testing and the increase in curricular standardization, particularly in schools where end-of-year tests are linked to students' graduation (Journell, 2010). This situation, Journell (2010) found, was exacerbated in schools that had struggled to meet proficiency requirements in previous years. Teachers in subjects that are even more frequently tested than social studies may also be concerned about how to "fit in" teaching about current events with mandates looming over their heads. The testing regime also has long-term impacts on educators, considering that new educators have themselves been educated entirely in the era of high-stakes assessments. As they move from "tested students to testing teachers" (Dunn & Certo, 2014), many preservice teachers lack civic knowledge and dispositions because they, as K–12 students, "experienced a lack of substantive discussion of political and social issues" in their own social studies classes (Journell, 2013). As a result, they find themselves largely unprepared to teach current events in their own classrooms. Lo (2019) cautions that ignoring these topics has short- and long-term consequences, arguing that a "civic debt" disproportionally affects students of color in low-income areas. This is not a "gap" in civic learning and understanding, Lo explains, much like the achievement gap is rather an "education debt" (Ladson-Billings, 2006). Marginalized youth "exhibit less political knowledge, skills, attitudes, and behaviors than their wealthier White peers. This means that youth of color engage less with the political system, not simply because they know less about politics but because they perceive the system to be less responsive to them" (Lo, 2019, pp. 112–113). This civic debt is intimately connected to discussions of so-called controversial issues because "one education-related cause and consequence of civic debt is a lack of discussion about race and inequity in the classroom" (Lo, 2019, p. 114). Many teachers continue to avoid talking about race, despite evidence that discussion of controversial issues is a best practice in civic education and beyond. Because so many days after moments bring to bear race, racism, and white supremacy, we can also argue, then, that avoiding days after conversations contributes to the civic debt that Lo so powerfully charges us to work to eliminate.

Despite their concerns, there are still many teachers within and beyond social studies who engage in teaching current and controversial events, including on days after. Payne and Journell (2019) point out that elementary teachers can teach contentious political issues by creating critically caring relationships anchored in identity recognition. Teachers can support students in using their personal experiences as assets to interpret issues and develop empathy. They emphasize the importance of engaging in these discussions purposefully and recursively. Setting aside time and space, such as morning meetings or regular discussions of news articles, creates a classroom community where a day after won't be the only time that justice-oriented topics are discussed. → little bit of time

Teachers who teach controversial issues in a justice-oriented way know that the idea of "open" and "closed" issues is fraught with complications (Hess, 2004). While teachers are often the arbiters of what is open and closed in a classroom space, they should not make these decisions without explaining their rationales to students (Journell, 2011, 2017). When it comes to controversial *identity* issues—such as those about race, gender, or sexuality—teachers need to handle these with more nuance. Teaching identity issues as "open," even if there is ongoing political debate, conflicts with a commitment to justice and equity. Some teachers may consider these identity issues to be "taboo," even on days after, but avoiding these discussions does more harm than good. What is *not* said in the classroom is just as important as what is said. Overall, avoidance (especially by white teachers in predominantly white schools) leads to teachers "missing an opportunity to engage their students in transformative discussions about White privilege, sexism in the United States, and American attitudes toward non-Christians" (Journell, 2011, p. 380).

Sometimes this avoidance can be couched in claims about neutrality, yet, as discussed in the last chapter, silence and neutrality are deeply problematic in how they maintain a harmful status quo. Choosing not to discuss controversial issues or disclose one's personal opinion about those issues is not "neutral," as it is still a choice. In the case of justice-related issues, it is a choice that harms marginalized groups. It's also a mirage. Research shows that teachers attempting to maintain neutrality nevertheless exhibited their political leanings, and teachers who did not disclose were more likely to influence their students' beliefs than teachers who did (Journell, 2011). Sometimes, neutrality can be a "shield; when faced with intolerance in the classroom, [teachers] could fall back on the idea that 'teachers are supposed to be neutral' and avoid taking sides. While doing so might protect them from having to reveal something of themselves, it could also leave young people without an adult to defend them from incidents of racism, misogyny, or transphobia" (Geller, 2020a, p. 198). In thinking about engaging in discussions of current and controversial issues, especially on days after, Geller (2020b) powerfully concludes,

> Some issues we discuss in classrooms (e.g., immigration) may make discussions more interesting, but they have serious, real-world consequences for young people in our classrooms. How teachers leverage their own opinions can have consequences for marginalized youth. Teachers often look for topics that are relevant to students' lives. That relevance can be helpful, but it can also mean that students are more vulnerable to intolerance from their peers. If teachers draw on issues that touch on the lived realities of oppressed and marginalized groups, they must be particularly thoughtful about the impact that their words—and their silences—may have. Teachers should think about how disclosing can make classrooms safer for marginalized youth. (p. 40)

By disclosing, teachers can model how people authentically participate in democracy (Geller, 2020a; Journell, 2011). We can see an example of both disclosure and a push against neutrality in a study about teachers discussing a local current event that they actively protested (Swalwell & Schweber, 2016). Teachers who protested against a budget bill in Wisconsin found that "teaching in a balanced manner meant counteracting some of the false and negative press the protests were garnering. It also meant disclosing political beliefs if teaching in largely Republican districts or participating in a 'charade of non-disclosure' if teaching in largely Democratic ones" (p. 304). Teachers engaged in a "curiosity-driven curriculum," because, even when directly ordered by administration to not discuss the protests, they could not avoid it because students were so curious. Disclosing her personal experiences with protest helped one teacher dispel misinformation about the protests. Furthermore, teaching about a current event as it was unfolding led some teachers to politicize their teaching of history in future years.

TRAUMA RESPONSIVENESS AND SOCIOEMOTIONAL LEARNING IN THE CLASSROOM

Socio-emotional learning faces the risk of becoming white supremacy with a hug if we do not apply an anti-oppressive, antiracist lens.

—Dena Simmons (2021)

"Trauma responsive" and "socioemotional education" have become buzzwords in recent years, with more educators and administrators going through "trauma-responsive trainings" and "socioemotional learning (SEL) professional development." The challenge with most of these initiatives is that they are often divorced from the rest of the school day and seen as "add-ons" or "extras," rather than as inherently intertwined with the key mission of teaching and learning. Indeed, in the wake of the 2020 attack on the Capitol, I heard from a teacher who was told she could only address it with her students during "SEL time," which was once a week. Any school that has a set-aside "time" for socioemotional learning, whether it is once a day or once a week, is doing socioemotional learning very wrong.

Typically, psychologists define trauma as the emotional and psychological response to an upsetting or disturbing experience or event, which then leads to distress, anger, anxiety, or fear. In children, we might see these responses in the form of "increased negative behavior, less emotional regulation, increased fighting, withdrawal from peers, anxiety, difficulty concentrating and/or completing tasks (Cook-Cottone, 2004). Further, the stress associated with poverty and systemic racism are experienced similarly to post-traumatic stress; cumulative effects of these traumas have exponential and confounding effects on student outcomes (Cole et al., 2009)" (Dunn, Sondel, & Baggett, 2018). As Thomas, Crosby, and Vanderhaar (2019) explain, "Using a trauma lens when handling difficulties with students means shifting the question from 'what is wrong with you?' to 'what is happening with you?'" (p. 428). Instead of focusing on the child's behavior, educators should think about how they respond to the behavior in ways that do not add more harm. As Shalaby (2018) writes, "It isn't the behavior of the children that threatens community; it is the response to that behavior, the use of exclusion, that threatens the community" (p. 162).

When educators realize that trauma can affect their students and begin to implement practices to respond sensitively to this trauma, they move toward trauma-responsive or trauma-informed education. According to the Trauma Responsive Educational Practices Project at the University of Chicago (2017), an educator who is trauma responsive "(1) Realizes the impact of trauma on all aspects of schooling and understands potential paths for recovery; (2) Recognizes the signs and symptoms of trauma in students, families, and staff; (3) Responds by fully integrating knowledge about trauma into policies, procedures, and practices; and (4) Resists re-traumatization by recognizing how classroom/school practices can trigger trauma histories."

Venet (2021) cautions us to not see trauma as something that only happens to children and only happens outside of schools. Seeing trauma through "a structural lens means that we stop seeing trauma as a problem affecting only certain children. Instead, we start recognizing the role that schools have to play in causing and worsening trauma because of the role of schools in perpetuating oppression" (p. 8). This structural lens to trauma, Venet argues, is vital for imagining how schools can shape "social, historical, and political factors . . . in pursuit of a better world" (p. 9).

There is not one common trauma-informed or trauma-responsive program or "intervention" currently in use, however; Thomas et al. (2019) identified 33 studies that elucidated 30 different frameworks, and there was little empirical support for these interventions. "There is a noted trend-like nature among educational initiatives that are ever-changing and at times overwhelming to educators," the authors explain, "Trauma-informed practices in schools should not be perceived just as 'another thing that will come and go'" (p. 445).

Too often, however, trauma responsiveness can perpetuate racism and white supremacy culture when implemented uncritically. As Blitz, Anderson, and Saastamoinen (2016) argue, even when staff demonstrated concern about students' trauma and toxic stress, there were still some who insisted on color-evasive discourse and were resistant to professional development about culturally responsive practices. Beyond the individual level, Bloom (2010) found that, in some trauma-responsive programs, attempting to "control" the trauma led to "policies and practices that are progressively structured and rigid. These practices, however, inhibit the flexibility and creativity needed to manage secondary trauma [experienced by teachers] and students'" trauma and toxic stress (Blitz et al., 2016, p. 535). Any trauma-responsive plans that do not include attention to issues of race and cultural responsiveness can, in fact, exacerbate trauma for students of color. Instead, "a culturally responsive, race-conscious, trauma-informed process may better support students in developing relationships of trust with school personnel" (p. 538) and will help school personnel move beyond feelings of frustration and deficit perceptions. In a thorough and detailed book about equity-centered trauma-informed education, Venet (2021) writes,

> Some of the strongest critiques [of trauma-informed education] have come from advocates for educational equity who wonder if "trauma-informed" is just another distraction for schools avoiding the larger work of equity, such as ending racism in schools (Gorski, 2019). Indeed, I have observed firsthand that some schools proudly claim to be working on becoming trauma-informed but refused to engage in discussions about equity, especially as it connects to racism. Why is trauma-informed education an appealing topic for professional development, but ending the things that *cause* trauma is not? (p. xvii)

Social justice scholars emphasize the importance of linking this trauma responsiveness to students' analysis of systemic inequity as a way toward healing. Love (2016) argues that to ignore the trauma caused by systemic oppression or fail to prepare students to resist that which causes trauma would perpetuate spirit murdering, or "the denial of inclusion, protection, safety, nurturance, and acceptance because of fixed, yet fluid and moldable, structures of racism" (p. 2). When teachers bring up days after events in their classrooms, it is first important that they attend to the tenets above if they are concerned (or their students are concerned) that the event was traumatizing, and then they can implement a Days After Pedagogy that moves toward healing.

For the purposes of this book, when DAP intersects with students' experiences of trauma (which is often), it is important that educators remember that *equity-centered trauma-informed education* (Venet, 2021) is

1. Antiracist and against all forms of oppression.
2. Asset based and doesn't attempt to fix kids, because kids are not broken. Instead, it addresses the conditions, systems, and structures that harm kids.
3. A full ecosystem, not a list of strategies.
4. Centering our full humanity.

5. A universal approach, implemented proactively.
6. Aiming to create a trauma-free world.

Socioemotional learning (SEL) can be seen as one component of a trauma-responsive pedagogy, in that it aims to support youth in "experiencing, managing, and expressing emotions, making sound decisions, and fostering interpersonal relationships. The Collaborative for Academic, Social, and Emotional Learning (CASEL) defines five core SEL competencies, including self-awareness, social awareness, self-management, relationship skills, and responsible decision making" (Simmons, 2019b). There are now abundant SEL training programs, interventions, and even "SEL periods" of the school day. Yet, despite the promise that SEL "can help us build communities that foster courageous conversations across difference so that our students can confront injustice, hate, and inequity" (Simmons, 2019b), SEL is often implemented devoid of explicit attention to the sociopolitical and sociocultural contexts of schools and society. As renowned educator and SEL expert Dena Simmons argues (2019b), "Recoiling from topics that divide us—when SEL skills could help us get along better—diminishes SEL's promise. Why teach relationship skills if the lessons do not reflect on the interpersonal conflicts that result from racism? Why discuss self- and social awareness without considering power and privilege, even if that means examining controversial topics like white supremacy?"

Like trauma-responsive education, SEL can be an important turn for schools that commonly focus on academic knowledge and skills without attention to how students are relating to each other and the world around them. Each of these strategies—such as teaching on days after—"has tremendous potential to create the conditions for youth agency and civic engagement and, ultimately, social change. We owe our students an education that centers on their lives and explicitly addresses the sociopolitical context. This will not only prepare our students to engage civically and peacefully across difference, but also to become the changemakers and leaders we need" (Simmons, 2019b). However, it is important that teachers be effectively supported in developing socioemotional competencies so as to support these same competencies in their students. As Warren, Presberry, and Louis (2020) write, transformational socioemotional learning for Black students relies on teachers who (1) co-create and co-construct socioemotional norms that support belonging and engagement, (2) nurture young people's agency (which requires teachers to perceive themselves as agentic, as well), and (3) have a strong sense of personal identity and purpose. If SEL is done in a race-evasive way or devoid of commitments to equity and justice, it "only aims to protect white comfort" (Simmons, 2021).

As Melissa, one of the teachers who you will meet later in the text, observed, her students pushed back when a counselor came into their classroom and told them that the fears they had (in this case, around the election of Trump as president) were unfounded. "Her concern was like, 'I don't want them to be sad or scared.' But they have to understand both the precarious position they're in *and* that people recognize that and care. We can't dismiss it and make it go away, or pretend like it doesn't exist. I think it's interesting that with all the focus on SEL, we're still trying to push people's feelings under the rug" when their feelings bring up political or justice-related issues.

In Melissa's case and many others in this book and beyond, it would be helpful to expand and reframe current ideas about trauma-responsive education and SEL. To do so would mean to place equity at the center of this work, rather than as an afterthought (if that). Venet (2021) again offers helpful ways to "shift" understandings of trauma, and these shifts align with a critical approach to teaching on days after. We should shift from being reactive to proactive, from seeing teachers as saviors to seeing teachers as "connection makers," from placing the responsibility for trauma responsiveness on individuals toward taking a schoolwide approach, and from "focusing only on how trauma affects our classroom to seeing how what happens in our classroom can change the world" (p. 15).

CONCLUSION

Days After Pedagogy, like other asset-based pedagogies, is not a commitment or a practice that can be implemented the way in every school or classroom. It is not an "easy fix" for a way to talk about current or controversial events in a social and political climate that is often divided and divisive. It is also not a way to introduce trauma-responsive pedagogy and socioemotional learning devoid of an understanding of how schools themselves are sources of trauma. Instead, Days After Pedagogy is an opportunity to extend commitments to asset-based pedagogies that center students' humanity and work to make school relevant and sustaining, especially for children of color. Days After Pedagogy offers educators who wish to talk about current and controversial events—including beyond social studies classrooms—a structure for thinking about how to do this in equitable and thoughtful ways that consider the contextual factors shaping every classroom, especially who our students are and who we are as educators. Knowing this, how can we work against oppression and for justice in moments when injustice is so apparent?

THEORIES IN PRACTICE: A LETTER FROM A
TEACHER TO HIS STUDENTS

The stories in this book illustrate how educators turn the theories above into classroom practice. One beautiful example is this letter from middle school English language arts educator, Chance Howard. Chance teaches in Atlanta, Georgia, and he wrote this letter to his students on August 27, 2020. "It was sort of difficult teaching today, but I managed," he explained, "I wrote my kids a letter to let them know how I was feeling."

To My Dear Students, Old and New:
        The word civil (adj.) is defined as "not deficient in common courtesy," while Webster defines the word right (n.) as "a moral entitlement." The Civil Rights Movement ended in 1968. Or at least it was supposed to.
        Fast forward. The day is July 13th, 2013. It was a Saturday night. My best friend and I were counselors at a local summer camp. We were allowed to live on the camp grounds because neither of us had an apartment in Atlanta at the time. There was no cable, no air conditioning. There was an old Xbox and very, very poor WiFi connection. A chilling rain began to fall that night. It was almost as if it were a sign of what my best friend and I could literally FEEL about to come. Lightning would flash sporadically as we sat in front of the old desktop computer in one of the camp offices. CNN was live streaming on their website as presumably the entire country was watching. "Not guilty." They said. The jury on July 13th, 2013, found George Zimmerman, murderer of Trayvon Martin, not guilty on all charges. As a barely 21-year-old man at the time, this was the moment it finally hit me. "I could be killed one day, and it wouldn't mean a thing." There was outrage. There was anger. But nothing was done.
        August 9th, 2014, something else happened. This was the fall semester after I had just pledged my fraternity. Most guys would be getting ready for parties and throwing events. But instead, my frat brothers and I marched through a rain-filled downtown Atlanta. A march we walked alongside the late Civil Rights activist and Congressman, John Lewis. This time for the life of 18-year-old Michael Brown. Not to mention Eric Garner, who was choked to death not even a month before. Once again, there were protests. But nothing changed.
        April 12th, 2015. This time it was Freddie Gray. I'm now 22 going on 23. Freddie Gray was 25. My thoughts begin to race. "Man. That's really close to my age. That could've been me." Baltimore was irate. I can still see the burning CVS building that became so infamous that night. Fox News saw it as a symbol of "ignorance and stupidity." CNN was a bit more delicate and saw it as a symbol of "revolution" and strength. I saw it as sadness. My mentee at the time was staying with me that night. As a matter of fact, he was about your age. Finishing up his 7th-grade year. I sat him down in front

of the TV and we watched the outrage together. He asked questions. Most of which I didn't have the answer to. But I gave him what I could and hoped it was enough to keep him informed. Once again, there were riots. But nothing changed.

And then there was . . .

Sandra Bland. Terence Crutcher. Atatiana Jefferson. Aura Rosser. Stephon Clark. Botham Jean. Philando Castille. Alton Sterling. Akai Gurley. Tamir Rice. Breonna Taylor. George Floyd. Rayshard Brooks. Elijah McClain. Ahmaud Arbery.

Jacob Blake. And so many more in between.

There are so many instances of blatant racism against Black people living in America that I literally forget some of them. Think about that. How many times do you think it takes to do something that you lose count of how many times you've done it? How many times have you brushed your teeth in your life? How many showers have you taken? How many skittles have you eaten? How many times have you gone to the park to play with your friends? How many times have you been driving around with your parents? These are things you literally can't count because you've done them so many times. THAT is the extent of this massive plague of a disease that is racism in America. Black people are not cared for in this country.

There's a lyric from hip-hop artist Pusha-T that states "CNN said I'd be dead by 21." There's another from Kanye West that goes "Wasn't supposed to make it past 25. [The] joke's on you, we still alive." Today, I am 28. My life was expected to end 7 years ago. And then again, 4 years after that. Somehow I've managed to make it past TWO expiration dates in my lifetime. But the harsh reality is so many people that look like me, Black people, men and women alike, don't get that privilege.

The time now reads 12:59 am on August 27th, 2020. Despite this overflow of words, I am truly speechless. I only have thoughts. I think about the time I was pulled over for speeding, and there were no street lights around for anyone to see what was going on. Sometimes, I think in hypotheticals. I think about my nephew or my future child just running on the playground and some prejudiced neighbor thinking he's doing something mischievous. I think about my best friend going to Target to purchase a TV and security tries to restrain him while they wait for the police to arrive because they thought he stole it. I think about taking out a life insurance policy so my loved ones will have the means to bury me. Bluntly speaking. I think about death. Often. And by no means is it because I want to die. My life is beautiful and I love to live it. And even though I don't know them, I'm sure the people listed above loved to live their lives too. But I think about death so much because every day I wake up, I know there's a possibility that there's someone who will see me as a threat. No matter how many homeless people I feed. No matter how many community services projects I create. No matter how many students I teach. There's a person who knows nothing about me, but because they don't like the color of my skin, they feel they have the right to harm me. I'm tired. There's like this massive weight of trying to navigate through two completely different worlds. One world where I have to work a job, pay bills, hang with friends, go to the doctor, dance, or just simply sleep. And then there's the other world where I have to do all of those things and watch my back at the same time because my existence is unacceptable for some.

It seems as though the world we live in is growing more cruel by the day. For Black people, it is. And every day I try to wake up and find just a little bit of hope somewhere. But I honestly think I'm running out of places to look. It's hard looking at people being happy when it feels like I'll never receive the common courtesy that I'm morally ENTITLED to. It's hard to even BE happy because the thought that "something bad is about to happen" sits in the corner of your mind and 9 times out of 10 when you think it, it's justified with a new hashtag being created.

I want a better world for you. I want a better reality for you. Because the reality I live in is surreal. To be the victim of oppression for 400 plus years just doesn't seem . . . real. I am so proud to be Black. It gives me a sense of pride. A sense of strength. A sense of purpose. But that has been a threat since I have existed.

I honestly don't know what's to come. The year 2020 has truly tried to outdo itself at every checkpoint. Be informed. Feel your feelings. Take care of yourself. Take care of one another.

Love, Mr. Howard

Student Spotlight: Days After Community Turmoil

The filled auditorium remains divided as I calmly sit with my hands clasped, my brown braids gracing my shoulders. A man approaches the podium. Shuffling papers, he reads, "You . . . trained a student *suicide bomber* and then . . . set her loose. Have you seen the videos on YouTube where your *suicide bomber* practiced her skills under the tutelage of one your progressive leftist teachers? Where your *suicide bomber* was nurtured and indoctrinated into her leftist ideology? We have. Just go to 'Soapbox' on YouTube." The crowd roars to my left. Peers and community members rise to give their standing ovation. To my right, people angrily shout, "Get him out!" "He has the right to say whatever he wants," the chairman of the Marquette Senior High School Board of Education passionately states into his microphone. The man was talking about me. On January 6, 2020, I was metaphorically described as a terrorist to my community.

Marquette, Michigan, a tourist town on the south shore of Lake Superior, was split on a controversial issue: The removal of Marquette Senior High School's "Redmen" mascot/nickname. Community members had contentiously debated the morality of the high school logo for over 20 years until October 2019, when two high school students painted their faces red with "war paint" at a football game. Indigenous peoples are 2% of both the U.S. population and the Marquette County population. In Marquette, the largest racial group, by far, is white, making up 93.2% of the county residents. It's important to question why people continue to hold biased beliefs about Indigenous peoples.

I had attempted to do just this as part of directed study for my senior year. The goal of my research and writing was, through education, awareness, and art, to increase visibility and accurate representation for Indigenous peoples and their cultures. Ultimately, my goal was to nurture a more accepting society within Marquette/the Upper Peninsula. As a part of my new academic endeavor, I participated in the Project Soapbox Mikva Challenge, a competition to promote civic engagement through 2-minute speeches about pressing issues in our country. Growing up as an Indigenous student reclaiming her Indigeneity, I learned many inaccuracies about my own history. I started to notice the relationship between the falsified history of marginalized people and the ignorance that perpetuates hate toward people of color, most prominently in my life being the derogatory "Redmen" mascot that crowns my high school. Thus, I challenged the narrative of my 93% white town with a speech titled "Moving Beyond Whitewashed History." I won the competition.

Afterward, I attended school board meetings to deliver public comments about the psychological, social, and cultural harms that derogatory Native imagery and nicknames inflict onto Indigenous youth and communities. However, the majority of my town continued to believe the "Redmen" nickname generated a positive, honoring school environment, and the issue exploded. I became the face of the "Redmen issue." Not only was I broadcasted as a *"suicide bomber"* to my entire community, but the school board failed to do their job: protect their students. I felt violated. Although I remained externally obedient, I left the meeting with more fire and drive than ever. I was motivated to positively change the narratives of the Indigenous peoples in my community while combating now glaringly evident, preexisting, lies.

The following day, I emailed the Marquette Area Public Schools Board of Education and expressed, in detail, my utter disappointment with the way in which the board members failed to protect me and my interests as a student. Out of the seven school board members, I received one response. The school board member asked me, "Why did he call you a suicide bomber? What was that in reference to?" The obliviousness that plagued the school board added to my disgust.

In thinking about the day after this meeting, I remember only silence. The incident was widely known across my school but was never discussed in any of my classes. The minimal support I received was private apologies from a few educators in between and after class.

There was just one teacher who supported me in the long days after. A few weeks later, one of my teachers reported to me that he had attended a Board of Education committee meeting to express his disappointment in the board's failure to promote a safe learning environment for students by remaining inactive on the mascot debate. My teacher voiced that he believed it would be a good idea for me to attend the next school board committee meeting because it would be a smaller, less-broadcasted setting where I would be less scrutinized by outside members of the community. In doing this, I would also be able to express—and even demand—my need for an apology from the school board on their failure to protect. I agreed.

My teacher helped me print off the Board of Education's antiharassment bylaws and policies. I highlighted the sections that the school board failed to implement at the January 6 meeting and the policies they had (and are) violating by championing a racially derogatory and psychologically harmful mascot within the school. We printed off five copies of the bylaws, one for each of the attendees at the meeting. I skipped class to attend the committee meeting and to deliver my public comment.

When it was time to share my voice, I first handed each member the highlighted Board of Education policies. I asserted that the mascot is in direct violation of the race/color harassment policy, as racial slurs and nicknames implying racial stereotypes are "strictly prohibited." Additionally, the policy explicitly states that the board will "investigate all allegations of unlawful harassment" and will take necessary steps to "remedy its effects." This did not occur. The only time the board intervened was when the president of the school board said that the community member had the "right to say whatever he wants."

After voicing my concerns about the various violations of bylaws, I asked the board members for an apology. None came and the meeting concluded. The committee members did, however, ask me to stay and chat. One of the members undermined every policy I brought up, claiming that the comment made indirectly toward me was not in violation of anything by "legal standards." This committee member claimed to have been in contact with local attorneys who had expressed this same sentiment. Then, the other committee members delivered inadequate, lackluster apologies, with one of them stating that "there are other Indigenous students who attend the school" so they "didn't know who the January 6th public comment was directed towards." Three of the board members stated that they were "sorry that had happened," but "there was nothing they could do to prevent the situation." Notably, because all of this discussion happened after the meeting had officially concluded, none of their even halfhearted apologies are on public record.

I swallowed my pride as I realized there would be no further action, no reconciliation, no reparations, and no justice resulting from communication with the Marquette Area Public Schools Board of Education. There was no further action taken by staff and administration. This was my final interaction with the Board of Education and one of my last days of in-person education in the Marquette school district as the COVID-19 pandemic began. In the words of Ojibwe and Michigan-based educator and poet Lois Beardslee in her essay, *What One Says, and Doesn't Say, to White Educators*: "How did sacrificing children to preserve the reputation of a school district or to prevent inconveniencing its public employees become the norm?" This is what my teachers did on the days after—they sacrificed me and my Indigenous peers by not publicly discussing anything that had happened. Their silence spoke volumes. Today, the "Redmen" nickname remains a vexing topic in my hometown. However, I will not let others impede my self-worth while I advocate for educational equity for people of color. This experience, which was intended to tear me down, was one of the most eye-opening experiences of my life and one that will forever leave a lasting imprint on me—and I hope how I acted in return leaves an even greater impact on my community.

Remaining strong and incredibly motivated with my braided hair shielding me and my ancestors guiding me, I will rise above.

(The quotes included at the beginning of this paper are direct quotes from the January 6 school board meeting. The Board of Education meeting was broadcasted by our local news station on social media and is still available to watch on their Facebook page.)

Author Bio: Bezhigonoodinkwe nindizhinikaaz. Marquette, Michigan nindoonjibaa. Migizi nindoodem. Miskwaabekong ojibwekwe nindaaw. Roxy Mashkawiziikwe Sprowl is from Marquette, Michigan. She is Eagle Clan and a citizen of the Red Cliff Band of Lake Superior Ojibwe. Roxy is a sophomore at Michigan State University studying social work, American Indian and Indigenous studies, and law, justice, and public policy. As a reconnecting Anishinaabekwe (Ojibwe woman), Roxy is a strong advocate for reformed, accurate history curricula in America. Additionally, as a survivor of the child welfare system, she values the power of sharing voices and experiences in order to change inequities and inequalities in American institutions. In Roxy's free time, she enjoys writing and performing poetry, beading, biking, and reading.

CHAPTER 3

Toward a Purpose for Freedom
Why Teach on Days After

> Education is always *for* something and *against* something else. . . . Education
> is not and can never be neutral. . . . At the deepest, most fundamental level,
> education stands either for human freedom and liberation, for enlighten-
> ment, or it stands for subjugation.
>
> —William Ayers (2005, p. 10)

When June heard about the walkout, she knew that her students would
want to be involved. But how, exactly, would that work? Her students
represented a wide range of identities and abilities, all high schoolers at
a school for students with disabilities in New York City. She was a social
studies teacher and team leader, supporting other teachers in their own
goals and pedagogies. Would it be possible to get them to Washington
Square Park, where thousands of others were expected to protest? Would
it be too difficult or dangerous? But, she reasoned, wasn't that the purpose
of the walkout in the first place: to address the difficult and dangerous
things happening in schools today? A school shooting in the United States
almost every week. This time, it was after Parkland.

In February 2018, a gunman killed 17 people and wounded 17 others
at Marjory Stoneman Douglas High School in Parkland, Florida. In the
weeks following the tragic event, student activists from the high school
(as well as the parents of those killed) launched a social media campaign
with the hashtag #NeverAgain. They also planned a mass school walkout
for that April, and thousands of youth around the country made plans
to march in solidarity. "There's something powerful in the fact that the
people who will have the deepest scars from the events of February 14—
people who would be expected to, say, be resting at home and mourning
lost friends," wrote *The Atlantic* journalist Isabel Fattal a few weeks after
the shooting, "are stepping up to do what, in their view, adults in the
political sphere aren't." Back in New York City, June's students wanted
to step up, too.

Reflecting on the choice to support the walkout—and not just to
support it, but to *explicitly* teach about it in class—June got teary-eyed,
as so many educators did while talking about these powerful days after

experiences. She laughed when I told her she was the third teacher I interviewed who had cried that day. "I guess that makes sense," she said, "this passion and these unexpected moments are what I love about students and what I love about teaching. I just wish it didn't have to happen this way." The story of June's students and their walkout is the answer to *why* engage in teaching on days after and why embrace it as a form of justice and equity-centered pedagogy.

Every semester, when I teach a class on power, privilege, and oppression in education, my students tell me that they have rarely talked about "these issues" in their previous schooling. "I learned more in 15 weeks than I did in my previous 15 years of schooling," a student once wrote on an evaluation. And while I am glad they learn so much, I am deeply grieved that so many reach 18 years without having had a classroom experience centered on dialogues about the most important things in our world: themselves and each other. But it doesn't mean they didn't talk about "these issues" with friends, just that they didn't do it in the facilitated space of a classroom. Gemma, a middle school English teacher, sees this reality as a prime reason to teach on days after: "Students are going to have the conversation whether we make space for it or not, but if we're not making space for it, then the conversation happens on the bus, in the hallways, and in the locker room, and it's not facilitated. I feel really committed to making sure that my students have a facilitated space for conversation. I won't pretend to make my space safe because that's out of my control, unfortunately. I would love to say, yes, our classroom is a safe space, but I honestly think that's a lie, because for some students, they feel their emotional safety is threatened every day at school. Trying to make facilitated spaces and brave spaces feels important."

This chapter argues that teaching on days after is a pedagogy of justice and equity. I describe the purpose of Days After Pedagogy (DAP), including that it supports students' agency and voice, that it works against oppression, that it is trauma responsive, that it offers a space for transformation and transformative learning, and that it is sustaining for students' and teachers' identities.

DAYS AFTER PEDAGOGY SUPPORTS STUDENT AGENCY AND VOICE

Teaching on days after gives students a chance to see themselves as active in the world and gives them models for how to respond to challenging issues. This pedagogy supports student agency and voice in that students are the driving force behind what is happening in the classroom. Some teachers fear that too much student choice can lead to conversations that are "too political." When I asked her what she thought about the argument that teachers weren't supposed to be political, Ann, a middle school teacher who I taught as an undergraduate, responded, "Well, here's the thing, and I learned this from you. I just ask why. Why do you think this? It's not like, 'Hey guys, we're going to go out and we're going to protest this and we're going to do that.' I'm like, 'Oh, you know, here's some ways that has been handled. What does that make you want to do? Want to learn more? Okay, good. Well, here's some resources for you. . . .' I am giving them that student-led choice to let them be powerful in their own agency."

Today's students are often consumed by test-preparation and teach-to-the-test models of instruction that focus more on outcomes than on the process of learning (Au, 2007; Kumashiro, 2015). Even though Freire wrote about it decades ago (originally in 1970), the banking model of education is alive and well, where teachers deposit knowledge into students' heads and they memorize and regurgitate it without much critical thinking, self-reflection, or engagement (Freire, 1972). Agency, on the other hand, occurs when someone can "intentionally make things happen by one's actions" (Bandura, 2001, p. 2). When students have agency, they are demonstrating their "capacity to act in ways that exhibit their own choices in their learning, informed by their beliefs and careful consideration, self-regulation, and self-reflection about their ability to control and take ownership of their own learning" (Moses et al., 2020, p. 2). Students with agency are "empowered thinkers who take initiative in their learning and do so purposefully" (Robertson et al., 2020, p. 2). Teachers nurture this empowerment in myriad ways, often through social justice–focused and asset-based pedagogies that offer students a chance to be agentic, such as culturally sustaining pedagogy, critical pedagogy, and participatory action research (Paris & Alim, 2017; Barton & Tan, 2010).

Days after are opportune moments to make space for student agency in the classroom, to make space for what students are feeling and want to know more about. While I argue later that DAP is also important even if students don't think they need to know (especially when students are from dominant identity groups and may not understand the relevance of a topic of injustice for their communities), at its heart, teaching on days after is about allowing students to make choices for their learning in the service of their current and future humanization.

From Observers to Participants:
A Student Walkout and Protest in New York City

June has been teaching for 14 years and has been at her current school for students with disabilities for the past 10. Although she was prepared as an elementary educator, she now relishes the opportunity to teach high school humanities and support other teachers in her administrative role. The students at her school are predominantly students of color. June is white and in her late 30s, and she sees it as her "responsibility to help students make sense of the world around them: the printed world, the human experience, and how we react and respond to different events." June shared a story about a meaningful experience about teaching on days after school shootings. Because she is not sure how many families share with their children about tragedies like this and because of the vast array of abilities represented in her students, she is often cautious about bringing it up in class initially. But then, the spirit of activism that swept the nation caught her students' attention in the wake of yet another shooting at a high school in Parkland, Florida. June recalled, "There was a lot of student interest in the walkouts that were happening. I felt it was very important and I wanted to hear some of the initiation from students. That was the whole point. Students [were] the center of the protests. So the moment I realized that we had students who wanted to bring it up independently, we made sure that they had the ability and the tools to participate. I felt my responsibility with my team was to be able to make this event accessible to them and make sure that, in whichever way they wanted to participate, we were there to make that happen and support them."

June went to the administration and got their support for broadening the scope beyond her single classroom, for "a whole school opt-in opportunity," as she called it. This meant that all social studies teachers were teaching about gun control, gun violence, and governmental rules and regulations. June remembered, "We knew that not every student had the same foundation of knowledge to make an informed decision of whether or not to participate [in the walkout]. We significantly altered our curriculum for that time period to make sure that our students had the facts and then they made their own informed decisions. Every student had an access point to this topic."

"The students were able to also choose at what level they felt most comfortable participating," June explained. "About 55 percent chose to walk out, and most of them wanted to walk to Washington Square Park where we knew that there was going to be a gathering of other schools. When we got there, our students immediately joined in the 17 minutes of silent protesting and holding signs." For other students who "expressed a hesitation about a large group setting," June and her team helped "brainstorm alternative ways to protest. They could still be included in the experience, but also accommodate some social anxiety. Those students did a march right near the school building and created their own smaller protest."

When June began reflecting on the experience, she started to get emotional. "One of the memorable pieces of the whole thing was when students came back with this sense of amazement that strangers were thanking them and commenting to them. There's still such a misunderstanding of special education and individuals with special needs, and there's just a lack of patience, generally speaking, for people who 'look different' or 'act different.' The whole community immediately recognized what their mission was and I felt like they saw them as students first, not as kids with special needs. They knew what they were standing up for. It was about their rights for safety and more from their government. And it was just awesome."

I asked June about parental support for the walkouts and teaching about these topics. Many new teachers, especially, express fear of ramifications if they address topics like this in their classroom, and I was curious how parents reacted. "We told the families, your child has the right to choose to participate tomorrow. We informed the families that students would be offered the choice. We did not ask permission [to talk about it]. Parents reacted very positively. They also reacted very positively to know that there were options other than Washington Square Park. I did plan for potential worst-case scenarios to make sure that we had plans for in case it became a target [for more gun violence]. That was a big concern, so we planned for the worst, and the best happened."

What was even more impressive about this particular example of DAP was that it was not done in isolation, and June and her students were able to build on this "ton of momentum" to create sustained justice-oriented efforts, all aimed at supporting students' civic agency. As June said, "Students were able to utilize their own strengths." A critical component of giving students agency in their learning, as demonstrated well in this example from June's school, is that DAP informs what happens in and outside the classroom. The pedagogy goes beyond the classroom walls. First, June created an extracurricular group called Student Activists for Change (SAC). SAC had monthly lunchtime meetings and included both students and teachers who were "so excited to be involved." At one meeting, students made postcards to mail to local representatives. At another meeting, students practiced making phone calls to elected officials. Other students made signs to hang up around the school about a second walkout, organized by SAC. A month later, students walked out of class again and marched around the neighborhood. June remembered, smiling wistfully, "Students were chanting again. People were leaning out of their apartment windows, joining in the chants. Later, the kids were talking about the trucks honking at them in support, and it just was amazing."

Importantly, June's students had a say in whether or not this issue was addressed in class, and they had a say in what was done and how it was done. As a result, they were able to feel agentic in their learning—as students and as citizens. June noted that, while the purpose of teaching on days after is not to meet standards, it certainly does achieve the goal, as well, referencing civic engagement learning standards. "We have our standards to back up what we're doing, if anyone were to question it. It's not an agenda; it's a life skill."

Critiquing Criminal Justice: Student-Led Research on Days After

Toby has also been teaching for more than a decade. A self-identified cisgender white man, Toby is a model for other white men for how to engage in antiracist and critical pedagogy in the classroom. Teaching on days after is one way that Toby takes up his antiracist practice. As a high school English teacher in an urban-emergent city in Colorado, Toby sees many opportunities to use DAP to advance student agency and voice. One example is what happened in his classroom in the wake of the shooting of Michael Brown in Ferguson, Missouri. Brown, an 18-year-old Black man, was shot and killed by a white police officer while unarmed and walking home one evening in August 2014. Massive protests began in Ferguson and elsewhere as part of the Black Lives Matter movement's demands for racial justice and an end to police brutality and killing of Black folks.

In his 12th-grade English class, Toby taught a media literacy unit (one that was "already out there" that he adapted for his students) on media reports that speculated about the reasons that the officer would have had for killing Brown and what he might have been doing before he was stopped. The coverage was dehumanizing for Brown, his family, and other victims, and there was wide social commentary on the racist coverage that followed, treating Black victims worse than white killers. Students were engaged and interested in the topic, so Toby followed it up with a "mini research unit where they jumped off from one of the things that we talked about that they were interested in learning more about." For the follow-up project, Toby recalled, "A lot of my Black students wanted to do more research on police brutality and police shootings." This made Toby "a little wary" because he knew that other teachers might assume that having Black students in class means "they must want to read this article about police brutality and police shooting cause it's an issue that would affect them. But the uncritical part of that is how some teachers don't think about why would students want to read about things that are very violently real, existentially threatening to them. It's a fine line." In this particular case, Toby offered the students agency in their choices and "a lot of them actually did want to take that opportunity to read more about what was happening."

On other days after, Toby takes a similar approach by allowing students to lead the inquiry. He relayed one memory that "really stuck out" to him when the class was discussing the verdict in the trial of the police officer who shot Laquan McDonald. McDonald, a young Black man living in Chicago, was 17 years old when he was shot 16 times and killed by a white police officer in 2014, just several months after Michael Brown's murder. The officer and 16 others were later charged with conspiracy to cover up the killing when they lied and said that McDonald lunged at the officer with a knife, despite video that showed that the officer opened fire mere seconds after pulling up behind McDonald walking down the street. It was 4 years later when the officer was finally convicted. In Toby's class, one Black student began to do additional research during this day after discussion, and he found out how long the officer was sentenced to jail: 6 years. In class, everyone was astonished. "My uncle," the student shared, "Got way more than that for weed possession." Toby remembers that the student "had this moment where he's sitting back at his desk and just asking me, 'That's the amount of time he got? For shooting this kid 16 times? And my uncle. . . . '" Toby's voice trailed off sadly before he explained that, even in Colorado where marijuana is now legalized, the student's uncle was convicted before that, so is still in prison. The student then chose to engage in further research not just about police brutality but about inequality of prison sentences based on race.

He especially remembers his undocumented students asking, "Did you hear about this? Can we talk about this in class?" on days after events related to immigration, such as when Trump canceled DACA (Deferred Action for Childhood Arrivals), a program established by President Obama to allow those without documentation to remain in the country and have temporary legal status, and later when Trump instituted a travel ban on seven Muslim-majority countries, banned entry for Syrian refugees, and significantly delayed entry for other refugees. For them, "It isn't something that *happens* to come across their social media timelines or they *happen* to catch on the news. It's something that's obviously very, very real to their lived experience," so it's especially meaningful for him that they "have been the most vocal with following up and saying, 'Thank you for giving us a place to engage.'"

DAYS AFTER PEDAGOGY WORKS AGAINST OPPRESSION

Many teachers who see themselves as committed to justice and equity are still anxious or fearful about teaching on days after because those days seem, often, to be too politically charged or partisan. They are worried that they will be perceived as biased by administration, parents, students, or colleagues. Yet because Days After Pedagogy cannot be done well in isolation, there is hopefully nothing "new" that would come up about a teacher's identity and positionality on days after that students should not already know. The concern that a teacher's stances and personal beliefs are suddenly going to be revealed on a day after negates the fact that they have likely already been revealed before, *if* the teacher is truly teaching for justice and equity. Students should not suddenly discover that their teacher cares about trans students on a day after. Students should not suddenly realize that their teacher supports Black Lives Matter or the right of all children to learn in healthy and safe spaces on a day after. Students should already know their teacher's position on these issues, even if it has never been explicitly stated.

One of the foremost purposes of Days After Pedagogy is to work against oppression, or the continued marginalization of some groups over others based on socially constructed identity markers. As discussed in Chapter 2, oppression occurs when "polices, practices, norms, and traditions . . . [are used to] systematically exploit one social group (the target group) by another (the dominant group) for the dominant group's benefit" (Sensoy & DiAngelo, 2009, p. 345). When we talk about oppression, we are not talking (only) about individual acts of prejudice, but rather prejudice plus power (social, ideological, and institutional). Teaching on days after is a way to fight against oppression and to highlight for and with students the opportunities they have to join in the struggle. It is not enough to "recognize" that oppression is happening, although that is certainly a first step if you are teaching students from a dominant group who have been taught and socialized to not see injustice if it does not directly affect them. As Kumashiro (2015) writes, "Challenging oppressions requires more than raising awareness about more progressive perspectives on the world. The reason we fail to do more to challenge oppression is not merely that we do not know enough about oppression, but also that we often do not WANT to know more about oppression. It is not our lack of knowledge but our resistance to knowledge and our desire for ignorance that often prevent us from changing the oppressive status quo" (p. 27). Teaching on days after pushes against this resistance.

In Sophia's elementary classroom in New York City, part of fighting against oppression is teaching students how to navigate "the system" of oppression and work against it. Sophia identifies as a mixed-race Puerto Rican Latina and has been working as an inclusion teacher for 22 years. She teaches all subjects for 4th- and 5th-graders in an urban school. Sophia ensures that her students know that school itself is part of the system: "Teaching is political. We can't say that it's apolitical because politics controls everything: what we can teach and what we can't teach, who determines what's acceptable. Systemically, this education system wasn't necessarily set up for everyone's success. I need to teach my students to be critical. I need to show them this is a system. It isn't broken. It works exactly the way it's supposed to work." Beyond that criticality, however, Sophia also believes that supporting her students within an oppressive system means teaching them the structures and skills needed to succeed in what currently exists. Gutiérrez (2009), a scholar in math education, would call this "playing the game to change the game." In thinking about her students' future, Sophia sees the need for immediate and long-term work against oppression: "How do we navigate the system, right? There are some things that we can do to kind of play the system, as well. How do we put those two things together where we're critical, where we're learning stuff that is really meaningful, but also learning the things that we're supposed to learn so that we can navigate the system? Because our students don't have time for us to change the system. I'll keep working on changing the system by disrupting it. But they only have 8 to 12 years before they have to move on. The system isn't going to change in 8 to 12 years. So I've got three jobs: critical learning, play the system, while I change the system. That's my job, not their job; although, as we're doing this critical learning, I'm hoping that they'll join."

Some days after lessons that work against oppression do so on a very local scale, like the lessons described by Chris, an elementary school teacher in a small city in New England. Chris, a white man in his mid-30s, has been a teacher for 4 years. He teaches a bilingual class with newcomer immigrant students and talked with me about a lesson on transgender identity and pronouns. (For more information on gender pronouns and why they matter, there are great resources for all ages at www.mypronouns.org.) This was borne out of conversations after their classroom math tutor, a volunteer college student, had come to class with several different forms of gender expression. When the students and families asked questions about this, Chris decided it was time to address it the next day. Because Chris did not want to put the burden for educating the class on the tutor himself, he chose to address "baseline important issues" like the person's name and pronouns. He told the students "I'm going to call him 'him' and 'he'" because that is how the tutor had introduced himself and connected it back to the four community agreements of the class. These agreements, posted in the classroom in both Spanish and English, were respect diversity, celebrate growth, work to the max, and share peace. Indeed, Chris had already heard a student referencing the agreements when the math tutor was present. "I heard one student say to another, 'Respect diversity. We don't have time for that rudeness because this is a rule.' In some cases, that's all a 10-year-old needs to know: people are different. We have lots of differences here and outside in the world. Let's keep learning math." So to prepare for the tutor's next visit, Chris supported his students in learning specific things about trans identities (like pronouns) and built on "tons of curiosity about learning about stuff that matters," as well as their personal connections to transgender people in their lives. In discussions like this, "we do the work of helping to affirm that trans people are great and cool," Chris added. Importantly, these days after lessons are tied to Chris's vision for a classroom rooted in social justice and antioppressive learning, echoing ideas of leading scholars like Freire, Muhammad, and Ladson-Billings: "I feel like I get to do the work of social justice when they are not just the people who I am doing the work *upon*, but doing the work *with*, and they get to think through their own values."

DAYS AFTER TEACHING REDEFINES "RELEVANCE"

Some of the stories that did not make this book are from teachers who said that they did not think that many days after events were relevant for their students, either because of age or identity. When asked why they would teach on days after, they said things like, "If it's relevant to their lives, I'd address it." On the surface, and in some cases, this is a logical statement. Aiming for "relevance" is something that, in fact, we empha-size in educator preparation programs via culturally relevant pedagogy (Ladson-Billings, 1995).

Too often, however, ignoring the vast body of literature on what it actually means, "relevance" is reduced to issues that the students already know about or want to know about. This reinforces norms that there are certain things students can discuss and certain things they cannot, which stigmatizes those topics that are perceived to be untouchable. But what happens when your students don't know what they don't know? What happens when a group of white upper-middle-class students don't know about police brutality and the ongoing murder of Black and Brown individuals in communities not that far from their own? Relying on this reductionist definition of relevance maintains inequitable power dynamics and oppression because those in privileged communities who do not *have* to know about injustice may not *want* to know about injustice and thus may deem it "irrelevant."

DAP does not have to be something students already know or care about to be important. Too often, teachers use this as an excuse to avoid talking about difficult topics with students whom they fear may be re-sistant to those conversations. For example, too many white teachers of white students say these things don't matter for their students. However, white teachers need to teach for justice on days after not just for their stu-dents but for their colleagues of color who should not be the only people tasked with talking about these issues.

Maya, a high school journalism teacher in a suburban district in the Midwest, reflects on this challenge of making days after events relevant to her primarily white, middle-class student population who see themselves as disconnected from the realities of many marginalized communities. Maya, a white woman, had been teaching for 6 years. She pondered what she would do if a student was dismissive during a days after conversation that related to a larger social issue. Such comments, Maya noted, could be considered racist "because if you're not concerned about, for example, attacks on mosques, you're accessing your white privilege because you don't have to think about it. It doesn't directly impact you." She won-dered aloud about how to deal with students who say they are so sick of talking about this. Because "they don't have a person" they know who is affected, in their insular white communities, Maya "can see their point.

I can see why they would think that: 'I don't have Muslim friends, so it doesn't matter to me.' But look, they're humans! So how do I convey that importance to them?"

For Gemma, this is where what she calls radical empathy comes in. Gemma is a white woman in her 30s and has been teaching for 9 years in the same state where she grew up in a very small city in New England. She currently teaches 6th-grade English and social studies. In reflecting on teaching against oppression on days after, she first notes that "if I know that I have students in the classroom that occupy an identity under threat, we make time. I think about my own education growing up and I feel like, how did I not know these things were happening? I feel kind of a responsibility to have my students not walk away in that unknowing space. If it's an event that happens and there's national conversation about it, I want us to have a conversation about it." This means Gemma is leading her students in discussions that may not seem immediately "relevant" to them. To a teacher who might question this strategy, Gemma "would first have some questions and wonderings about the identity of that teacher. That's not something that I hear my colleagues of color say. I hear it most often from white teachers who don't feel the personal impacts themselves. I think the first place I might go is a little bit of a reflection around identity and the privileges that allow that statement to be said aloud. Then look for some radical empathy. Increasingly, I'm recognizing that I will never truly understand the deep emotional labor, trauma, and perspective of folks who experience daily racism and anti-indigeneity in this country. Putting radical before empathy comes with that level of recognition that there's this attempt to get to the root of larger systems that I really can only ever understand from my position within that system." This approach to DAP combats false empathy because it requires action and not just white savior-type statements and supposedly antiracist stances. In later chapters, we return to Gemma's classroom to see examples of how this stance translates into practice.

DISRUPTING WHITENESS:
PUSHING AGAINST "TWO SIDES" ON DAYS AFTER

The middle is a point equidistant from two poles. That's it. There is nothing inherently virtuous about being neither here nor there. Buried in this
is a false equivalency of ideas, what you might call the "good people on
both sides" phenomenon. When we revisit our shameful past, ask yourself, Where was the middle? Rather than chattel slavery, perhaps we could
agree on a nice program of indentured servitude? Instead of subjecting
Japanese-American citizens to indefinite detention during WWII, what if we
had agreed to give them actual sentences and perhaps provided a receipt
for them to reclaim their things when they were released? What is halfway
between moral and immoral?

—Tayari Jones (2018)

Multiple educators spoke at length about the importance of using
days after to disrupt whiteness at the individual, institutional, and
ideological levels (Matias, 2016). As discussed in Chapter 2, working against whiteness means critiquing how whiteness has come to be
normalized in society and then finding ways to disrupt that, to make
it seem not the only "normal." For these teachers, they saw working against whiteness as a critical component of working against oppression: naming racism and white supremacy and refusing to debate
other people's humanity. Some things are just not debatable; there is
no need to find "common ground" or the "moral middle," as Tayari
Jones (2018) writes: "There's nothing virtuous about finding common ground." Such is the case for "debates" about white supremacy
and racism. Gemma and Toby feel strongly about their stance on this
issue, and I include our conversations here at length to illustrate the
power and nuance of Gemma and Toby's thinking about this particular element of teaching on days after. In Chapter 5, other teachers share their stories of how their own identities and positionalities
relate to DAP.

First, Gemma and I were discussing whether or not a teacher sharing
her perspective with students was working for or against oppression. I
asked her this in response to seeing a tweet of hers that mentioned the importance of students knowing teachers' politics and beliefs. It seemed she
was advocating for teachers to disclose to students (Hess, 2009), a view
not shared by many educators (and definitely not many administrators or
policymakers).

Alyssa: What do you think about sharing your perspective with your
students?

Gemma: You know, I think students already know. . . . We're not
fooling anybody. I think our students are deeply aware of our
politics. I think they're very intuitive. And by politics I mean both
big P and little p. I have been very clear that the classroom is not a
space for bigotry, and that the language that is used by the person
occupying the highest office [President Trump, at the time] is not
language that I accept in the classroom. In moments like that, it
becomes pretty clear to students where I fall. I've also had honest
conversations about why I don't use debate in the classroom.
I know students love debate as a format. It's so fun, right? It's
competitive and there's a winner. It plays into so many ways of
being, especially in early adolescence, that kids just love. But I
talk pretty openly about the fact that I'm not going to create space
for students' humanity to be debated. And it's too often in issues
like immigration, for example, it becomes a debate about "who's
allowed to be here," and that's just not acceptable.

Alyssa: And what do students say when you tell them that?

Gemma: It's on a rare occasion that a deeply conservative student—and
we have many—will go back and forth with me. I don't want to
center those students in relationships, because honestly I think
they're centered in every other classroom. There are times when
I'm like, "Oh, this space might be deeply uncomfortable if you're
a white cis male student with privilege." And then I think, "Oh,
but every other space is comfortable. So that's probably okay." I
struggle with that a little bit. I had a student a few years ago who
was really willing to kind of go back and forth with me, and we
did a little bit of that in front of the class 'cause I wanted them
to see us engage in what that looks like. And then I would also
pause and say, "You know, it sounds like we're going down a
tangent. This conversation is of value to me. Let's circle back to
it in the break, and anyone's welcome to join us." It is interesting
to be in the position of teacher because there's a power imbalance
there. I recognize that the things that I'm offering and saying
in my classroom are automatically coming with the weight of
my position. That's tricky. I also am comfortable wielding that
position in power to continually try to decenter whiteness in my
classroom.

I asked Gemma what decentering whiteness looked like in practice in
her classroom, especially on days after. For her, it meant "really disrupting who we're reading, following the work of #DisruptTexts, and making
sure that, as a white woman, I'm constantly trying to bring in voices that
aren't mine into my classroom." She reflected on the high national aver-
age of teachers who are white, which was even higher in her rural New

England town: 97.1%. "For most of my students, I look like every other teacher they're going to have. So both for my students of color but also for my white students, I think it's critically important that they're hearing from other people."

Across the country, in Colorado, Toby feels similarly about the importance of not debating the "two sides" of some issues and the importance of fighting against oppression on days after. On the day after members of Congress were advocating for the Equality Act as a means to "push back against a lot of the anti-LGBTQ legislation coming from the Trump administration," Toby recalls working with his 9th-grade class on a news article. Originally introduced in 2015, the bill, passed in 2019 by a Democrat-controlled House of Representatives, aimed to extend civil rights protections to those identifying as LGBTQ. During class that day, "a student asked me if we were going to 'read anything from the other side.' I didn't think that she meant the question maliciously because actually I know that she is part of the school's Gay Straight Alliance. I didn't believe that her question was from the viewpoint of like, 'Can I express what I feel about the LGBTQ community in a negative way?' I think it actually was more from a standpoint of curiosity. . . . But it became an opportunity for me to frame this: There are some issues that we'll read about where maybe there will be a 'some people believe this, but some people believe this, more than one side sort of thing.' But with LGBTQ rights, the starting point isn't going to be whether or not we would agree with the person's identity. We're not going to call into question people's identities. We're going to assume the humanity of those whose lives we are reading about and move forward from there in terms of what's the best way to affirm these lives." Toby recalls that such a stance "felt like a helpful framework" for the students to understand why they were reading some articles that were "unapologetically one-sided" and "why that is an okay stance for them to take."

As with other teachers, I asked Toby if he ever got pushback to the idea of teaching "only" one side or talking so explicitly about disrupting white supremacy. "There was a particular parent who was upset with my curriculum a couple of years ago and was accusing me of it being heavily biased. That's how she framed it: 'Your curriculum is too political.' But my response to her was that choosing to teach only dead white authors is also a political choice," Toby remembered. "She did not have a counter-argument. I think that that was the first time that she considered that kind of take. She asked, 'Why are you teaching James Baldwin, Toni Morrison, and Gloria Steinem?'" It was Toby's first semester of a new doctoral program focused on social justice, so he was making concerted efforts to "push things, as far as the voices that I wanted to have in my classroom." He knew that his students—high school juniors—had already been thoroughly exposed to the "dead white guy literary canon" in 9th and 10th grades, so he wanted to "use [his] position to select texts that were going to be things that they weren't getting elsewhere." Toby chose some of these texts on days after, in the form of articles that critiqued white supremacy and argued "unapologetically" for one side. Toby was similarly unapologetic in his commitment to social and racial justice.

By disrupting whiteness in their classrooms, Gemma and Toby demonstrate what it means to make Black lives matter at school: "Some educators have been accused of politicizing students by daring to hold discussions about institutional racism. But students are already having these conversations: in hallways, on playgrounds, in lunchrooms, and online. Now more than ever students need to be encouraged to have these discussions in the classroom. Educators must ask themselves whether they will encourage open exchange about racial justice or if they would rather have school be a place that marginalizes the main concerns of their students' lives" (Hagopian, 2020, np).

DAYS AFTER PEDAGOGY RESPONDS TO TRAUMA IN A MEANINGFUL WAY

"It was as if we had entered an alternate universe," Brandon told me, "And our teachers there didn't know about anything that was happening on our planet." What was happening on his planet was that Trayvon Martin had been murdered while walking home with a bag of Skittles and an iced tea. Martin's senseless murder and the subsequent claims that he was killed in self-defense, despite a 911 recording telling neighborhood watch member George Zimmerman not to approach him, spurred a movement: Black Lives Matter. Although older now, Brandon had been Trayvon's age at the time. "No teacher talked about it," he continued, "So I wasn't sure if they just didn't know, or if they didn't care, or what." When I asked how this made him feel, he answered quickly and decisively: "It was traumatic." He elaborated, saying that, as a young Black child, "both what happened *and* that no one cared to talk about it—both were traumatic."

Far too often, I hear teachers saying that school is meant to prepare students for the "real world," as if school is not part of the real world, as if the real world is not already happening around our students both in and out of the classroom. We cannot pretend that students' lives are not deeply affected by the world. Indeed, is there a realer world than the one of the classroom, in which students are learning to find themselves, to discover who they are in concert with others, to learn about what matters to them, and to develop as people? Sophia summarizes this tension well, reflecting on what she used to think as a new teacher: "I was like that earlier in my career, thinking that math and writing and the school were a safe haven from the real world. But school is part of the community. We *have* to be part of the community, and what the community is dealing with are these real-life situations." Days after teaching responds to real-world trauma in a meaningful way in that teachers who use DAP refuse to ignore the potential emotional responses that students may be having to world events.

DAYS AFTER PEDAGOGY IS A FORM OF TRAUMA-RESPONSIVE TEACHING

After the 2016 presidential election, my colleagues, Beth Sondel and Hannah Carson Baggett, and I undertook a research project to investigate teachers' pedagogical decisionmaking. We anticipated perhaps 40 or 50 responses to a questionnaire that asked teachers what they did and how they felt about it. We were surprised to get over 700 responses from teachers all over the country, and this told us that teachers needed a chance to talk about what happened in those days. Many of their responses were full of emotion and struggle. The responses that resonated the most with us were those that described teachers' attempts to respond to students' deeply felt and emotional reactions to the news that Donald Trump had been elected president. For these educators, we found they engaged in a "pedagogy of political trauma." (For more information on trauma-responsive pedagogy, see Chapter 2.)

The teachers I interviewed for this book shared similar experiences, as you'll read in later chapters. Indeed, the day after the 2016 election was the most frequently discussed day after across all of the interviews. There could be many reasons for this—the number of years participants had been teaching, the communities in which most of them taught that would make the election a salient event, or the mass media coverage of the event overall—but one thing is for sure: There was no escaping the emotional impact of the election in many classrooms across the country.

In Scarlet's 5th-grade classroom in New York City, the trauma was palpable. Scarlet, a white woman in her early 30s, had been teaching for 9 years. Before she saw her students that day, her principal called a staff meeting. In general, leading up to the election, there had been "an assumption in the community that I'm working with, both in terms of the students and the families and most of the teachers, we kind of went without saying we're all on the same page, that this [Trump's candidacy] is not a good thing." At the staff meeting, in a circle with colleagues, Scarlet's principal let teachers cry and then "invited us to make space for that in the classrooms, as well." While Scarlet said she "didn't necessarily need the invitation," she appreciated that her principal—a Haitian woman of color and career New York City educator—was explicitly supportive.

Indeed, as our research showed, this was not the case for many teachers around the country who were told not to talk about the election (Dunn, Sondel, & Baggett, 2018; Sondel, Baggett, & Dunn, 2017). Scarlet and her co-teacher had already been implementing "circle time using restorative justice practices" and had briefly talked about the election.

That morning, Scarlet, her co-teacher, and their 10- and 11-year-old students of color sat in a circle and began a conversation. There was "not a lot of structure to it; we just held a space for them to chat." It was an emotional conversation, where both teachers and some of the students were crying. The students were confused, Scarlet recalls, with some of them saying, "We've joked about Trump, but now it's, Oh my God, this really is happening." In particular, Scarlet talked about one African American student speaking up: "I remember him distinctly [saying], 'I'm just afraid I'm going to get shot in the street.'" Scarlet remembers "feeling this tension" of not knowing exactly what to say, of wanting to legitimize the sense of fear and vulnerability but also wanting to assuage his fears and say, "No, you're going to be okay." But she couldn't do that, because she knew the reality was that she could never promise him that. In the end, Scarlet agreed that that was the "reality of our country" but that "Trump coming into office, especially here in New York City, doesn't mean our day-to-day reality is going to change immediately right now." In later conversations throughout the year, Scarlet returned to this moment. She wanted her students to recognize both the danger of his policies and that he was "symbolic of what is a deeper issue in our country." In these later social studies units, "I wove in more civics lessons around things like Congress and House of Representatives because I really wanted the kids to see that Trump is not the only issue here. He is part of a bigger system that is creating this sort of oppression."

But on that day, after the election, big civics lessons were not to be had. It was focused mostly on supporting students through the trauma of Trump being elected. Another meaningful part of the day for Scarlet was collaborating with a 1st-grade teacher who "wasn't sure what to say to her kids. She knew that I was more comfortable with restorative practices and having these tougher conversations. She was wondering if the fifth graders could do something." So, with the help of Scarlet and her students, at the end of the day, the 1st- and 5th-grade students met up in the dance room, one of the school's bigger spaces. They sat in a large circle and Scarlet "made the fifth graders intersperse, spread out, with the first graders between [them]," acting as "hosts." Following a little chime, the 5th graders then modeled for the 1st graders some breathing exercises, and a dialogue began like it had earlier in the morning. Only this time, the 5th graders led it. "It was really interesting to see them," as they repeated some of the things Scarlet had said to "ease them" earlier, making it "kind of their version to the little kids." Hearing this was powerful for Scarlet, as it showed they heard her and that it resonated with them. Although the trauma was still present for all ages on this day, likely this DAP made a positive difference for them.

Trauma-responsive DAP can also be more localized. For example, in later chapters, we will hear how other educators responded to local hate crimes and community devastation. Sometimes these moments that start out as local then become national, as in the case of Eric Garner, killed in 2014 by police after a confrontation outside a convenience store where he was selling loose cigarettes. In the video that later went viral, spurred on the Black Lives Matter movement, and inspired a hashtag and rally-ing cry of activists, viewers could hear Eric Garner gasp his last words: "I can't breathe." In 2019, the police officer who killed Garner was tried and found not guilty. At the time, Sophia was teaching 2nd grade in New York City, close to Garner's home in Staten Island. Sophia described what happened the day after the not guilty verdict came out. "I remember feel-ing crushed to the point where I was going to call out of work." Instead, she made a decision as she headed to school: "I remember walking to work, as a woman who is Latina but fair skinned, which has certain privi-leges." She remembers thinking that she did not know what it would be like to be a Black man, so, on this day, she had to "make sure that I don't take up that space. So my decision was not to talk about it at all."

But, as many teachers know, on days after, sometimes what we want doesn't actually matter at all. The students often have other plans, as Sophia's did that day. When they arrived at school, they were carrying the free newspapers they received on the subway, "waving the newspaper at me, saying 'Can you believe this?' And at that moment I realized, holy crap, right? I wasn't planning to talk about this because emotionally, you know, 'me, me, me.' But it looks like these kids want to talk about this. They want a space where they can understand what's going on, but also to voice what they're feeling." So Sophia did what the best teachers do, and she changed her plans for the day and responded to the trauma her students were experiencing. She invited them to a morning meeting and wrote "Not Guilty" on the board and "just had them talk." Students said things like, "I don't understand; they didn't find any cigarettes on him" and "If he was saying, I can't breathe. . . ." Sophia's voice trails off as she's telling the story. "It was almost therapeutic," she continues, and I'm not sure if she means for the students, or for her—and it's likely both. Their conversation continued as the students brought up Black Lives Matter because "a lot of them could hear from their windows at night, you know, the chants of the protesters. Some of them participated in the Black Lives Movement." During that discussion, Sophia recalls a powerful moment between two students who she described as a Latina girl and a Black boy. The young girl said, "But it shouldn't be Black Lives Matter. It should be all lives matter because all lives do matter." Sophia was about to respond because she did not want her Black students to have to defend themselves, but another student spoke quickly, "turn[ed] to [his classmates], and said, 'Yes, all lives do matter. But the police are killing people who look like me.' Oh my God. In that moment, you could see her understanding, right? There was this mutual respect and this mutual love for each other."

In discussing why responding to students' trauma on days after matters, Sophia thoughtfully reflected, "Even in moments where I don't want to talk about things because I'm still healing, I need to understand that when I go into that classroom, those kids, they need to heal. They need to be heard. They may or may not have spaces at home to talk about this and to develop it and to write about it and to advocate for it. We want them to be agents of social change. I can't do this by myself. And they want to be part of it. This is part of their community. This is part of their history. In a couple of years, they're going to be reading about this in history books or their children will, and it's like, why didn't we talk about this when I was in school?" Sophia illustrates here a powerful example of how DAP can lead to healing, learning, and taking action.

DAYS AFTER PEDAGOGY OFFERS A SPACE FOR TRANSFORMATIVE LEARNING

Educators have much to learn about learning itself.

—Patel (2019, p. 4)

On days after, there is a unique opportunity to make a classroom a space for transformation and transformative learning. Teachers, by explicitly addressing issues of inequity and injustice, have a chance to nurture students as active agents for change, empowering them with skills, strategies, and dispositions for future days after.

Transformative Learning Overview

Although developed to describe adult learning, the theory of transformative learning (Mezirow, 1997, 2000) also describes how youth learn. For the purposes of this chapter (and book), let us assume that children are capable of much more than we give them credit for, even if not in the most cognitivist, positivist, "measurable" ways. Children are, in fact, capable of everything that Mezirow (2000) outlines in his theory of transformative learning, which is his term for "the process by which we transform problematic frames of reference (mindsets, habits of mind, meaning perspectives)—sets of assumptions and expectations—to make them more inclusive, discriminating, open, reflective and emotionally able to change. Such frames are better because they are more likely to generate beliefs and opinions that will prove more true or justified to guide action" (p. 42). In particular, the process of transformation looks an awful like what we see happening when youth are exposed to social-justice, critical pedagogies in the classroom. As Mezirow (2008) describes it, transformative learning includes

> reflecting critically on the source, nature and consequences of relevant assumptions—our own and those of others . . . arriving at more justified beliefs by participating freely and fully in an informed continuing discourse; taking action on our transformed perspective . . . [and becoming] more critically reflective of our own assumptions and those of others. (p. 94)

Transformative learning may happen in a moment, a major recalibration of one's previous ideas and understandings—what Mezirow calls "epochal"—or it can be cumulative. Again, although Mezirow is writing about adults, any teacher knows these moments can also occur for people of all ages; we have seen this in our classrooms. Indeed, transformative learning sometimes looks like the "aha" moments that teachers spoke about striving for in the book's Introduction. We know that children are capable of "reflection and action upon the world in order to transform it" (Freire, 1972). DAP offers spaces for this critical reflection, discourse, and action to occur around issues of justice and equity.

Transforming Beyond the Standards

Transformative learning might look like what happens in Ann's 8th-grade English class. Ann has been a teacher for 3 years at an urban middle school in the southeastern United States. Ann relayed an instance where her administration told her that she needed to "be more conservative" in the current events topics she was discussing with her students. However, the following year, the school's focus was on "student choice," so Ann used that to her and her students' advantage and offered students a choice about what news articles they read. Many that they selected were the same things Ann herself would have chosen on days after. "It's not just them looking through, pulling out the standard. It's them being engaged and getting pissed off and wanting to do something about it. And it encourages them to go home and talk to their parents, to be like, 'Oh my gosh, did you know this happened?' It's more beneficial." Even though Ann has been reprimanded by administration for her curricular choices, she has persisted in teaching on days after because she believes it leads to transformative learning for her students. As a white woman, she thinks using her privilege in this way is especially important. Reflecting on this reprimand, she notes, "Honestly, it didn't make me angry because I was just going to keep doing it. It just made me feel like there was a disconnect between what admin thinks our students know versus what they do know and what they're exposed to." Ann remembered teaching about the 2016 presidential election and the subsequent immigration ban, moments that she took "cues from the kids" and tried to "turn it into a teachable moment that inspires them." I asked her what she wanted to inspire them for or toward and Ann replied, "I want them to be able to look around and say, 'I like this. I don't like this. Here's how I *want* to change this, here's how I *can* change this.' I want to inspire them to look at the world around them and have it reflect who they are and let them know that their voice is powerful. The powers that be and the oppressors are counting on them not to know what's going on and be tripped up by big words. They're counting on them to be busy."

Penelope, a veteran teacher who teaches in a suburban community in the Midwest, considered the transformative learning that happened in her classroom on the day after the 2016 election. Penelope identifies as a white, Jewish, cisgender woman. The area where she teaches is one of the wealthiest districts in the state, with troublingly close proximity to the poorest-funded and poorest-resourced district. While her advocacy efforts are centered in this major city, her teaching takes place in a school that, although increasingly racially and ethnically diverse, is still predominantly white and conservative. She has been teaching for 19 years and considers herself a "bit of a radical." The day after the election, Penelope found her high school students experiencing vastly different reactions. "I had my international students crying; they were afraid that they were going to be deported. I had LGBT students just fearful for their lives. I had African American students crying, and I also had a room full of people that were super happy about it. They were wearing MAGA hats. So what do you do? Because now you have a room full of strong emotions at opposite ends, right?" Penelope wanted the MAGA hat-wearing students to think more critically about what that stance might be doing to their classmates. Her approach: talking about safety. "I think you can always bring everything back to issues of safety, because if you look at Maslow's Hierarchy of Needs, it's just step two, right? You got your food, water, shelter, and then the next thing you need is that feeling of security. The worse things get, the more fundamental I go in. We boil it down to safety." For students on both sides of the political aisle, Penelope sees at the root of their beliefs a fear for their safety. Whether or not she *agrees* they have reason to be fearful is beside the point: "You can start to dissect and decide whether or not the *causes* for that fear are valid, but you don't invalidate the fear. The fear is real. The *cause* might be some sort of misunderstanding, but the *fear* is real. When we take questions that get down to that root of fear, then you see people in a room looking at each other with commonality because everybody deserves a feeling of safety. That's what I do when it's the worst sort of polarizing tragedies." Penelope said that it was "really powerful" to see her students open up to each other more after that common understanding of a concern for safety: "I saw kids view their hats a little differently. Take some of the hats off, look each other in the eye and realize where [their peers] were coming from. Everybody matters. And the safety of everybody matters because it doesn't get more important than that." The transformation that happened in that moment sprung from a recognition of each other's humanity.

Transformation Beyond the Day After

Transformative learning can also go beyond the day after. That is, students' interests or ideas may be piqued on that critical day, transforming how they think about the world and their place in it, and that may come up again later in the school year or beyond. Scarlet remembered how one student in her 5th-grade class did just that. In Scarlet's class, students do their final project on an issue that matters to them. She recalled a young Muslim student whose interest in gun control was piqued in the wake of a day after event. After the mass shooting in Parkland, the class had discussed the shooting and followed up with "all these lessons on gun control." This included reviewing 20 to 30 different laws and proposals in Congress that could "possibly help mitigate gun violence that they [Congress] don't do anything about." Fast forward to the end of the year, and the student was still very passionate about this issue. So, for her final project, she wrote a letter to President Trump "to say that she wanted him to put pressure on the NRA and to ban automatic guns." Surprisingly, a few months later, the student received a response back, in the form of a generic letter about "young people giving their opinion is what makes our country great." By then, the student was headed to middle school, so Scarlet called her dad and told him the letter was at the school. They joked about how they couldn't believe it, and maybe she should burn it (the student was clearly not a Trump fan), but her dad came to pick it up for her anyway. Scarlet notes that "that end of year project and letter was directly an outcome of us talking about the school shooting from February. That sort of work is what drives me forward because, I'm like, 'Yes, you guys, turn your attention to whatever you want to turn it to and then make those connections and be critical.'"

Allowing their students to voice opinions directly to decisionmakers was a way that Sophia and her co-teacher also aimed for transformative learning in their classroom. Sophia reflected at length on what happened the day after the shooting at the Pulse Nightclub in Orlando in 2016. There were 49 people killed and 53 wounded during a mass shooting at the gay nightclub, a hate crime against the LGBTQ community who spent time there. She remembers that it happened over a weekend, and she reached out to her 4th-grade co-teacher, Brian, who identified as a gay man. "As a woman of color, I always felt that I had to always speak up. I didn't understand that I also have some privileges. I didn't learn that for a very long time. So wherever I feel privileged, I also understand that I need to allow other people to be heard," Sophia said, and because she strives to be an accomplice to the LGBTQ community, she wanted to make sure he was okay and to see what he wanted to do on Monday. "It was our first year together, but he understood this was the kind of thing I did anyway. We started to brainstorm some things that we could possibly do. We could read articles; we could listen to a couple things." They decided to include a speech from Lin Manuel Miranda when he won for best score in Hamilton: "He gave that amazing speech, that love is love is love is love. And I was like: right there. That's it. We're going to incorporate this in some way." Brian and Sophia were a bit concerned because Sophia had to be out on Monday for a doctor's appointment, and they didn't want anyone to think that Brian, because of his identity, was teaching about the shooting because of a "gay agenda." Despite their apprehensions, they made plans for him to go ahead on Monday because they realized, "You know what? This is not about me. This is not about Brian. This is about the kids having the right to learn about their world and read about their world and write about their world."

Brian did start the lesson on Monday, but it did not go as planned. He started by asking the students, "What's going on? What do you know? How are you feeling?" But then, in the news at the time, was "the first twist, that apparently the person who did the shooting called and said, 'I pledge allegiance to Islam,'" so the media were calling it a terrorist attack and not a hate crime. When Sophia returned on Tuesday, the class was still talking about it, and Brian and Sophia decided to extend the lesson even longer. They discussed and read news articles from *News ELA*. They did, eventually, listen to Lin Manuel Miranda's speech and talk about "what does he mean by love is love is love?" But they also followed students' questions about how the media were framing the crime and "we unpacked the difference between being Muslim and being a terrorist. The two are not synonymous. And it came from them, really, because a lot of them know someone [who is Muslim]." A Muslim student in class shared, "Actually the people I know who are Muslim are very peaceful and loving." The class deconstructed where that characterization started and dialogued about it.

Beyond the issues of religion and sexuality that came up because of the Pulse shooting, the students were also very interested in learning more about gun laws: "that was big, that was the core" of what they seemed to care most about. They were upset at the current laws, "so we wrote to our local politicians about changing gun laws. We found the names of all of our local politicians: councilmen, district reps, all the way up to the president. Each child was assigned a politician and they had to learn a little something about that politician." The class then wrote a group letter based on what they had learned about their individual politicians, and each letter was signed with the teacher's and student's name. The students learned how to address an envelope and "what snail mail is because everything's via email these days." Just as in Scarlet's class, some of the students did receive letters back the following year, and it made clear the importance of including student voice and writing in days after lessons. "We always do writing. We always write for a purpose," Sophia said, her voice eager with passion. "We try to make sure that, you know, not every piece of writing is going to be as impactful, right? Sometimes we just mean it for a publishing party and for our peers to read. But this writing was more. This had impact."

But the transformation didn't stop there. Sophia also recalls that, the following school year, students had a week of kindness. Inspired by what they had learned about hate crimes and antigay bullying, they decided to raise money for an antibullying organization. As 5th graders then, they sold bracelets and bookmarks made from materials found around the school and donated the proceeds. "That was just that one incident [the Pulse shooting] and it kind of grew over into the following year." Transformative learning at its best.

DAYS AFTER PEDAGOGY IS SUSTAINING FOR STUDENTS AND TEACHERS

Teaching on days after is especially important for helping students feel part of a classroom community on difficult days. It is vital to create a space where they can be themselves, be open, and be vulnerable. Chapter 2 explains, in much more detail, how teachers can use both culturally relevant and culturally sustaining pedagogy. Here, participants share how DAP allows them to sustain their students' identities and advance aims of justice and equity. Teachers also describe how teaching on days after is sustaining for their own teacher identities and allows them to connect with their more ideal teacher self.

Sustaining Students' Identities

When Scarlet thinks about the positives that come along with teaching on days after, she immediately thinks about the interconnectedness that is possible when addressing these events in ways that sustain students' emotions and connect to their humanity. "When these events happen, whatever it may be, it's so interwoven with everything we talk about at school because the curriculum that we had and created was so intertwined with social issues and social justice activists. It would be impossible to think of these things as isolated. I just really want them to see how interconnected it all is. That's the biggest thing, 'cause I feel like if they can start to make those connections across issues and problems they see in the world, then they're able to look more critically."

Leah, a white woman in her early 30s, also points to the necessity of sustaining students' identities on days after. In her science and social studies elementary classroom in metro Detroit, she sees days after teaching as linked to the school's mission of relevance. She has been teaching at this school for 3 years since she returned from living and teaching abroad. "Our whole mission is to be place based and to be responsive to our communities. Our school is so community focused, and we're so aware of the social emotional learning of students and we build that into teaching." When issues of injustice or inequity do arise, for Leah, "It's pretty hard not to take the time when those things come up, because I feel like to not take the time to talk about those things, to talk about what's wrong about what's currently happening, I think it's denying a part of the students' humanity. It's denying a part of their social emotional processing." Leah acknowledged that some of these issues are controversial and difficult and that "some people would say that that's the parent's job," but to her, that was a "funny thing." To these families, she would say, "No one learns in isolation. You don't. We're not trained animals who are in this one space and so we act this way, and learn this way, and think this way. And now we're in this other context and we just don't." In Leah's classroom, teaching on days after sustained the connection between students' home and school lives. Echoing Scarlet, Leah concluded, "All of our learning is so interconnected."

A peek in Bethany's classroom offers a concrete example of how Days After Pedagogy can be sustaining for students who need and want the space and time to be open with their feelings. Bethany was student teaching in 9th-grade English on the day after the 2016 election. She is a white woman in her early 20s, and she was teaching in an urban high school, working with a group of students who identify as Black, Mexican, and Muslim or, in her words, "basically anyone who had been outwardly victimized" by Trump in the leadup to the election. Bethany remembers going to sleep the night before "without checking the results," and then waking up the next morning to the news. "My first thought was, 'We can't do what we were supposed to do today. They're going to have things to say and I need to give them space to do that.'" Bethany, who was lead teaching at the time, scrapped her lesson for the day and instead told her students, "You all know what happened and I know since we've been talking about it. Leading up to today, you've had a lot of feelings, so I'm just going to sit here. Raise your hand and contribute and feel free to talk about how you're feeling or if you want to add something or whatever." Bethany moderated the discussion in each period for the rest of the day: "That's what we did the whole day. They just needed the space to be heard, and it was really great. It feels like they had no space to do that and they were surprised that I was letting that happen." Bethany remembers that her students asked her, surprised, "Really? This is what we're doing today?" She told them that "this is what we need to do so this is what we're doing. And I think they really appreciated that, that I wasn't just going to sweep it under the rug or pretend that it wasn't happening because it *was* happening and it was upsetting."

At the same time, Bethany wanted to ensure that her students knew where she stood, but as a first-year teacher, she was worried about answering their questions about who she voted for directly. "I don't know why or where I got the idea, but I feel like just to outwardly say who you voted for is taboo, like you're not supposed to do that," Bethany recalled. Instead, she told her students, "Well we're having this conversation right now and do I look happy? I need to have this conversation, too. I'm a woman and [there are] things that he wants to do that wouldn't be good for me as a woman." Bethany is confident that her students knew what she was implying and it was important to her that they did. "As the only white person in the room, I kind of felt like it was my responsibility to say I don't agree with him [Trump]. They already knew to an extent, because I would listen to them but I didn't really engage too much because I didn't want to get too involved or cross any lines or whatever. But that day, I really needed them to know that I was on their side and I was gonna listen and not judge and not be the most important person in the room. I felt like it was my responsibility not to pretend like everything was okay when it wasn't okay." Even the 60 minutes they had in each period was not enough, although Bethany is grateful that her cooperating teacher did not interject when she told him her plans for the day. "I felt like it needed to happen. So it was gonna happen. I was pretty adamant that this is the way things are going to be run today. I don't think I would have even been able to put that aside. I don't think it would have been productive for any of us to pretend."

Bethany reflected on how teaching on days after, particularly this day, tied into her efforts to sustain students' identities in the classroom. "I'm a huge believer that you shouldn't hold in things that you're feeling, even if it seems trivial or embarrassing. And I don't feel like just because you're in school you have to pretend you're not a person with feelings in daily life." That day, she was also teaching "children of Mexican immigrants, and they were very upset about things that he was saying at that time and they would bring it up to me all the time. This is what they're going through. They're afraid their parents are going to be leaving them. I'm not gonna say you can't feel that way just because you're in school."

In Scarlet, Leah, and Bethany's classrooms, their culturally sustaining pedagogy and Days After Pedagogy intersect in important ways. As bell hooks (2000) said, "When we love children, we acknowledge by our every action that they are not property, that they have rights—that we respect and uphold their rights" (p. 30). Indeed, one of these rights is a place to be fully human in a school setting.

Sustaining Teachers' Identities

Just as Days After Pedagogy can be sustaining for students' identities, it can also help sustain teachers. Many of the teachers I spoke with said that teaching on days after reminded them of who they wanted to be in the classroom. That is, it allows them to be the teachers they want to be, teachers who do not care about standardized test scores that they know do not accurately measure what their students know and can do. Teachers who don't rely on scripted curriculum or mandates from the district office about what, when, and how to teach. "It makes me feel less like a robot," one educator recalled, echoing the sentiments of many teachers who feel their teaching of late has been forced into smaller and smaller boxes of test-prep pedagogy. Especially because this role shifting has a large influence on teachers' burnout and morale (Dunn, 2014, 2015), even though it is emotionally difficult, teaching on days after is also a space for them to turn the theory of "care" into a pedagogical practice, and that is what many educators for justice and equity want deeply to do every day.

Carrie, who we met in Chapter 1, finds DAP to be more aligned with her personal and professional self than traditional and standardized curriculum. For example, as Carrie remembers watching the news as major events unfolded, "I'm not just thinking about them as Carrie, I'm more thinking of them as Ms. X. Sometimes I get really excited, and sometimes it's like the weight of the world is on our shoulders because I want to help care for my students, give them a place they have comfort and feel empathy and acceptance, while at the same time I gotta teach something." Even though this can feel like pressure, it's also who she wants to be as a teacher.

Rocio, a teacher of newcomer immigrant students, talked about one year when there was a lot of news coverage of Día de los Muertos (Day of the Dead), a Mexican holiday to celebrate and remember those who have died. It was popularized into the white American social consciousness in the Disney movie, Coco. As a Mexican woman herself, Rocio wanted to bring this topic into her class. By collaborating with the Spanish teacher, she was able to extend her students' learning in two classes. "I did a unit on comparing and contrasting Día de los Muertos to Halloween. After learning everything about the two holidays, my students got to make a little sugar skull. The Spanish teacher created an altar in her classroom, and the students all helped out with that." This was important for Rocio, who sees developing relationships and being culturally sustaining as two key goals as an educator. "Since my students didn't know what it was," she remembered, "I wanted to bring my culture into the classroom to show them what my family does." When thinking about the teacher that she wants to be, Rocio remarked, "I really want to be remembered as a teacher that really cared for the students, not only their academics, but their emotional needs as well. Being from my background growing up as a Latina, it was very hard to get through school sometimes, and rare to have a teacher to say, 'Hey, I see you, I hear you, I'm here with you.' I really want to be that advocate for my students." Teaching for justice and equity on days after allows her to be that advocate, to be her imagined and hoped-for teacher self.

CONCLUSION

One of the very first lessons I learned in an undergraduate education course was that "we teach children, not content." Children come first; content comes second. If we align our pedagogy with this now-truism for many educators, then how can we *not* teach for justice and equity on days after?

If we care about children, we care about what is happening in their lives and in the world around them. If we care about children, we can put aside our planned lessons for a day or more to address the most critical issues of our time. And if we care about children, we know that ignoring the issues does more harm than good. Even if it "protects" teachers in the moment, it risks students' and teachers' humanity.

Student Spotlight: Days After Parkland

After the tragic school shooting that occurred on February 14, 2016, at Marjory Stoneman Douglass, high school protests and vigils swept the nation. People from all over came out to show support for the Parkland community and the progressive gun legislation movement that students created. During this, a friend of mine asked me to help her plan a walkout at our school.

Marquette Senior High School is a school of about 900 students tucked quietly in Michigan's Upper Peninsula (UP). Often Marquette is thought of like the blue dot in the red sea of the UP; however, it is not as progressive as people think. So when the school administration got word of a student-led walkout, they instantly were concerned about how the community would react. Because of this and concern that the event could get out of hand, the administration became involved in the event planning. Over the next week, the group of us planning and school leaders went back and forth on specifics. The event was organically meant to be by and for the students. To show solidarity and the power that young people have. Ultimately, none of that ended up happening. Because the administration took over and a plan was never fully solidified, the day was full of confusion and disrespect.

On the day of the event, students and teachers were told that for about 10 minutes of our advisory time, students would be *allowed* to walk out. However, there were no education materials provided about gun violence, nor was there any space given for the people who were supposed to speak. The entire message was utterly lost in an attempt to "keep the peace" and avoid community backlash. While some used the time for silence to respect the lives taken, others made posts on social media using "gun-like" hand gestures, joking about the event. What was supposed to be a student-led event to show support and empower students to call for change was turned into a mockery.

I will never forget going home and feeling so defeated, unheard, and, above all, disappointed. Thankfully, though, we did not give up, and instead, one of my classmates took charge and began reaching out to community members to plan a march in our town's square downtown. People from the city donated toward an effort to bus us to Washington, D.C. for the national March for Our Lives protest at the Capitol, but we decided the money would better be used to plan a local march. Our local march took place in tandem with the D.C. march and sister protests around the nation. We walked the streets, chanted, gave speeches, and finally walked down to our state representative's office and left him a letter encouraging him to pass school safety and gun reform legislation.

While the off-campus protest went well and jumpstarted my activist work, the true message of this piece is how the administration handled the original event. The administration took control of the walkout, which led to the event being turned into a joke. Taking control of a student-led project is highly problematic and teaches students that their voices do not matter. Rather than feeling empowered and supported, many of the organizers felt discouraged and silenced. Ultimately, this only made us fight harder; however, that is not the case for everyone. Treating students in this manner does not create a safe environment, could lead to a distrust of authority, and ruin students' ambitions. On top of taking control, the event was mishandled, causing the purpose to disappear. The opportunity to watch students educate and empower each other was lost entirely. Lastly, while I understand the need to balance community and parent opinion with the students', the students' interests should always come first. Fearing backlash is no reason to not support your students. Because, at the end of the day, the students are the future; the students matter.

Author Bio: Deidre Gorkowski is a sophomore at Michigan State University in the James Madison College. She is studying social relations and policy and secondary education. She credits her outstanding mentors and teachers as the reason for her chosen education path. Deidre was born and raised in Michigan's Upper Peninsula, spending her time appreciating nature and engaging in activist work. She enjoys spending time with her family, friends, and pets; staying active; listening to music; and making art.

CHAPTER 4

Putting Students First
Who We're Teaching on Days After

> When teachers shy away from intersectionality, they shy away from ever
> fully knowing their students' humanity and the richness of their identities.
> Mattering cannot happen if identities are isolated and students cannot be
> their full selves.
>
> —Bettina Love (2019, p. 7)

Travis loved to cook. When he was little, he would watch Chef Emeril
Lagasse's television show and giggle loudly at all of Emeril's funny antics
and phrases. He liked making apple pie best because he could use his
mom's kitchen gadgets like an apple corer and peeler. Once, when he
tried to follow the instructions on a box of brownie mix, he misunderstood what beating the batter meant and started hitting it with his hand,
rather than stirring or using a mixer. Of course, after he learned the right
meaning of the word, he did a great job on those delicious brownies, and
it became a funny memory. With Travis around, there were many funny
memories because he was a really funny kid. There was the time he taught
his little sister to pee while standing up on the back porch (it worked!) and
the times he boobytrapped his room with string tied to the doorknob, to
the bunk bed, and to the dresser to keep his older sister out. The middle
child between two sisters, Travis—who everyone called Travey—was always well loved by his friends and family. They trusted him with their stories and respected his opinion; he was an old soul, wise beyond his years,
and had many mature conversations with elderly family members. But
even more than the elderly, Travey always loved babies. Whenever he saw
a baby in public, he would ask his mom, "Do you think they would let
me hold their baby?" And, because he was Travey, of course they would
let him. He wanted to be a teacher.

When Travey was in kindergarten, he met his best friend, Joey. They
both loved sports, especially football, and the outdoors. Every year, they
went camping with Joey's dad, caught crawdads, and cooked them over
a campfire. The boys would dare each other to eat crazy things; Travey
even once tried venison liver but later told his mom that, while he was
glad he tried it, he didn't ever want to try it again. They went everywhere

[handwritten margin note: sounds like something my brother would do]

and did everything together; they were best friends their entire lives. They even looked alike: the same haircut, same gaps in their front teeth. It was uncanny. Whenever you talked about one of them, you always talked about the other. It was always "the boys."

In 2003, Travis and Joey were 14-year-old freshmen at a rural Michigan high school. They were numbers 82 and 83 on the football team. And, tragically, on one October night that should have been like any other, these well-liked, joyful boys died in a car accident. They snuck out after dark, took Travey's sister's car, and drove too fast on a rural road before crashing. For this one small high school and the surrounding community, that following morning became a day after. The high school hosted the funeral services for both boys at the same time.

All these things I know about Travey I know because of the strength and grace of his mother, Terry, who shared her memories with me. Terry, although she describes her son as the one with blonde hair, hazel eyes, and a big heart, could easily be described the same way. When she talks about Travey, her voice wavers between strong and wistful, between laughing in memory and breaking in sadness. It is a grief that I cannot comprehend, and hope to never have to.

Terry, as well as Joey's parents, were at the high school on the day after the accident. After a hunter found the boys' car in the woods, they had to identify who was Travey and who was Joey because they looked so much alike, even wearing the same T-shirts, jeans, and Adidas sneakers. That Monday, the school opened the auditorium for any students who needed a space to process what happened. When I asked how she could be there when she was grieving herself, Terry stated the reason as simply a fact: "We thought that we would be able to comfort them. These were kids they went to school with their whole lives. I didn't know what to do, but I knew they would need comfort." In the days after that, Terry kept going to the school. She went to the pep rally at the end of the week, where the class homecoming float had Travey and Joey's pictures on the back, showing their beaming smiles while proudly wearing their football jerseys. She went to graduation 4 years later, when there were five empty chairs on the stage because, in an unfathomable series of events, the same graduating class lost three more students in the next year.

But in the classrooms, there was little attention paid to the tragedy. Today, over 15 years later, what Travis and Joey's friends remember is silence, canned statements, and lack of concern for the students' well-being. In such a small community, everyone knew everyone else. This meant the teachers were deeply affected too, unsure of how to proceed even as they were told what to do (and not to do). There is nothing that can prepare you for the loss of a student; this is what I tell practicing teachers, usually my own former students, every time they ask me about dealing with the death of a student for the first time. This is not something we can "how to" our way out of in teacher preparation or professional development. All the while, more and more students face mental health crises and die by suicide. The rates of gun violence and mass shootings in schools and other public places continue to rise. Politicians and lobbyists refuse to act. This type of day after is, unfortunately, not going away.

Brittany was a first-year math teacher at the time, working at the adjacent middle school in this moment of "significant community trauma." Brittany acknowledges that her memories have faded from that time, importantly noting that "the family members of the children do not have the luxury of these memories fading." In thinking about the day after, she remembers "the sadness, the shock, the grief, the 'how did this happen here?' and the unknowing." "I didn't know what to do," she recalled. "My colleagues didn't know what to do. My principal—despite telling us what to do—didn't know what to do. The district didn't know what to do. What stands out to me now, with about 15 years of reflection, is how incredibly unequipped I felt to be supportive of my students." Unfortunately for her fellow teachers and her students, "my principal, who was generally a kind and sympathetic person, essentially put a gag order on the teachers talking about anything. Instead, he directed us to send students to the school counselor on an individual basis if they seemed to be struggling. The 'business as usual' model was explained and rationalized because his idea was that most kids weren't connected or aware and by opening up our classrooms for conversations, we would make more kids upset than were currently upset."

Even though Brittany says she could "partially see the logic" at the time, she now knows that the principal's decision "sent a message—intended or not—to grieving, confused, sad, and unsure adolescents that their emotions did not have a place in our classrooms and school." In fact, Brittany hopes that some teachers ignored the principal's directive and did talk with their students, but "being a relatively young and new teacher, I did what I was told. I wish I had not. I wish I'd had more knowledge. I wish I'd had more resources. I wish I'd had permission to be empathetic to my students during that time. Perhaps now, as I am nearing 40, a mother, and have had many more years of teaching and educational experiences, I would have handled this differently. I certainly hope I would have. But then, I lacked the understanding of what I could do." Brittany also reflected on what it must have been like for Travis's sister to keep going to school during this time: "Can I imagine losing a sibling during middle school? No. More importantly, can I imagine that trauma and having to go to a place where my emotions were *not* accepted and allowed? No! And as a mom, would I want that for my children? Absolutely not."

Thinking back to that time, Brittany still has a lot of unresolved questions: "What would have been different if I had a bit more knowledge and understanding of social and emotional health? How could I have helped my school community if I had known how to facilitate, or at least engage with, difficult conversations around trauma, loss, and grief? How could I have better helped my students by prioritizing their emotional selves rather than following my administrator's gag order?" She's not certain there are clear answers to those questions, Brittany acknowledges, but "what I wish was that I had some resources, some practice, some education, and some permission to honor and value my students' mental health at a time when that would have been incredibly helpful to many."

This chapter discusses more about the necessity of a Days After Pedagogy. First, teachers talk about how they need to know students deeply in order to engage in DAP and that DAP allows teachers to know students more deeply—a cycle that offers a space for student identity exploration and development. Second, this chapter demonstrates that DAP is also appropriate for all ages and all content areas, disproving the myth that these topics and this pedagogy only work in certain subjects like social studies or English, or only with older students. Finally, I argue that DAP advances student-centered and humanizing lessons.

DAYS AFTER PEDAGOGY IS ABOUT KNOWING STUDENTS DEEPLY

How can you love someone you know so little about?

—Bettina Love (2019)

An important part of Days After Pedagogy is knowing your students deeply, knowing them well enough to know that something needs to be addressed. The power of days after events, however, is that they can also be inciting incidents for knowing your students even more deeply. That is, you can't engage in Days After Pedagogy without already knowing your students as full people, and you will come to know them even more in the days after, when they and you are tested in new ways as learners sharing the same space. But what does it mean to actually *know* your students? What does *knowing* look like?

For Adam, a New York City elementary teacher, this means he gets to know "who they are outside of school as much as who they are as mathematicians, readers, writers, historians, scientists. I think it's important to get a sense of: what are their pleasures outside of school? What do they enjoy? If I were to choose three words to describe this child, what would they be? Would my three words align with what the parents say? This changed a lot for me once I had my own daughter. It's so important as educators to understand that your students are not only your students; they're someone else's child. They're someone else's pride and joy, which means that someone else sees them as a whole, complete, valuable human being. And as educators, you need to do the same thing."

Scarlet talked about what knowing looked like in her classroom. While there are *collective* days after, there are also *individual* days after, such as the day after the death of a family member. Scarlet remembered a previous teaching job working with 3rd-graders. During their daily morning meeting, "I remember a student had a program from his grandmother's funeral from over the weekend. He stood up and put it under the doc cam and then read the entire thing to us. Just sniffling." Morning meetings were always a time to share "what's on students' minds, both formally and informally. . . . Sometimes it was a team-building activity. Sometimes it was just sharing something—silly stuff from the weekend." On this day, however, it was different, because sometimes "there was definitely [a need] for more substantial, vulnerable sharing." That day, her student needed to process his loss with his teacher and classmates, even through tears. His classmates encouraged him, even though Scarlet wasn't sure if he should keep going: "The class was just like, 'It's okay, keep going!' It kind of reached that moment as a teacher where you're like, 'Do they keep going?' He wanted to read the whole thing to us, and we let him because that's what he needed." Offering this space likely supported him and others to be more vulnerable during other critical moments, as well. "If you can get them to share with each other in that way," Scarlet reflected, "if we're all more human, then it's much, much better."

As Scarlet's story illustrates, striving to know students is especially important on days after tragedy. Kelly, a teacher of high school English, feels similarly about the importance of being responsive to students' needs in traumatic moments, which she has sadly experienced multiple times over her career. In particular, she talked about what happened when a student's death from a drug overdose was discovered right before school one morning. Kelly remembered what it was like to teach that day and the day after: "Kids were finding out as they were getting to school. It's a small enough district that you know the name of any kid. . . . I came in during second or third hour and realized really quickly this was a large group of kids who had known him because they just were all shellshocked. They just sat there." That day, and on days like it, Kelly noted that she would "share what information we're allowed to share to make sure everyone has the same info. Facts are always a mess at the beginning." Then she would give them a variety of options for things to do: homework for another class or a review packet or other "easy assignment" for her class. "But for kids who just aren't in it," she continued, "I always have those color sheets around. So I tell them like, 'Color or put your head down.'" She wants students who might need to disengage or go to the counseling office to not worry about what they're missing in class, so overall, "I usually just let that day be just kind of do what you need to do. But they almost always end up in a group needing to talk."

Kelly emphasized how important this space to talk was to her and her students, comparing her approach to colleagues "who just soldier on no matter what. Maybe they'll have a day where every teacher does this. But if they don't have it, they have to go next hour to calculus and focus on calculus. At least they've had this reprieve" in her class. In instances like when their classmates die, Kelly was concerned about their ability to process what was happening and wanted to provide an opportunity for them to grapple with some big questions and deep concerns in her classroom. "For some of them, it's the first time they've ever dealt with death," she recalled, "so there's always that element, too. There's always some conversation about what happens next? What is a funeral like, and how do open caskets work? There's always some kids who don't have any idea. Will we all go to the funeral, because a rural school usually closes if there's a funeral, you know." From the logistical to the philosophical, DAP nurtures a place to know what students might need.

Finally, part of knowing students deeply and getting to know them better through DAP is also checking in with them after an immediate response, to see how they felt about it and how a teacher might improve the next time. Chris, a middle school teacher, talks about this in terms of getting students' feedback the week following a major event. He plans for structured feedback sessions with "table presidents" because his class-room is divided into small groups and there is one leader per small group table. He posits that, should an event happen on a Friday, for example, "Next Thursday, I'll talk to them about it and ask, 'How do you think that went? What feedback do you have and how would you have done it differently?' I try and engage the students as stakeholders in conversations that are important for us." For Chris, such feedback is vital, especially if he feels like his DAP didn't go as well as he had hoped: "Sometimes, like when I make mistakes, I really try and find a way to be honest with my kids and talk stuff out and ask for their feedback."

DAYS AFTER PEDAGOGY IS FOR ALL AGES

One of the most interesting things I found when talking with teachers was the incredible variety of opinions about the "right" age (if there was one) to engage in DAP. Even among people who taught the same grade level, there was such variability in responses. There were elementary, middle, and high school teachers who all said their students were too young. While I don't wish to diminish these educators' concerns or fears, I still wonder, what does it mean that one teacher of elementary students can say they are not old enough and another can say their students are perfectly capable of handling these discussions? To me, this points to a critical component of Days After Pedagogy: So much of what happens on these days depends on the comfort, criticality, and capability of the teacher rather than the students.

It also points to the tendency for white educators to engage in "protection" for their white students, much as white parents do, but the idea of protecting white children's innocence just perpetuates the cycle of white ignorance and privilege. As one teacher in this study said, "If there are kids forced to live in detention camps, my kids [students] can learn about detention camps." Indeed, as a popular meme on social media extorts, if Black children and other children of color are old enough to experience racism, then white kids are certainly old enough to learn about it. If Black youth like Tamir Rice can be killed for playing in a park, white youth can learn about it. If Ayanna Taylor can be shot as she slept in her bed at 7 years old, as police conducted a "raid" on her home, then white youth can learn about it.

Research has also shown the importance of teaching critical issues in early childhood and elementary classrooms. For example, even though teachers are "leery about venturing into such serious topics" (Boutte, 2008, p. 169), we know that "children learn to negotiate meanings and find their place in this world. They learn quickly what is valued and not valued, and what to love and what to hate. Much of this learning takes place in school, where children spend most of their time" (Agarwal-Rangnath, 2020, pp. 2–3). This socialization happens from birth, and by preschool, we know that children can internalize, appropriate, and manipulate racist discourses (Hawkins, 2014). The same is true for harmful discourses about gender, sexuality, ability, religion, and other identity markers. Engaging in these critical discussions also allows young children to develop their agency, connect to their families' and communities' histories, and engage in activism for themselves and others (Chao & Jones, 2016). DAP works similarly; these critical moments offer opportunities for teachers to support students' agency and identity development while giving them a safe place to explore big questions and potentially difficult topics. Such dialogue can also destigmatize people from communities that are not like their own or those from marginalized groups, modeling an asset-based and humanizing approach to learning about others.

One exceptional example of DAP with young children was covered in news media in 2018 as Brett Kavanaugh and Dr. Christine Blasey Ford both testified ahead of his appointment to the Supreme Court. Educator Elizabeth (Liz) Kleinrock, who runs a popular Instagram account called "Teach and Transform" and often shares her social justice pedagogy with her over 130,000 followers, wrote that "everything about Kavanaugh in the news has been making me HEATED. So whenever I get frustrated about the state of our country, it inspires me to proactively teach my kids to DO BETTER. Today was all about CONSENT. We even explored the grey areas, like if someone says 'yes' but their tone and body language really says 'no.' Role-playing is a great way to reinforce these skills, but they MUST be taught explicitly!" Her students were 3rd-graders. Kleinrock shared images of the giant Post-it Notes in her classroom, with a big question at the top: "What does it mean to give consent?" There were subsections for "What does consent sound like?" (Yes, sure, yes please . . . "must sound positive and enthusiastic"), "When do we need to ask for consent?" ("Giving hugs, borrowing things, touching another person, kissing . . ."), and "What can you do if you do not give consent?" Then followed a list of phrases students could use in that situation: "No! . . . I don't like that . . . I don't want that . . . Nah, I'm good right now." In another corner of the poster, there were "What if . . . " scenarios. "What if you really want a hug but the other person doesn't . . . the other person says no, but they're smiling . . . you're in the middle of a hug and the person changes their mind . . . the person let you hug them yesterday, but they don't want a hug today?" The answer, in bright red capital letters: "NOT Consent." During an interview with CBS News (Brito, 2018), Kleinrock discussed her rationale for DAP: "While her lessons have nothing to do with sex, she cited recent examples in news—such as the Kavanaugh allegations, #MeToo movement and Catholic Church abuse scandal—to illustrate the need for children to verbalize their boundaries and how to voice it if they're wronged."

The founding of Woke Kindergarten, an outstanding educational resource, is also a story of justice and equity pedagogy with young children and the emergence of days after pedagogical resources. On Inauguration Day in 2017, Akeia "Ki" Gross was teaching in New York City. Reflecting on the day, they shared the following in an Instagram post:

As the end of the day approached, I informed my kids that 45 was officially sworn into office. This was met with boos and sighs. They were visibly upset, so I said, "I understand that you guys are feeling upset, and it's okay to feel how you're feeling. I feel upset too. But what can we do to help people understand how you feel? How might you show people that you can resist?" Then one of my kids raised his hand and said, "I know . . . we can have a protest and say, 'No Trump!'" Then the child who created this sign [referencing an image of a protest sign] said, "Yeah! We can have a protest! Good idea, Darren!" And so K201 Chelsea had their very own protest, inspired by their own beliefs and feelings about Inauguration Day. Many of these children went to the polls with their parents. We even had our own mock election many months before, so this didn't surprise me any, but I did feel a profound sense of hope in this moment. All I did was grab some cardstock, markers, popsicle sticks, and tape. Then I showed them what types of signs people held up at different protests (none concerning 45). We had previously learned about protest before. I didn't write his name, I didn't show his picture. I simply let them take the lead.

Their signs, shown in images on Ki's Woke Kindergarten Instagram account, include words and pictures saying, "No Trump!" "Boo Trump Boo!" Ki's reflection on the moment continues in their post: "As they finished, I taped the sticks to their signs. Then I looked over and noticed a group of kids marching in circles with their signs, chanting 'No Donald Trump! No Donald Trump!' Inspired, I suggested we take it to the halls. And we did. And it was glorious."

[handwritten margin note: I don't think bashing people is a caring thing to do or support.]

Since then, Woke Kindergarten has become a tremendous resource for educators and families. Describing their philosophy, Ki writes, "Liberation is the goal. Abolition is the journey. Woke Kindergarten is a global, abolitionist early learning community, creative expanse and consultancy supporting children, families, educators and organizations in their commitment to abolitionist early education and pro-Black liberation." This includes "Woke Read Alouds" posted on social media channels and YouTube, which include Ki reading aloud a text with an explicitly justice-oriented focus, asking questions, and leading a virtual dialogue about the text and its implications for children's lives. Beyond this, Ki creates "60 Second Texts," which are short virtual texts with words and images about "big concepts for little people." Many of these texts are created on days after and are amazing examples of the possibility of DAP to advance justice and equity. For example, Ki has created "60 Second Texts" after Black Lives Matter protests, the deaths of John Lewis and Chadwick Boseman, the murder of Breonna Taylor, the success of Stacey Abrams in campaigning for voting rights in Georgia, and the attack on the U.S. Capitol.

In many communities, teachers may be the first ones to discuss issues of injustice with young learners. For example, Isabelle recalls teaching in a middle school with a predominantly white and Latinx population and talking about Trayvon Martin's death in the context of a unit on civil rights and the murder of Emmett Till. Isabelle wanted to put the two injustices "in conversation with each other, discuss them not in isolation, but in a context of racist killings and how white killers often do not face consequences." These conversations were challenging for Isabelle to facilitate because "it's hard for the students to get it, unless your [students'] families have these conversations, and a lot of these families don't."

Young Learners

Mackenzie, a white woman, has been an English educator in a suburban area of the Midwest for 13 years. She has taught 6th through
12th grades. She recalled the importance of talking with young learners
on days after, especially given how much they are exposed to by the
news and social media. "More students care about that kind of stuff,"
she mused, "It is probably because it's more readily available to them,
through social media, and they see a lot more of it that way than just by
watching the evening news or reading the newspaper. They're invested
in it a little bit more, even in sixth grade." The difficulty comes when
teachers are asked to remain ideologically "neutral," as discussed in earlier chapters, a notion that Mackenzie finds "ridiculous." Especially for
English teachers, "When we're talking literature, it's hard not to show
some of what you believe in and feel politically when things happen.
We're talking about the children at the border who are being detained.
It's hard to talk about those in a neutral light. I don't know if we should.
I don't know how anybody can say they're doing the right thing by
detaining these children at the border or away from their parents, not
taking care of them and feeding them properly. How can anybody say
that our country is doing the right thing right now?" As a teacher, it
was hard for Mackenzie to rationalize what was happening to children
the same age as her students, and it was also hard to rationalize how
she was supposed to be "neutral" when discussing those topics with her
6th-graders.

So what does it look like to talk with 6th-graders about these controversial and difficult issues? To Mackenzie's memory, "A lot of them come
in knowing more about the actual incident than I do. They're really good
about asking questions and informing others. I was always surprised with
the maturity that they handled themselves with in the discussions and
[with] the knowledge that they had. If we had questions, we'd Google and
see what we could find."

When I asked her about how she'd respond to someone who said
her students were too young to handle it, Mackenzie got straight to the
point: "I think that's stupid. I really do." Clarifying a bit, Mackenzie acknowledged, "At one time, I probably would have thought that, too. But
having worked with them for so long, they want to be involved and they
want to know more and keeping them away from it is silly." Mackenzie
understands that some parents "or even some teachers think that we need
to protect the students from information when really they just want more.
They want to know about these things, the stuff they hear whispered in
the hallways. They want to be in a place where they can ask real questions
and get real answers."

Younger Learners

What about those learners even younger than middle school? Just like their older peers, elementary-aged students are also hearing news from family and each other; some may have access to the Internet on their own or others' devices, and some may have social media. Such was the case in Scarlet's 5th-grade class. Responding on the day after a local tragedy, Scarlet and her students addressed the issue head-on when a student's apartment burned down and her family lost everything. While the student was absent for a couple of days, Scarlet's remaining students continued to bring up the fire and "really wanted to do something." The students ended up getting the whole school involved to raise money for the family, and Scarlet says, "I remember being very impressed by their empathy skills." This is a critical component of DAP: believing in your students' ability to see the world through others' eyes—if the particular event doesn't relate to them immediately—and build empathy for others' situations and perspectives. If we think students are too young to do this, what opportunities are we denying them for reaching their full humanity? Believing that students are "too young" to learn about and discuss complex issues also contradicts asset-based components of DAP and other social justice theories.

In Sophia's case, her career in elementary schools has shown her that children this age are more than prepared to discuss what she calls "hard, heavy" issues. "I feel the kids are always ready. It's not a matter of them not being ready or it being uncomfortable for *them*. It's usually uncomfortable for the *adults*," she points out. "They can listen, they can formulate things. They can see a different perspective, hear different perspectives, share a different perspective." Yet it's also important to Sophia that the families of her students understand why she's engaged in DAP and how their children are being supported in the classroom. For example, if she had parents coming in to say, "I think this topic is too heavy," Sophia said she would "reassure them that I'm always meeting the standards. I always go back to the standards. That's what a lot of people want to hear." In 2nd grade, for example, the standard might be writing letters; in her classroom, they may use these days after events to write letters about a specific topic, or they may write to local authors and embed the authors' texts in the curriculum, as well. Second, Sophia reassures families that "what I'm hoping for is that kids question, that they don't take anything at face value, that they become critical consumers and critical readers, but also respectful of differing views. That seems to calm parents down a little." Sophia's classroom, you may recall from earlier chapters, is one where students were discussing LGBTQ rights, terrorism, bullying, and electoral politics, depending on what was happening in the world at the time. It's one where both the teacher and the students don't shy away from "hard, heavy" issues just because they are hard and heavy. Rather, they trust each other enough to know that they will learn and push through together.

The Youngest Learners

Teachers of the youngest learners "have the opportunity to create a framework for children, one that is grounded in inclusivity, understanding, empathy, and love for others. They can ground their teaching in social justice so children learn at a young age how to question and think about the world around them, better understand their identities, and stand up for what they see as unjust and unfair" (Agarwal-Rangnath, 2020, pp. 2–3). On days after, this social justice framework of questioning and understanding is deeply important.

It was in the wake of one of Trump's proposed immigration "bans" that Natalia pulled out her bilingual books on immigration to share with her 1st-grade class in New York City, the majority of whom are the children of immigrants from Mexico or countries in Central America. Many of her students crossed the border with their families. "Every child that I've taught in this school has seen immigration in one form or another," Natalia explained, "It's not introducing something to children that they don't know or understand, right? These kids, whether or not parents think they're listening, these kids know about border crossings, papers. . . . " One student's father had been deported; one student's father had been beaten in front of her while they were crossing the border to the United States. Natalia spoke sadly, "The girl is just a lovely child, but she lives in a perpetual state of distraction. [Think about] the trauma that caused her." So, Natalia wonders, with these children sitting in her room, where does she begin on days after that have the possibility of reactivating that trauma?

As an early childhood educator, for Natalia, it always comes back to the power of children's books. She starts listing the books she has used on days after events related to immigrant injustice: "*Mis zapatos y yo: Cruzando tres fronteras (My shoes and I: Crossing three borders)*, by René Colato Laínez; *Dreamers*, by Yuri Morales; *Pete and el coyote*, that one I'm still holding on and deciding when to read it." Reading these texts on days after opens up space for children to share their own immigration experiences, worries, and fears in the wake of Trump's ongoing rhetoric. "I read *Carmela Full of Wishes* and one of her wishes is that her dad gets his papers. One of my boys was like, 'Mi tío todavía está esperando por sus papeles y no puede salir de México.' [My uncle is still waiting for his papers and cannot leave Mexico.] Just like that. There was no explanation needed for what this meant. This 5-year-old boy who seemingly is on another planet half of the time just got it."

DAYS AFTER PEDAGOGY IS FOR ALL CONTENT AREAS

"My heart hurts about that," Emily said, touching her chest and sighing. She was remembering both a day of and a day after in September 2001. Emily was a student teacher in a rural placement, about 35 minutes from where she lived. That morning, like every morning, she left her house around 6:00 A.M. and got to school an hour or so before classes began. And also like every morning, she listened to National Public Radio, and her attention zoned in and out. There was a story about the Taliban, and Emily remembered thinking, "Who is the Taliban? Why should I care about this now?" It was a vivid memory for her, just like what happened during her 2nd-period class.

It was the class that Emily was responsible for as part of her student teaching requirements: 9th-grade math. About 10 minutes into the class, "a kid came in and told the teacher that airplanes had flown into the towers. My mentor immediately called everybody to attention; she didn't just tell me. She brought everyone together and her first response was, 'Let's turn on the TV and watch this.'" So they did. They watched the replays— and then more replays—of the World Trade Center collapsing. The kids were murmuring throughout, wondering if this meant the country was going to war. "For a ninth-grade class," Emily recalls, "They were quick to catch on to implications of what this might mean." But then, before the end of the period, Emily's mentor "helped me find the words to bring everybody together and focus on math again. It was not this idea that we could listen to kids, hear what they were thinking. Granted, this is all before iPhones. They were only getting info through us. We were able to clamp down conversation and get them focused again."

So, for that day and the day after, that was it. That was the only time Emily (and her mentor) focused on what was happening around them. They did not talk any more about it. "There was a sense in this rural context that it wasn't the teachers' role to help them make sense of what was happening. It was compounded by math teachers always feeling the pressure of getting through content. There's so much that [students are] expected to learn that we don't have the time. It feels like a luxury almost to just stop and have a conversation," Emily admits, shaking her head. "It hurts me now to think about that, even though I can make sense of why it happened. It's so clear to me now. They may have memories of us trying to get through it, but it wasn't the right thing to do."

Emily can think of another day after that was a missed opportunity, 20 years later. She is a faculty member now, at an institution that has been deeply affected by a sexual abuse scandal in the university and community. "That was another case where I felt that people, me included, were hiding beyond math. I didn't take the opportunity to bring it up, and they didn't ask. I didn't even stop to ask my class, 'How is it for you?' That's on me. I also just feel like there's some cultural norms around math, and being able to ignore the reality of life when you're dealing with these abstract ideas. Even talking about it now, I'm doing it again. My students as mathematicians are so easy to fall into that, too. But they are whole people. I appreciated being reminded that we couldn't ignore it when I saw other faculty's efforts."

These two missed opportunities in some ways define Emily as a teacher on days after. They are visceral memories for her, so much so that she volunteered to talk to me about it, even knowing that it would mean sharing what she feels are her past mistakes. Would she do it differently now, I wondered? "Yes," she replied confidently, "I'm reforming myself from getting caught up in thinking that curriculum is the most important thing. This has been a learning curve. I'm working toward it. I'm probably likely to make missteps, and I don't want to say I'm perfect at it. But it matters deeply to me and now I'm more comfortable just to make space for what's going on. Sometimes math can even help us understand things about it, but it also doesn't always have to be about math."

I share Emily's story here not just because I appreciate the vulnerability of her sharing but because of the common misconceptions that she identifies in her story: that it's too hard for some content areas to stop curriculum and talk about these events, or that the events have to be connected to the subject area in order to merit discussion. To be sure, Emily is not the only teacher who shared this perspective; many teachers did, even if they were committed to justice and equity. "I don't know how to find the time," another participant said. "There isn't any time to begin with and it doesn't relate to our subject." Others, even in the subject areas that one might think are "most" connected, like social studies and English, didn't think DAP was necessary. Thankfully, there are plenty of other teachers who know this is not true and who provide thoughtful examples of what DAP can look like in all content areas.

Middle School Science

Fiona knows that there is a certain time of year when DAP will be particularly important in her middle school science and STEAM classes: hurricane season. Generally, on these days after, Fiona will introduce the discussion by asking if anyone has heard about the hurricane, what they know, or if they have any family or friends who were affected. Even though they are far away in the Midwest, she wants them to understand the importance of being aware of the news around the globe and developing a human connection to an environmental disaster. "We have to at least have a conversation about it," Fiona believes, "especially once we get to middle school and high school science, because sometimes parents can struggle to have those conversations with kids just because there's not a ton of parents who are in science." When she brings up the topic, typically some students will have heard of the storm and others won't. She then shows several videos from the news to ensure that all students have at least a basic level of understanding of the particularities of the disaster. "I know not a lot of middle schoolers watch the news," Fiona remarks, "so I think it's important for them to be able to see it and hear from people who are getting interviewed." Then students will look up additional information using their school-provided Chromebooks. Depending on the event, they may make a short PowerPoint presentation to share with their classmates, or they may talk in small groups about what they found: "They're middle schoolers, and they like to talk, so they can share with each other about the stories they read."

In August 2017, this meant talking with students about Hurricane Harvey, which brought catastrophic flooding and damage to Louisiana and Texas. Over 100 people were killed, and it was the worst recorded disaster since Hurricane Katrina. As part of her DAP, which unfolded over several days as the hurricane and its impact continued to spread throughout Texas, they discussed how "the damage was so costly because Houston was a very large, expensive city." They also brought up J. J. Watt, a professional football player who became involved in the recovery efforts. Even though their discussion was happening in science class, for Fiona, it was about a lot more than the science of a hurricane. An excerpt from our conversation points to Fiona's overall commitment to DAP:

> *Fiona:* We also talked about some of the things that families are experiencing down there, like flooding. I showed them a video of someone wading through the water or boating through it. And then they laughed and thought it was funny. But I was like, "There's things we have to consider. There's a lot of garbage in there and trash and there could be bacteria and downed electrical lines." At the middle school level, it's hard for them to sometimes really relate and connect to what these communities are experiencing. So I tried to at least give them a little bit of information to put it into perspective.
>
> *Alyssa:* So what is your goal behind wanting them to understand what the families are experiencing, 'cause some people would say, "Well, that's not science."
>
> *Fiona:* Ultimately, it's for them to develop empathy with others. And it's not science, but it's also teaching to the whole student. It's teaching them about respect. These are gonna be things that they will be seeing often in the news. And I want to connect my classroom to things that are going on outside. That's why I talk about it.

World Languages

Yet another example of a content area where many people think DAP is "not doable" is world languages. What do you do when your students do not know much of or have an "academic vocabulary" in the target language? Can you teach about injustice in Spanish if the students don't speak Spanish? Can you teach about inequity in Mandarin if the students only know words for hello and goodbye? Can you teach about the 2016 presidential election in English if the students are just learning English? Indeed, you can, as teachers around the country illustrate every day. Even in districts where there is a "target language only" mandate, meaning that the language of instruction is always the target language and you cannot use a student's home language as an educator (a practice that has been roundly critiqued as damaging for both students' identities and their linguistic development), justice-oriented educators are finding ways to make this happen. One teacher is Chris, a white man who teaches newcomer immigrant and refugee youth in an English as a Second Language (ESL) program at a public school in Connecticut. In Chris's class, students tend to move in and out throughout the year, depending on when they arrive or if they migrate to another city with their families. When we spoke, all 14 students were Spanish speakers from Puerto Rico, the Dominican Republic, Mexico, Guatemala, Ecuador, Columbia, and El Salvador, a "magically small" class when the class caps were normally much higher. Many students from Central America were undocumented, and many from Puerto Rico had arrived in the aftermath of a major hurricane, Maria, that devastated their communities. So, the day after the 2016 election, given Trump's policy plans and rhetoric, was "heavy." Chris knew that he had to talk about it with his students but "had no idea what the heck I was supposed to do. My class and I hadn't gotten political. We hadn't gotten there yet; we hadn't talked much about the election. But it was so obvious to me that the conversation had to happen. I didn't know what that meant." He considered his options: read an article, watch a video, watch the news, "or just cry together? I really didn't have a sense." Then someone online shared an article from *The Huffington Post* on "what do we tell our kids?" about the election results. Chris decided to start there.

Chris and his 14 students sat at a large wooden table in the back of his classroom. He translated the article from English to Spanish to make sure all students understood. He asked students to stop him along the way if they had questions or responses. And, unsurprisingly, they did: "What does this mean for my family? Am I going to have to go back? What can we do about it?" Chris remembers that he did not have to "do much more than say 'the table's open' for the conversation to start." His students knew what was happening because their families had already talked with them about it, and they were "carrying heavily what was going on."

Some cried through the whole discussion. And then, it was time for gym. What was Chris to do now? "We cried, we hugged, and then went to gym. Okay, normalcy for a bit." While they were in gym class, Chris was "wracking [his] brain" about what to do next. On a "normal" day, it would have been math period.

As it turns out, Chris didn't need to have a plan at all. His students had come up with one for him, for themselves. When Chris returned to pick up the students from gym class, one student said to him in Spanish, "You have to fix your face because my mom says that if you make yourself look sad, then you're going to be sad. We came here to learn and we can't cry all day. Can you please fix your face so that we can go upstairs and learn math?" For Chris, this was "some sort of video game injection," giving him the boost he needed. Upstairs they went to learn math.

As Chris remembers it, this shift, motivated by the students' own choices about what to discuss and how much to discuss, illustrates "the power of resilient students, the incredible strength that they have" to hold such a heavy day in their hearts and also want to learn math, to move forward in the moment. Because Chris is an educator who understands that DAP is not just confined to a solitary moment or day, this didn't mean the end of the conversation, though. The dialogue that day served as a "jumping-off point for us to do a lot of engagement work," such as when students wrote skits about how to interact with ICE. They later performed their skits in several different community forums. But, on that day in November, as Chris remembers, "we had each other, and that was enough."

In this section, we see two teachers in a math classroom on the day after a major event. Yet their approaches were different, and only one (Chris) modeled Days After Pedagogy. While Emily pushed through with the content without acknowledging the significance of the moment, Chris, on the other hand, responded to what students needed. First, they needed to process, and then they needed math.

DAYS AFTER PEDAGOGY USES STUDENT-CENTERED AND HUMANIZING LESSONS

There are no savers. There is only a village, a community, and a goal: protecting children's potential.

—Bettina Love (2019, p. 82)

While DAP is appropriate for all ages and all content areas, it does not mean that there is some magic checklist or slide deck that can be used verbatim with all students. A key component of DAP is making discussions and lessons individualized to particular contexts. Aiming for student-centered and humanizing lessons requires knowing the students whose experiences you want to center, knowing what humanization looks like for the particular youth in your classroom. By humanizing here, I draw from Freire (1972), who sees humanization as the way that students and teachers engage in dialogue to become more fully human, or more fully and completely themselves in a classroom space. DAP supports students in challenging the dominant paradigm of "studenting" in that they can actually focus on being real, whole people instead of "doing school" and performing certain types of skills and behaviors merely to pass tests and please adults (Patel, 2016, p. 54).

In Karissa's music classroom, her students were having trouble concentrating one day, rightfully so, she acknowledges, because it was snowing. Seattle rarely gets snow, so this was an exciting moment. She knew that the students were not going to be able to focus on her plan for the afternoon. So she changed her plans for a bit: "We did a snowflake song because they needed to talk about snow. [When they finished singing it once], we went to look at the window to see how the snowflakes were moving." Then they sang the song again, this time moving like the snowflakes. "When they got that out, they had the space to think about other things. They could put their brain in other places," Karissa remembered. This might seem like a trivial example, but for Karissa, it's deeply relevant for how to make DAP student centered and humanizing. Like with the snow, "if they're thinking about these things that are happening in the world and they don't have the space to talk about that, then their brain just stays there and they have trouble focusing on whatever else." Karissa's choice to engage in DAP when she notices that something is "taking up their brain space" shows that she is not willing to push through the pre-planned content if it is clear that her students need something else. This is especially important that she listens to what her students need because, as a white educator working with predominantly children of color, she cannot know firsthand what they are experiencing.

Rocio, a Latinx educator in Connecticut, shared her experiences creating student-centered and humanizing lessons in a special elective class called Latinos in Action. This class was designed to "create leaders in the community through community service and excellence in education." Rocio, as a community leader and skilled educator, was the perfect choice for teaching such a class. One effort toward humanization that Rocio made intentionally was countering the language that students were hearing from President Trump in his speeches about immigrants and refugees, in particular a speech he made about "building the wall." Rocio recalls what listening to his anti-immigrant and white supremacist language meant to her, as a Latina woman. "Seeing how impacted I was, just seeing how events like that hurt me . . . I just can't imagine not really exploring" these topics with her students. She did not want her students to hear such language used about their communities and "ingrain this within themselves." Ever so skillfully, Rocio also connected these discussions about the power of language to harm or liberate to things she had heard her own students saying. "There's been things I've noticed in the hallway, where students are being called certain words," such as slurs for LGBTQ people and disabled people. "That's not something that I want my future leaders to be saying, so I have to have lessons about how hurtful words like that can be" and why students should not use them. In this way, Rocio worked toward humanizing students both inside and outside her classroom.

Leah, a middle school teacher in an urban district of Michigan, also worked to humanize days after lessons in the wake of the school shooting in Parkland, Florida. Leah discussed what happened in her "advisory group," a homeroom section for 6th- and 7th-grade students. Leah created a space to talk about the school shooting during their circle time. "I cried in front of my students. That was pretty emotional. That's a thing that sticks out to them. I think when adults cry in front of them, they're like, 'Oh, that has my attention.'" Leah also talked with her students about the student walkout, coordinated by Parkland youth, and taken up by many thousands of youth around the country. She recalls telling the students that "if they were interested, they were welcome to let me know or to organize themselves." Students did not bring it up again, with the exception of one student who wrote a paper for another class about how teachers should carry guns in school. In the 8th-grade homeroom, however, "students were really interested in doing the walkout. I think some of them had older siblings who were going to be doing it at other schools." The administration approved the walkout, which Leah noted "is kind of not the point necessarily of the walkout, but it was fine." The 8th graders made signs and "walked around the block a couple of times." Unexpectedly, Leah remembers that her "students who hadn't organized themselves and saw the other students doing it got really mad. They were really upset that they weren't included in the walkout." What Leah realized was that, although she had thought she told them it was up to the group to organize themselves, they thought *she* was going to do it, that even though it was clearly a student-led walkout, the adults were going to tell them what to do and where to be. Meanwhile, the 8th graders generated leadership and organized the effort. Leah calls this "a learning moment for everyone" because the students had to come to terms with their disappointment and think about what they might have done differently. Leah does not let herself completely off the hook for this missed opportunity, however. "It was an interesting learning experience for me, too. How do I make sure that the conversation we have is empowering them to take action on their own? How do I ensure they don't only rely on hearing an adult tell them the plan of what we're going to do?" What I appreciate about Leah sharing this story is that the students were able to discuss what happened: an important part of DAP. But she realized later that there was a missed opportunity of moving from discussion to social action. This is not because she didn't think such action was necessary or that her students were not interested. This shows that even the smallest moments matter on days after; there will be so much communication happening, so many feelings to share and process. It is easy for things to be missed, to slip through the cracks. This doesn't mean that DAP was a failure, by any means. It is never too late.

CONCLUSION

When I give presentations about teaching on days after, I am often asked what "the most important part is." I usually say that all components are important and must be carefully considered and intentionally enacted. But what I've come to realize is that there *is* a most important part and it is this: the *who*. The students. First, because, what are we doing this for if not for our students? It certainly doesn't make our jobs as educators easier to teach for justice on days after. But it is also the most important because to teach on days after requires a deep commitment to student connection; this connection is both a *prerequisite* for DAP and an *outcome* of DAP. None of the other components of DAP truly matter if you don't know your students or if you rush into trying to teach for justice on days after if you don't carefully consider who your students are (in relation to who you are, as well, as discussed in the next chapter).

The teachers' stories in this chapter demonstrated what it means to know students deeply. They also shared compelling stories about why DAP is not only appropriate but also *necessary* for all ages and all content areas. Knowing students means knowing that their lives don't stop once they get into the classroom, and they definitely don't stop between English and math class. Teachers hold such an important role in processing life moments of loss, of uncertainty, of injustice.

Consider for a moment how many teachers are facing classrooms with, as Rick Ayers (2015) writes, "an empty seat in class." How many communities have lost their own Travis and Joey this week? Knowing our students deeply means that it will be even more painful if we lose them. This is a risk we have to take.

Within my schooling experience, most of the major events that have taken place haven't been spoken about directly. Most vividly, I remember the 2020 election and the 2021 Inauguration Day. For most of my fellow students, these days were pretty significant in our lives, and we all held decently strong opinions. In school, even though we were in virtual class, these events were not discussed. I remember feeling like there was a clear tension between the teachers and the events taking place. It almost felt like they were trying to avoid the conversation because we saw election news everywhere else on our phones, computers, newspapers; even outside you could spot signs for each presidential candidate, but it wasn't mentioned in school. Any time a political matter has been talked about in class, my teachers are quick to make it clear that they're not "claiming a side or party," and they have trouble navigating these conversations, so they're quickly shut down. Especially if a student were to mention the election or ask to discuss it, my teachers have always responded back awkwardly, with a silence of them searching for what to say. Sometimes they stutter and it's clear they get nervous.

While I can understand how uncomfortable these conversations can be, I still think they should be talked about. We didn't even have to talk about the politics directly, but it would've been nice to have our teachers acknowledge these significant events and ask students if they're feeling okay or if they're stressed about it. Since the official results of the election took much longer to be finalized, there were multiple opportunities for teachers or administration to reach out, but even during vote recounts, none of my teachers brought it up. If they happened to bring it up, they didn't necessarily have to make a political comment; there was an opportunity just to mention how different this election has been from the others. In fact, I think it was a bigger deal to me that the teachers didn't talk about these events. It would've been as simple as making a Google Form, which can be anonymous, and asking students if they're feeling all right because the election and Inauguration Day could've been a huge part of their lives. To me, it was inconsiderate to the students who may have depended on the election, like students whose parents may be undocumented. They were most likely fearing for their lives during the election.

Also, for most of us, Inauguration Day was a huge deal, whether you were against or for our presidential candidate. Unfortunately, we went through the school day without speaking of the inauguration, and most students missed seeing it. It was quite disappointing because I would've liked to see our first female, Black and South Asian vice president get sworn into her position. It was a moment of history being made, and we missed it because we were at school. The worst part is, we didn't even talk about it that day or the day after!

Another event I remember was when COVID-19 started taking its toll on the country. Our teachers were ordered by administration to talk to students about the virus, in hopes of spreading some knowledge and helping students who might've been scared. These conversations BARELY happened. Every teacher I had, from every hour, was supposed to address it at the start of class, but I only had two teachers truly bring it up. One teacher spoke her opinion on how getting in a car crash was more likely than catching the virus, which at that point was not only inconsiderate to students who may have health risks or are scared in general, but also we didn't even have enough information on the virus in March 2020. My other teacher briefly addressed it at the beginning of our class, and she was our health teacher, which made sense. While she kept her personal opinions out of it, she did run through the precautions, telling us to wash our hands thoroughly and use hand sanitizer whenever possible. COVID-19 changed students' lives, but it was another event that was not expected and also not addressed. It would have been nice to speak more about it in the school environment, before COVID-19 took that resource away from us, too.

When we returned to school, we had to follow mandatory precautions, like wearing masks and social distancing. It was an odd feeling to return because everyone surrounding me had masks on, but we still didn't discuss COVID-19 in our classes. We didn't discuss how it has significantly changed all of our lives and the impact COVID-19 has left on communities of color. Only one of my many teachers addressed the anti-Asian racism that's been caused by COVID-19. At the beginning of class, on her Google Slides presentation, she had a picture inserted that said, "#StopAnti-AsianRacism," and she mentioned how upset the hate crimes have been making her feel.

I'm fortunate to attend my school because we have great resources, and my opportunity chances are a lot higher here than at other schools. However, it's been disappointing to attend a school that is so hesitant to address social and RELEVANT issues because they're worried about their reputation, how the school will be viewed, and community backlash. For a school that claims to be highly diverse, conversations that'll support and address all students' situations tend to be avoided. We can all do things to better ourselves and help those around us. I believe having these conversations is something we can do to improve as a school, as a community, and as individuals.

Author Bio: Sudeshna Flores, who goes by Sue, is in the 11th grade in Okemos, Michigan. Sue is cisgender and Latina, and she was born in

Texas, which she claims as her true home. Sue enjoys journaling and activities that help her self-reflect. She finds a lot of joy in studying astrology and the zodiac chart. Lastly, she loves having conversations with people where she gets to know them on a deeper level, talking about their life, politics, and society.

* * *

The last day of school before quarantine: It was a Thursday, and I barely even knew what COVID-19 was, much less that it was even in the United States. None of the teachers talked about it. The only time anyone mentioned it whatsoever was during my last class of the day, when my English teacher said that we probably wouldn't have school the next day and to make sure to bring home things that we didn't want to be left at school until the following Monday. I remember thinking, "Wait, what?" completely confused. I had no idea what was going on, and I was scared. On Thursdays, I always went to the school library for a while to hang out with some friends before robotics, which wasn't until 8, because I didn't want to walk home in the cold and then all the way back to school. When I went to the library, however, the lights were off, and the librarian who was packing up said that all after-school activities were canceled. Usually, when we had a snowstorm on the way, they would do this, but I hadn't even been notified that this was happening. So not only did they not mention COVID-19, but they barely even mentioned that the school was closing. I went downtown with some friends for a while after that, and we put on the masks my parents had me bring to school just in case, despite back then how everyone was saying that masks wouldn't help. I went home afterward, and that was when I heard that we wouldn't be going back to school until Monday, just like the English teacher predicted. No one talked about it at all. Looking back, that was probably because everyone was just as scared as I was. I tried asking my friends and teachers, but they didn't have any answers either. Everyone just kept saying, "You'll be back on Monday," then on Sunday, they said it would be a week. A week turned into two, and so on.

Throughout the entire time, school did nothing to teach us about what was going on. If it hadn't been for the news, all I would have known is that a virus was keeping us all from going to school. At first, it reminded me a bit of the flu season, when many kids would be home sick, except this time it was the school keeping everyone home, and we had no idea who was sick, and it lasted a lot longer than simply mid-to-late winter. We didn't learn anything in school about what COVID-19 was, where it came from, what it did to you, whether it was deadly or not, nothing at all, until recently. It's been almost a year since the day we all went home, and it wasn't until now that in science class we learned the most basic information; COVID-19 affects your breathing. If it weren't for the news and my parents, I wouldn't have known any of this. I think it's really important that, although it was very late, we did eventually learn the bare minimum about COVID-19 in school. However, to this day, they have not gone into detail about it. They tell us the things we need to know about the disease itself and the precautions we need to take if we decide to come into school for the hybrid model, but that's it. They never mentioned the political side of it, for example, how some people blame it on China. Teachers already talk about other issues that have become controversial, like climate change and Columbus Day. If teachers are capable of talking about past controversial events while still allowing us to form our own opinions, then they should be able to talk about current events, too.

Author Bio: Ava Rizzico is a high school freshman in Massachusetts. As a member of the LGBTQIA+ community, they believe that equality for all individuals is very important. They enjoy sailing, robotics, and dance. Ava hopes that someday the world will become less polarized and instead start working together to solve larger problems.

CHAPTER 5

Educators: Who Is Doing the Teaching on Days After?

As Sophia tells it, everything changed, as things tend to do, when she became a mother. But for Sophia, things changed for her professional identity in addition to her personal one. Sophia is a bilingual, Puerto Rican woman. She has lived in the same community in New York City for her entire life. It is forever home to her. It is where she now raises her family and where she wants to start a community organization if she were to ever leave the classroom. But it wasn't until she had a child that she realized that her experience of this place was not as universal as she thought.

One might not think that teaching on days after could be so affected by becoming a parent. Sophia recalls what her classroom looked like before motherhood: "When I started teaching, I was 22 years old, and I was going to teach a lot of children how to read and how to do math really, really well. . . . Teaching in a dual-language classroom for me was really powerful because of what my grandmother was told not to do here, not to speak Spanish. Instead, I was encouraging bilingualism and biliteracy. And then September 11th happened. We ignored it." They ignored it even though they were also in New York City. "I was teaching kindergarten that year and said, 'We're not going to talk about it. This is a safe place.' And that kind of became what my classroom was like": a classroom that felt "safe" on the surface but where critical issues and moments were not discussed.

But then Sophia went through a major life event that changed everything. "And then I became a mom," Sophia says, "Puerto Rican families run the gamut of skin tones, right? Police were never really discussed in my family. But in my husband's family, they were very much having these conversations." Her husband was afraid of what it would mean if they had a son and their son looked like him. "I didn't understand why. And he's like, 'Soph, you have no idea what it's like to live in this world as a Black man.' And I don't, right? So I still thought it was nonsense. And then I had my son and saw the experiences he was having in the playground and at school. That's really what shifted things for me a great, great deal." Sophia is quick to note that not every teacher needs to be a parent to understand the importance of addressing issues of race and justice in their classrooms, or that every parent–teacher inherently understands this at the moment of parenthood.

I start with this story because it illustrates the many nuances of educator identity and how these identity markers affect what happens on days after. DAP does not look the same for every educator, just as it does not look the same for every school context. When considering racial identities, for example, as a white woman, it is not my position to argue that teachers of color should and must engage in DAP if it means causing themselves or their students further harm. Nor is it my goal to say that all white teachers should engage in DAP if they are unprepared for these discussions; this lack of preparation, despite one's best intentions, may lead to more harm than good if they are teaching students of color. Rather, teachers from all identity groups must consider what they know to be true about their own preparation and identities, as well as their students' identities, in determining when and how to engage in DAP.

This chapter offers readers more insight into teachers' personal identities and feelings on days after, including their struggles and challenges. I highlight several key components of DAP, including the need for teachers to be comfortable with taking curricular risks and willing to be vulnerable with their students. Teachers discuss what challenges and fears they have related to DAP and how their own positionalities matter in these critical moments. This chapter is about teaching on days after in spaces that often make it feel hard to do . . . and the teachers who do it anyway.

DAYS AFTER PEDAGOGY REQUIRES TEACHERS TO BE VULNERABLE

Teaching is a daily act in vulnerability.

—Parker Palmer

The first time I cried in front of a student, I wasn't much older than the student himself. I was only 18, serving as a classroom co-teacher in an all-boys' juvenile detention center in Dorchester, Massachusetts. I was a freshman in college, and this role was my placement for a service learning course. Twice a week, I would get in a van of college students—all white—and head from our predominantly white, private university to Dorchester, where the van driver would drop us at a variety of different community sites and organizations. I'd be wearing, according to the dress code for workers at the detention center, baggy clothes, no jewelry, no makeup. My hair had to be down. I was the only woman in the education wing. I was the only white person in the room. I had no idea what I was doing.

Supposedly, I was co-teaching poetry. But the co-teacher, the actual employee of the detention center, was rarely there. Most often, it was two security guards, 10 to 15 students from ages 13 to 21, and me . . . teaching poetry. The injustice of not merely their incarceration but that they were supposed to be learning from me, who was so clearly unprepared and unfit for this role yet who was automatically given a role of authority, still devastates me today, 2 decades later. I shouldn't have been there; I know that now and should have known it then. I perpetuated a system of injustice in the supposed "justice system."

Toward the end of my semester there, the students were writing their final poems. We were going to put them into a booklet, make photocopies, and bind them. One student called me over to his desk and asked me to read what he had written. It was a poem about how he felt like the caged bird in Maya Angelou's book, *I Know Why the Caged Bird Sings*. There was a drawing with it. I read it and cried, right there next to his desk. I knew he could see I was crying. I looked down at his desk, and sure enough, he was looking up at me, smiling. I was so embarrassed. My words caught in my throat, and before I could speak, he let out a big "whoo hoo!" I am sure I looked as confused as I felt, as he continued, "I knew I could do it! I knew it was good enough to make you cry!" I laughed awkwardly and asked why he had wanted to make me cry. He took the paper back and stared at it, proudly. "Aren't the most beautiful things supposed to make people cry?"

As teachers, we face the most beautiful things in our classrooms. And also the hardest, the saddest, the most complicated. The things that bring us the most unexpected joy and unbearable sorrow. We face all of these things that can bring our emotions to the surface. In these moments of vulnerability, especially on days after, being a justice-oriented teacher is not about "controlling" one's own emotions but about figuring out what it means to be vulnerable with one's students.

Vulnerability, or "a condition of openness . . . to being affected and affecting in turn" (Gilson, 2011, p. 308), requires a certain relationship with students. To be open with students is not something that can happen merely on days after. Like many of the elements of DAP, these cannot be developed in a vacuum and only deployed when discussing current events. Furthermore, vulnerability is accessible to different people in different ways, depending on one's identities. Moore (2020), for example, critiques the work of Brené Brown for this reason. While Brown's conception of vulnerability is one that has clearly resonated with many, it is also formulated without clear regard for how vulnerability can be operationalized (and weaponized) depending on one's race, gender, class, and more. Indeed, as Cole (2016) argues, "How we experience our common condition of vulnerability differs greatly. . . . This is a structural matter as well as an experiential one. People are subjected to or immunized from vulnerability in radically distinct, different and unequal ways" (p. 266).

In education—a profession replete with white women standing in front of classrooms—it is vital that vulnerability not be an excuse for "white tears," or a white person's response to being confronted with issues of race and their complicity in it. That response—which is often accompanied by anger, fear, hostility, shame, guilt, or the "emotionalities of whiteness," as Matias (2016) calls it—is a result of a lack of understanding of privilege, a weaponization of whiteness, and a lack of resilience in having race-focused conversations and experiences. We also know that "social institutions of power [like schools] continue to influence our emotions" (Matias, 2016, p. 6). So, to be clear, when discussing vulnerability as an important component of DAP, it is meant to recognize the nuance of how such an emotion is viewed by others, enacted by individual selves, and influenced by the institution of school.

Many of the teachers I interviewed talked about crying with students on days after. This is not the only way to be vulnerable, of course, but this is what stuck out to many of the teachers as they remembered these particular moments. Ann, for example, remembered her students once asking why she was crying. Her response to them clarified that being emotional and vulnerable about injustice and tragedy is important. She told them, "This is intense. That's something that we need to acknowledge, and it's okay to feel upset or bad or angry about it. It's okay to be emotional and passionate." Ann said that her own vulnerabilities as the teacher "help my students feel safe and passionate and help them make that distinction that it's okay to be emotional [about] events that happen." Karissa complicated this idea in her comments. As a white woman teaching students of color, she is careful to attend to when her own vulnerabilities might impede her students' learning. She remembered teaching in the wake of the Parkland shooting, when "all of the adults in the building were so tense. . . . It was on our minds all day, but the kids were just so unaffected by it." Even though she had planned to discuss it with them, when they told her they didn't want or need to, Karissa did not push it. Karissa remembers, "I cried during my prep period that day. I closed my doors and I took that time for myself, and I listened to some music that moved me. I let myself sit with those feelings and I had conversations with my colleagues away from the students, still finding those ways to let myself process, but not putting that on to them. . . . Just because I'm experiencing this trauma, that doesn't mean that they needed to." Importantly, Karissa is not suggesting that teachers do not feel vulnerable in the wake of yet another school shooting or other traumatic event, or that they completely bottle up their emotions when in the school building. Rather, she is pointing out how educators make difficult decisions about what to bring into the building and what to process as individuals or with colleagues.

Part of the willingness to be vulnerable is also being willing to admit to students that you do not have all the answers and, like many of them, do not know what to do or how to feel. Several described this as "flying by the seat of their pants." This is unchartered territory for many educators, since many teacher preparation programs (and, indeed, society in general) stigmatize vulnerability as "unprofessional." Carrie, a high school social studies teacher whose story was shared in the introductory vignette, counters these messages, however, challenging us to think about the connection between vulnerability and humanity: "If we can let students see our humanity and we can recognize our students' humanity and the complexity of that humanity, that's just such a bigger lesson. . . . You don't have to know [all the answers]. Society puts that pressure on public educators. But students appreciate hearing about you as a human." Carrie's thoughts echo Agarwal-Rangnath's (2020) exhortation: "Our current schools teach us to see the world in a way that undermines humanity" (p. 5).

Mackenzie remembers teaching the day after a student died by suicide. "The first trauma that I had to teach through happened 2 months into my first year of teaching," she remembered, noting that it was especially difficult to process this as a brand-new teacher. In her small school, there were about 900 students: a small enough community for everyone to know what happened when they came to school the next day. Mackenzie was teaching 10th and 12th grades. Pedagogically, Mackenzie made a quick change to her lesson by "just letting them talk and, if they had questions, I answered them the best that I could. Mostly I kind of just listened and let them talk about how they felt." Personally, however, Mackenzie had to do a lot more than make space in her classroom to talk. "It was definitely, really . . . [sighs]. It was not anything I'd expected. It was a kid whose family I had known for a long time. His dad had worked with my dad years before, and I'd known him since he was a little kid. He was one of my brother's friends. It was more personal for me." Rick Ayers (2015) writes powerfully about the vulnerability of moments like this, when you are faced with an "empty seat in class" after the death of a student: "To just sit down and begin to write, to try to begin to write, about the death of a student is appalling. Appalling that the deaths of young people have become a commonplace, even an everyday occurrence about which we need to have a dialogue. But also appalling is that losing a student is a howling nightmare, an unmitigated horror, leaving little more than a gaping emptiness and mystery, something beyond words. But words are what we have" (p. 5).

Finally, several educators talked about what it meant to invest their energy, time, and, indeed, hopes in students on days after and around issues of justice and equity. Aiden Downey and I explored this idea in our research (Dunn & Downey, 2017) about teachers who "bet the house," who invest so much into supporting students or engaging in school responsibilities that they struggle to disentangle those roles from

their sense of self. (Note that "betting the house" is not the same as
the white savior complex!) And yet, "betting the house" is often what
teachers are called to do. That is a vulnerable space for a teacher to be
in, to pour so much of oneself into a student. Especially when issues of
justice and equity are concerned, this vulnerability is amplified because
it causes teachers to question themselves and their success as educators. What does it mean if you don't succeed? What does that say about
you as a teacher? Gemma shared a powerful story about this form of
vulnerability, as she recalled her efforts to work with a conservative student in a way that supported his learning but also did not center his or
her own whiteness in the process. Gemma's thoughtful analysis of these
classroom moments is an illustration of not just her commitments as an
antiracist and justice-oriented educator—and, indeed, one who is deeply
successful in putting these commitments into practice in authentic and
powerful ways—but also of how vulnerability around race can come
into play for both teachers and students. These moments of working to
decenter whiteness arise frequently in days after discussions, like those
on Trump's Muslim ban. Gemma remembers these lessons where she is
"constantly trying to figure out what it looks like to help my white students deepen and develop understanding without keeping my students
of color in 101 conversations, and also without the 'turn to face the
Muslim student in the class after [a dialogue about] the Muslim ban.'"
Here, Gemma is referring to Michael's (2015) argument that, as Gemma
paraphrases what it means for her own practice, "students of color have
a calculus level of understanding [about race and racism] and white
students have an arithmetic level of understanding." In Gemma's classroom, as she works to close the gap between arithmetic and calculus,
she worries that "I'm further centering my white students . . . I worry
about those things that I know happen in a classroom and I haven't
quite figured out yet how to fully disrupt them. We name them; we talk
about them. But I think it's still a risk." One student in particular stands
out in Gemma's mind.

The student's divorced parents shared custody. On the weekends he
was with his father, Gemma noted, he was, "as my friend Shawn Dean
Garcia calls it, 'pickling in white supremacy.' He's just so deeply steeped
in that it soaks through [his] pores. That was his experience: pickling in
white supremacy and toxic masculinity, and it made for these really challenging outbursts in class." Gemma already had been working to develop
a relationship with this student because she knew his 1st- through 4th-
grade years had been spent mostly in the principal's office. In 5th grade,
his teacher "really shifted the trajectory" when she refused to kick him
out of class. Now, in 6th grade, Gemma wanted to live up to that challenge. She began attending all of his football games and working "hard to
be in a relationship" inside and outside of the classroom.

What that commitment to not kicking him out of class looked like in practice proved challenging, though. "It just kept bubbling up," Gemma explained, "when some of his statements would come out of his mouth that were just horrifying, I was really stuck between supporting this kid and having them stay in my classroom and the experience of my students of color in that class." He was "mad at me for my curriculum," Gemma said, in part because he viewed her as a "white race traitor."

Through lots of conversation with the student and his mother, Gemma developed a plan. During the lesson, he would write down his feelings and responses on a piece of paper, instead of saying them out loud, and at the end of class, he would decide if he wanted to share the paper with Gemma or not. "A lot of what he was spewing in the classroom came from his trauma background and his time with his dad and was so far from his personal control. It's so frequent and it's so sad how the racism that happens overtly is often rooted in pain that some of our white cis boys have experienced at the hands of white cis fathers and others in their family. It's really tough to grapple with not wanting to excuse the behavior because it's inexcusable. And also, what does it look like to hold their hand through it?"

Gemma's vulnerability in these discussions continued as she worked through how to best support her students of color without excusing this student, while also finding ways to support him. It was a year, she said, of "handholding and conversation and feeling like I was failing at my job." So what happened to him, I wondered? Gemma laughed, "It's ridiculous . . . in a such an incredible way!" At the end of the year, in the 6th-grade English language arts (ELA) class, students had to choose someone they admired to write about for a biography. And, lo and behold, this student picked Colin Kaepernick. "I don't understand how this happened. He loves football and he decided he was going to take a look at why Colin Kaepernick was kneeling. He finally allowed himself to ask the question instead of just saying he should never play football again. That was a remarkable situation."

DAYS AFTER PEDAGOGY PUSHES TEACHERS TO BE CURRICULAR RISK TAKERS

It is often said (and indeed I often say it myself) that it is better to ask for forgiveness than permission. For teachers who consider themselves to be risk takers in the classroom, this has become a standard mantra, alongside, "just close the door and do what you know you need to do." And yet, with teaching on days after, we should not have to ask for permission *or* forgiveness. Why are we asking for permission to ensure that students know what is happening in the world around them? Why should we ask for forgiveness for naming oppressive policies or white supremacy or racial violence? Although I understand this tendency and find it compelling to practice myself, I also wish to push back on the idea that either permission or forgiveness is needed in the first place. What does it say to our students, especially students from marginalized groups, if we need to get administrative approval to talk about the grave injustices of our times, injustices that threaten their humanity? Or that we apologize after the fact, even if it comes under duress or pressure from the administration? This is especially true for white teachers. We cannot be so complicit in white supremacy that we think it's okay to acquiesce to pressure to not do something or to apologize for doing it, just to save our jobs. At what point do our allyship and co-conspiratorship necessitate a stance of refusal?

One form of curricular risk taking is creative insubordination. Although she was writing about mathematics classrooms, Gutiérrez's concept is useful for teachers of all content areas. Creative insubordination is "the bending of rules in order to advocate for all students to learn" (Gutiérrez, 2015, p. 679). Sometimes, teachers know that rules, guidelines, and policies are either directly or indirectly harmful to students. Sometimes (many times) these rules need to be bent (or broken) in order to best serve students. But to do so creatively means that teachers have to figure out the nuance of how to "play the game to change the game." In her work with math educators, Gutiérrez argued that teachers found it worth it to take risks to support their students, to work toward changing others' minds or practices, to model advocacy for other stakeholders, and to embody an identity that they were proud of. The teachers in this book felt similarly about teaching for justice and equity on days after.

In this section, I share the stories of teachers who refuse to apologize, ignore, or be silent. I devote substantial space to this topic because I want to emphasize the multiple ways that teachers conceptualize what it means to take curricular risks on days after, as well as what they mean by creative insubordination. Some may teach for justice on days after without their administration knowing; others may deliberately ignore administrative edicts to not discuss days after events. In each of their stories, what remains constant is these educators' steadfast commitment to equity and a refusal to remain neutral in the face of injustice. In short, these are the teachers we need on days after.

Let's start with Zara. Zara is a secondary English educator in a small, rural town in the Midwest. As she describes it, it is an "incredibly faith-driven, Republican, conservative, white community." In a way, it is a lot like where Zara herself grew up, and her students remind her a lot of who she was back then but definitely not who she is now. When she talks about social issues with her students, Zara specifically brings up her own childhood: "I try to take my experience and reflection on myself as a naive, sheltered high schooler in a small town that didn't offer me a whole lot of exposure to diversity. I try to use that to expose [my students] to experiences, ideas, and questions that they wouldn't necessarily get otherwise. It's not necessarily wrong to believe what your parents say. It's fine. It's your job as an informed citizen to at least explore and question multiple views so that you can make your own informed decisions. And the informed part is the most important part." Zara and I had a conversation about teaching the day after the 2016 election and how it was a difficult day for her because she felt so differently about the election results than her colleagues and students. This didn't stop her from talking about it with them, however, and was also closely linked with her philosophy about teaching and her past days after experiences.

Although teachers in Zara's school were still displaying Trump and MAGA signs years after the election, she knows that her more liberal signs would not be welcome and would lead to a complaint from a parent. She knows this because parents have complained to school administration before when Zara has asked for students to provide evidence for claims they are making in their writing. She recalled her principal saying that asking for evidence "is too much because then I'm telling them they don't know what they're talking about, when really I'm saying, 'Sure, you can make that statement, by all means. Say what you're saying. But you can't say that without evidence. So give me some evidence to support what you're saying.' Then their parents call in and I have to sit down with the principal. I get called out for bullying their students for requiring them to have data." Zara "accepts now" that this will happen, but she does not stop asking for this evidence because she "push[es] my students from day one. It is not enough to say something's true. You have to prove it and you should expect that of yourself. And you should expect that of everyone who says something to you and everything you read. Because I say that's an expectation for every student, parents can't do anything about it."

Our conversation continued as I asked Zara to list some examples of things she has asked students to back up with evidence that, later, their parents have found upsetting. She rattled off a long list of topics students have wanted to write about: how immigrants are criminals, that socialism is communism, that gun control should be eliminated, that welfare should be eliminated because people don't need it and misuse it. The list goes on. What does Zara do in these situations? If they say something that she knows is not factually accurate, she will ask them if they have data or evidence to support their claims. If they don't, Zara says, "let me pull it up really quick. Here's a chart for you. What you're saying is different [than this evidence]. So prove to me that this chart is wrong." And when the students couldn't prove their claims were truer than the data-based evidence? Then, Zara says, "Then I got in trouble."

Alyssa: So you don't care about getting in trouble?
Zara: No.
Alyssa: Why?
Zara: Well-behaved women rarely make history.

Zara also shared a particular day after where she engaged in creative insubordination. On the day of the student-led walkout, a month after the shooting in Parkland, Florida, "our students were not allowed to walk out. They were allowed to attend a voluntary assembly in the auditorium. So you're allowed to walk out of class and come to this school-controlled thing. I think that was not the best way to do it. Because now you're silencing students' voices and you're making them sit quietly and be talked to at a time when they needed to speak." Zara's students weren't sure if they wanted to go or not. They had "a lot of dialogue" in class about questions related to if they would go to the auditorium, if they would try to leave the school against administrative rules, or if they would stay in their classrooms. For example, Zara and her students discussed, "What do you want to get out of it? What's your objective or your purpose? Will I want to walk out because of this rule? How do we make our goal still happen if we can't leave the school?" Zara had her own questions, too. "I wasn't allowed to leave the classroom for the assembly. I couldn't even go and support the students in what they were doing. I had to stay in my classroom. So I was wondering, how do I support my students? How do I create the opportunities for outreach and dialogue that was now being silenced? How do I amplify the voices of students who are being silenced?" Then the rules got even stricter. Not only was Zara confined to her classroom and the students who wanted to "walk out" required to only enter the auditorium, but teachers were then told they also had to "actually teach" during the scheduled assembly. The administration wanted students to feel like they needed to be in class as opposed to walking out. Other teachers took this rule and ran with it. Some teachers "made the assignment really important, like a 50-point task that, if you walked out, you are not able to make it up." Zara, however, did not want her students to miss anything. So, instead, she taught MLA formatting, "something that the kids already knew." Many students chose to stay versus attending the approved assembly, so they ended up having a discussion about school shootings and gun control, while MLA guidelines were written on the board. Zara technically followed the new rules, as did her students, but they still had an opportunity to discuss what was important to them that day.

Kelly works in a district just a few hours away from Zara, also rural, also conservative. And although they've never met, they would be good colleagues if they were teaching in the same school. Perhaps it might not make them feel like such ideological outsiders in their community to know that there are other educators experiencing the same pushback but responding in a justice-oriented way. Kelly, an English and sociology teacher, knows from experience that administrators are "not terribly supportive" of teachers if there is parental pushback, but she personally "has a good track record of explaining [her] reasoning. I'm better with humans than my principals are. There are plenty of times where they have thrown teachers under the bus, so I don't really count on their support. It would be shocking if I got it."

And yet, like Zara, Kelly doesn't feel she needs administrative support to take on days after conversations. Both Zara and Kelly's whiteness are surely at play here, as teachers of color may not be granted the same leeway from administration if they were in similar schools. "I just do it," she explains, "I spend a lot of time thinking about it and playing through in my head why I am doing this, so that if somebody called or I got a walk-through [principal observation] that day, I would know what my justification would be."

Kelly points to a crucial task here, to proactively anticipate pushback. This is not to make ourselves nervous about what is to come, but because all pedagogical decisions should have a clear rationale and purpose. A clear rationale and purpose is necessary for all teaching, and DAP is no different. Furthermore, as Patel (2016) powerfully argues, "As educators . . . contested engagement is an important part of our work. We must engage with each other, in part, where we each are, and push each other to reach beyond and differently, to unlearn so that we might learn differently" (p. 83).

Kendra and Carrie, as veteran teachers, are well versed in developing those rationales and resisting pushback. They are frequent teaching partners. Even before they tackled a lesson on the day after the Capitol attack in 2021, the story that opened this book, they collaborated on a lesson in the wake of Brett Kavanaugh's testimony ahead of his Supreme Court appointment. (More on the specifics of that lesson in Chapter 7.) They received some pushback from administration on this lesson, in part because a reporter from the *New York Times* found out about what they were doing (after Kendra tweeted about it) and called the school. The school leadership wanted Kendra and Carrie to wait to talk to the reporter until they had gotten clearance from the district leadership. This did not sit well with Kendra and Carrie, as you might imagine. "You wanted us to wait for the *New York Times*?!" Kendra recalls, exasperatedly, "Uh, no. We're not waiting." This constant need to adhere to district "protocols" was not surprising but still frustrating. Sometimes, days after were complicated by the fact that they knew administrators would not understand the need to shift their lesson from district pacing guides or standardized checklists of what "effective" teaching looked like. Carrie and Kendra weren't pleased with that either. Referring to the walk-through checklist of required standards for teachers to meet, Kendra noted, "You can check all the boxes. I did that and then some! You just couldn't figure out how to put this on your little sheet." Carrie continued, "You're gonna criticize a 30-minute moment in my classroom? When was the last time you came into my classroom or took a look at this awesome project we've been doing for 2 months? It's patronizing and insulting. It's clear you don't have any idea what I do. What we do that you can't see is work hard, think critically about what we say to students and about lessons we cover, find resources to use, and change them on the fly. Where is all that on the checklist?"

Donna, while teaching her high school social studies class in the Northeast, was once confronted by a parent who did not like that she was not teaching "both sides" in a discussion that connected the class content of Reconstruction to then-current political debates about racial justice. In particular, she brought in a *New York Times* op-ed by Charles Blow called "The Lowest White Man." Donna appreciated that the article allowed her to show "how the history of reconstruction and the civil rights movement are repeating themselves in the present day." After that class discussion, one of her white students took the article home, and "according to the dad, just slapped the article on the table and said, 'Look what we read today.'" The father then called an administrator. The next day, Donna was called into a meeting with the parent and her assistant principal. Donna recalls that the parent began the meeting by saying, "Look, I don't see color, I don't care if you're black, white, green, purple. I like you no matter what. So what's this all about?" A year later, remembering this comment, Donna rolled her eyes a bit. It was not the first time she had heard this color-evasive discourse. She knows that it is a privilege to say that "color" doesn't matter. She did not specifically address that in the moment, though, instead saying, "I'm not just feeding your kids propaganda by a left-leaning Black columnist. I use this source to teach historical content that your children need to learn." When the parent asked her to consider sharing "other perspectives," Donna refused: "I'm just not going to share a Richard Spencer [piece] in my class. It's my job to keep my students safe, so I have no interest in sharing that perspective."

As Donna thinks about this instance and others like it from other days after in her career, she notes, "I'm okay with standing by the decisions that I make even though I know they are politicized. And if that's what's going to take me down, then that's what's going to take me down. I mean, I obviously don't want to lose my job, but also I'm not going to start looking for middle-ground shit to use in my classroom." A self-described "rabble rouser," Donna is also very conscious of the privilege that comes with saying she is willing to risk her job over this type of teaching. She recognizes that her educational background and her whiteness make it more possible to take this insubordinate stance. "I recognize the privilege that I have when I say that, with me being a troublemaker saying 'if you're going to fire me over me being political in the classroom, then that's going to be on you.'"

One example of curricular risk taking is the idea of sharing one's own political views with students. Whether explicitly taught or not, many preservice teachers leave their teacher preparation programs thinking that this is hugely taboo. "It's just something we know not to do," a new teacher told me once. But how? Why? The research on this, as shared in Chapter 2, is clear. Disclosing one's personal views does not equate with pressuring students to align with them. Disclosing one's personal views does not equate with indoctrination or politicking. Indeed, I would argue that it's deeply important for our students to know our political views. Political choices represent our values. And if our values are aligned with a commitment to justice and equity, students should be able to see this in our classroom every day. Gemma spoke about this idea a lot in her interview. As a middle school humanities teacher, she emphasizes "conversation in the classroom" for many days after moments. Remembering how she structured classes on the day after the announcement of Trump's Muslim ban and the day after the shooting at a Pittsburgh synagogue, she discussed how her own views often came up during these days after dialogues. Typically, Gemma will use conversation protocols from the School Reform Initiative, such as "Save the Last Word for Me" or "The Four As," or use a discussion format like a Socratic Seminar or a Harkness Seminar. "I think in some ways my views are super transparent because of the articles I'm choosing to use and the questions I'm asking," Gemma reflects, although she does make sure to share her opinions if they are doing a discussion where everyone is sharing. "I do offer my perspective on the questions that we're asking, but I think students already know. . . . We're not fooling anybody. I think our students are deeply aware of our politics. I think they're very intuitive. And by politics I mean both big P and little p." As an example of how student might intuit her "big P" political leanings, as in her political identification, recall the earlier mention of Gemma explicitly telling students they are not to use the same bigoted language as elected officials (such as Trump, president at the time). In terms of her "little p" politics, Gemma offers another example of how these come into play in days after moments, such as in the wake of the Muslim ban when, as discussed earlier, Gemma did not allow her students to debate because it risked debating students' humanity.

To be creatively insubordinate is to know when to listen to administrative edicts and when not to. Toby recalls a story of when he knew insubordination was necessary. As for many educators, it was the day after the 2016 presidential election. As he started to recall this day, Toby grew emotional. "It still just hits me, thinking about the students who were crying and just devastated." He knew his students were going to be upset that day and, "immediately, we were able to start talking about it even through their tears. It came up that my class was the only class that they had that day where [they talked about it]." How could that be, I wondered? "None of their other teachers had actually engaged in it at all, beyond maybe some sort of muffled and muted kind of comments about the results of the election. We'd actually had a directive from our principal to not" talk about the election results. So his peers listened, but Toby did not. It was "one of those moments where I had to make a decision as a teacher to willfully defy that. [The principal] never visited my classroom that day. I knew that it would be an act of violence towards my students in a way to force them to be like, 'Sorry, we gotta read *Hamlet* today.'"

So there was no *Hamlet* that day. Instead, Toby opened up the class as "a space for students to express what they were feeling. I remember trying to validate the pain and the reasons why folks were feeling scared." Toby also tried to use the discussion "as a space to invite us to think about how we can be allies toward the people who would most be affected by the ideas" that Trump would enact as president. What made this discussion work, though, according to Toby was that "students came into my classroom already knowing that it was going to be a space that they could talk about it when none of their other teachers were even willing to engage in the rawness and, in fact, were explicitly avoiding it because of how political it was." Toby and his students had already read James Baldwin, Martin Luther King Jr., and Gloria Anzaldúa. They had already talked about campaign rhetoric and proposals during the election cycle, so that "talking about the news had already laid the foundation for and created that space for students to feel like they could be safe coming in to cry and express their hurt and pain on the day after. That's one of the biggest reasons to make it a consistent thing for me in my classroom, so that when a big thing does happen, students already feel that or know that about my class."

DAYS AFTER PEDAGOGY PUSHES TEACHERS TO WORK THROUGH FEARS AND CHALLENGES

Eliana was starting in a new role at the beginning of the 2014 school year. She had been teaching in a large, urban high school the previous year, but she was shifting to start in a new academy, or themed section, within the school, which was part of a district turnaround plan. The district had recently been placed under "state receivership" because of federal mandates about test scores. The school was opening earlier than usual, and just before they started the new year, across the country, Michael Brown was murdered in Ferguson, Missouri.

The timing was tricky, as Eliana "felt I needed to open with that, but I didn't know the students yet." Furthermore, even though she shakes her head at this belief now, "it felt heavy-handed" to start the year with talking about Michael Brown because "I myself was only just coming into my interest on race, racism, and race relations. It started out as a personal reckoning, and as I learned more, I realized I needed to do better professionally." Having grown up in the same town where she was teaching, and because she shared a Latinx background with most of her students, "I knew very well the messages many of my students had been hearing all their lives, about meritocracy, colorblindness, racial progress, and Latinx identity."

Additionally, this new academy role meant that her own workload had increased. Even though "I did think we needed to discuss it, I wasn't plugged into resources and had three brand-new preps, so I was short on time to prepare. On top of that, the new academy where I was to teach had a strict notebook policy. I was afraid that I didn't have the freedom to allow students to air their concerns and connect on a more personal level with the event and its implications." Eliana was teaching two new classes: psychology/sociology for juniors and seniors and world history for sophomores. She felt that it would be easier to discuss with the psychology/sociology class because of the alignment of class material, but she was also concerned she might have to "first establish a basic understanding of some sociological concepts [because] most students had never learned *explicitly* about societal structures, how people exist within and across institutions, what those institutions are. I had designed the course to start broadly with some Bronfenbrenner-type intro to the levels of analysis and then look at statuses and roles, until I arrived at identity. But that was weeks in!" Thus, what ended up happening was very brief and "did not elicit much student response." In her sophomore class, "it hurts me to admit that I don't think I talked to them about it at all."

When talking with teachers around the country, the worries that they have about teaching on days after are akin to the worries they have about teaching about other political or justice-related matters. These worries, they say, are heightened on days after because of the often hyper-focused media attention to what has happened in the world and what feels like increased administrative oversight. For the teachers who participated in this research, their fears and challenges were similar. They were worried about getting pushback from administration and parents (which might eventually lead to discipline or job loss), not having enough time, making a mistake in what they said or how they said it, and not having all of the information about what happened. They were further worried about not being able to do "enough." Many of the teachers I talked to recognized that there were ways to push through those concerns and still find ways to support students.

Curricular Challenges

Brittney remembered student teaching during the 2016 presidential election. "I was student teaching in my senior year, in an ESL classroom. I was at my placement the day after Donald Trump was elected," she shared. Before she got to school that morning, a key question was racing through her head: "How are we going to talk about these vocab words or their homework when these students were directly impacted?" Brittney was glad to see that her mentor teacher did shift the day's lesson, an important choice for the students and for Brittney. When it came time to employ her own DAP in her first year as a teacher, however, Brittney felt limited by the long list of standards she was supposed to cover in her classes. In her secondary Spanish classroom, "I struggled a lot last year keeping up with the scope and sequence of our curriculum. And so there really was no time" for talking about major events on days after. This was frustrating for Brittney because she felt like not doing this meant that her justice-oriented values were at odds with her teaching praxis. "I feel like after any school shooting or any shooting really in the U.S. that's racially motivated, there were things I wanted to talk about with my kids." The reality of being a first-year teacher was overwhelming to her, "and I just never could [utilize DAP] for fear of falling behind and keeping up with the curriculum."

Brittney was not alone in this concern; however, of all of the educators I talked to, the only teachers who expressed a fear of "falling behind" were teachers with less than 3 years of experience. Oscar, who has been teaching for 20 years, summarized one rationale that other veteran teachers echoed: "Am I worried about getting off my timing of the curriculum? No. Not at all, because the reality is that if you tried to teach that day, especially in the era of phones and social media, you wouldn't be able to. You might as well just talk about it. That's what the kids will need and want." This reflects, perhaps, one of many things that teachers learn to grapple with as they gain more classroom experience. There are many things that can "throw off" curriculum, not just major events. The flexibility and adaptability necessary for DAP are certainly a skill that may come with time. However, it is also a disposition that can be supported in teacher preparation and induction programs so that early career educators can see models of how (and why) it is not only acceptable, but encouraged, to deviate from the set and standardized curriculum in these moments.

Another curricular challenge was determining what was "enough." It was hard, many educators explained, to "choose which things to talk about." Scarlet summarized this difficulty: "I feel like if you had freedom from curricular pressure and state tests and standards, you could just teach based off the news. You could just literally take the newspaper and be like, 'All right, this is my lesson plan for the day and I'm just going to go with it.'" The reality looks different. "I always felt in my practice that I didn't address enough," Scarlet continued, "I always felt guilty. I would see a teacher friend who talked about something in their classroom and I'm like, 'Oh crap. I just did another morning of math!' It's hard. I don't think I ever did enough."

Fears of Pushback

By far, the biggest concern that teachers commented on was fear of pushback from their students' families, their school administration, or the public—or all of the above—if they engaged in DAP for justice and equity. Some teachers had personally experienced this, like when Violet was told to take down the decorations that her students had made for their Black History Month door decorating contest because a white student complained to their parents, and then the parents complained to the school that the door was racist.

Social media has exacerbated teachers' fears of pushback. For example, while this isn't specific to DAP, Brittney has seen what parents at her school do when they are upset about something a teacher said or did. In addition to emails or phone calls, "parents put it on the Facebook community page. That's my biggest fear. Parents typically post their complaints there. They will take a picture of an assignment or of the online grade book and completely berate a teacher" in a Facebook post. This is in contrast to the stories that make the news about racist and sexist lessons (Picower, 2021); instead, families might post about how they do not want their students talking about race at all in their classrooms or how they think social justice is "indoctrination." Even those outside the school community may respond if something is shared on social media. For example, Scarlet discussed what happened when her school posted a picture of a justice-related lesson on Twitter. A friend approached the assistant principal to ask if the photo was from Scarlet's classroom (it was) and why the administrator had not given Scarlet credit. To Scarlet's surprise, it was an intentional choice because "the number of hate messages we get about these lessons is off the charts." When Scarlet went on Twitter to see for herself, she found a photo of a bulletin board from her lesson on white privilege. There was another post about her lesson on gender as a spectrum. "There were so many white racist trolls," she said sadly. "There's 50 comments from people that have no affiliation with our school. They are saying, 'This is child abuse. You're creating snowflakes, and we should be teaching reading and math. School isn't about race and politics.' That was very jarring for me to see." In her New York City context "with likeminded educators," Scarlet had forgotten "that's not how everyone feels about it. It was quite a shakeup." Yet, in the end, their condemnation that Scarlet was "creating social justice warriors" was actually encouraging for her: "Great! That's my job! You're saying it derogatorily, but that's my goal of what education is for."

Other teachers had not seen any pushback or backlash in their schools, but they were concerned about it nonetheless. This had more to do with their understanding of the sociopolitical contexts of their schools and community rather than their personal beliefs. For example, William is a Black man who teaches 2nd grade in a racially diverse suburb in the Midwest. He explained that he thinks parents and administration would only be okay with him doing DAP if "I was unbiased in how I talk about those things" and if the parents agreed that "it was appropriate for kids their age." He struggled to know where this age-appropriate line was because he was also a parent. "I don't even know where to start with other people's kids. You know, we talk about things like that with our own kid. But it's a lot different when you're dealing with other people's kids." At the same time, he acknowledged that his students did often bring up major events like school shootings because "they are exposed to them on TV at home," even if it's not *discussed* at home. He wishes he had a better grasp of what was and was not "allowed" at school because he thinks DAP would help with his overarching goal for teaching: "I'm just trying to help them be good citizens and care about each other."

In a district not too far from where William teaches, Greta teaches middle school German and technology. Our interview was scheduled during Greta's planning period, so she was video-chatting from her classroom. It was good to talk with her because she also used to be a former student. Her first year was tough for many reasons, including that she works in a district where she feels like an ideological outsider. Her values and commitments to justice and equity are challenged by students' comments, parents' perceptions of curriculum, and harmful school policies. So when we talk, it is not an easy discussion. Greta knows that she needs to do more, but she isn't exactly sure how to do that in the current divisive political climate. This excerpt from our interview illustrates how much fear some new teachers have internalized.

> [*whispering*] I wanted to do something about Kavanagh and the hearings. God, I wanted to soooo bad. But I was just afraid of what parents would say if they found out, let alone if my principal did. I know you taught us about creative insubordination and all that, but I just didn't know if *this* was the time to be creatively insubordinate. I . . . hold on, I think they might be outside my door [*goes silent*]. . . . Okay, okay, it's fine. [*sighs loudly*] It's not them. [*laughs awkwardly*] I'm scared to even talk about talking about it. How silly is that? Or is it?

Several teachers talked about the conflict between "family values" and "school values," and how there were some things that parents were teaching their children that schools wanted to counter, as well as other things that schools were teaching that parents took umbrage with. One of these value conflicts arose for Gemma about the Women's March in 2017. Gemma had traveled to the march ("despite all of its faults around intersectionality, I was still glad to be there"), and when she returned on Monday, she did a days after lesson with her middle school students. Later that afternoon, she received an email from a parent about how her lesson had been full of lies. "I had broken down the wage gap, and I racialized it. We talked about what white men make, and then we went from white women to indigenous women." The student's mother wrote that "she had always told her daughter that she could be whatever she wanted to be. My lesson was disrupting that and sharing lies. . . . She was really frustrated that her daughter had heard" the discussion of the wage gap. In her email, the mother "acknowledged that her daughter really loves me and my class. She was frustrated because her daughter's teacher hero was telling her lies." Gemma considered how to respond: "I sat on it for about 24 hours because it was a pretty heated email with lots of accusations. I finally responded by inviting her in to have a conversation, which she did not take me up on. She didn't actually respond to the email at all. But we did come together for a conference for her child a couple of months after that. . . . When we started the conference, I was able to say that it's so clear that what we share is that we both care about this student so deeply. So let's focus today's conversation on how well she's doing, because I was worried the conversation was going to become about me, but we're there for her daughter."

DAYS AFTER PEDAGOGY NECESSITATES THAT TEACHERS NEGOTIATE THEIR POSITIONALITY

A key part of Days After Pedagogy is recognizing where you, as an educator, stand in relation to your students. As with every pedagogical decision that teachers make, reflecting on one's own positionality and identity is a critical component to ensuring that you are teaching for justice and equity on days after. Just as it is important to know students deeply, it is also important to know oneself deeply. While there are many identity markers that teachers would want to account for on days after—our race, ethnicity, gender, sexuality, national origin, religion, ability, and language, to name a few—the identity that most teachers in this project spoke about was their race. Teachers wrestled with how their own racial identity aligned with their students and with how they should take this into account when planning and implementing DAP.

Teachers of Color

Decades of research have demonstrated both the importance of and challenges for teachers of color in U.S. schools. As discussed in Chapter 2, teachers of color are severely underrepresented in classrooms across the country. This is despite ongoing efforts to recruit and retain teachers of color. However, as Kohli (2021) argues, "to understand and address the diversity crisis of the teaching force, it is necessary to move beyond discussions of racial representation. Teachers of Color are not simply vehicles for student success, but rather are whole people with professional goals and oftentimes dreams for their communities" (p. 3).

Furthermore, there are often "hostile racial climates [that] cause teachers of Color to leave their schools or contemplate leaving the profession" (p. 21). In Kohli's (2021) insightful text, she shares counterstories from teachers of color who navigate this climate by highlighting their experiences of "survival and resistance." In particular, she explores how teachers of color use their racial literacies, communities of resistance, organizing efforts in schools and communities, and critical professional development to "develop into the educators and activists they wished to be . . . [and] use their power and agency to resist policies and practices that exacerbate racial inequity" (pp. 21–22). The teachers below explain how they used similar tools to make sense of and fight for justice on days after.

Yolanda is the only Black teacher in her entire district. This means that she is likely the only Black teacher her high school students ever have. Yolanda thinks that she "brings a different perspective, different experiences, and it's my job to make sure I keep doing that even when it's uncomfortable for me." On days after, this can be especially challenging because, in discussions of justice and equity, her white students are often anxious and uneasy. "I have to teach my students that it's okay. We're easing into discomfort around here. I do it every day, and they should do the same." This doesn't mean that the discomfort comes easily to her, though. "I often wonder as the only Black teacher who sometimes pushes the limit, where will I be met with resistance?" Many of the topics that Yolanda wants to discuss with her students "have been historically off limits" in her district, meaning that she has heard from other teachers what things they "should" and "should not" discuss in class. While she feels she has "great administration in her building," if a white parent were to escalate their concern to the district level, Yolanda is confident that they would "not be as understanding" of her right to teach about justice and equity on days after. This is why Yolanda likes to "see how far I can go to find a way to sneak certain things" into the regularly scheduled curriculum, so that her students can be exposed to more social justice lessons *and* so that it paves the way for days after. One example Yolanda shared was on the anniversary of Nelson Mandela's death, which was around the same time as the anniversary of John F. Kennedy's death. She was teaching in a 1st-grade classroom in the same district, and the standards required teaching about historical figures like JFK. Yolanda's plan was simple: She would teach about JFK. But she would also teach about Nelson Mandela. She put up both pictures side-by-side in the hallway so everyone could see what the class was learning. In fact, she got recognized by her administration for teaching about JFK, but they never mentioned Mandela. "I didn't care, though," Yolanda said, "because I know that my students took away something greater."

Being the only Black teacher in her school "requires me to continually expose myself to microaggressions. It starts to weigh on me sometimes" when she has to teach about injustices and tragedies that "have happened yet again." It is also difficult when her students don't respond in the way she hopes they would. She said she feels like saying, "I've still gotta teach you. Now what do I do?" It is not that she wants her students to think exactly the way she thinks—which would be impossible because their experiences are so different—but she hopes that they "will be able to put their own ideas together and not just repeat what their best friend or parents said." Yolanda spends a lot of time "trying to figure out" how to push forward in a way that honors her commitments to justice, especially if she's not met with "openness or a response that they enjoyed or learned something."

Brittney is also one of the only teachers of color in her school and district. She is a second-year teacher working at the same high school she went to as a child, so she understands the environment very personally. Yet, it doesn't necessarily make a difference as she grapples with what it means to engage in justice work as a biracial woman in a predominantly white community. One of the things that Brittney always brings up when it happens is a school shooting. Or, if something "major" were to happen closer to home, she claims, "It would be a no-brainer" to talk about that on the day after. Talking about days after moments related to race proves trickier, however. Brittney thinks that "talking about a school shooting is safer than talking about race." That doesn't mean she would not have those conversations, Brittney clarifies, but it would be harder for her to be the one to introduce them. "If it's something my students brought up, I would never shy away from it or say 'we're not going to talk about that.' But I struggle more on how I would bring those things to their consciousness."

Like Yolanda, Brittney feels a responsibility to talk about race with her majority white students since their other teachers are also white and do not have the personal experience (or, in many cases, professional experiences) talking about issues of race, racism, and justice on days after. Her colleagues (middle- and upper-class mostly white women) do not view DAP as a component of their practice. "And even the ones that do,"

Brittney continued, do not know "how to have those conversations with students in an authentic way, and there's a fear that they will be spotted as a phony or somebody that's trying too hard to connect. It's gotta be real." Real, for her, also means being upfront about her positionality and privilege. "Being biracial, I have always, even still as an adult, not known where I fit in. My brightest moments are when I can check more than one box for race. I struggle, too, because I want to fight for the marginalized as a biracial woman, but I still have lived quite a privileged life. So I guess at times I still question myself on if I am even the right person to talk about this." As she struggles through these big questions about who she is and what types of pedagogical choices to make in light of her identity, Brittney works consistently to push back against her own self-doubt and fear because of the few students of color in her classes—so that they have an opportunity for their voices and experiences to be centered—and for the majority white students, so they learn more than what the biased curriculum teaches them. For her students of color, "their stories aren't always told, or they're misrepresented, they're stereotyped as 'disadvantaged'" in the curriculum. So, on days after, it is especially important to "get it right" and not perpetuate the media stereotypes that often, for example, portray white perpetrators better than Black victims in instances of racial violence. That is why it's important for Brittney to "take the time to talk about these things and teach them how to talk about these things without it being an argument or a debate. If we can talk about these tough things as students, then they're going to become adults talking about these tough things. And that's how we make change."

Dominique teaches in a very different context than Yolanda and Brittney. Her students are nearly all Black. So, on days after, the questions that she gets are also very different than the ones faced by teachers of color in predominantly white contexts. When she was teaching early elementary grades, her young students wanted to know why injustices keep happening and why people can be so cruel and hurtful to each other. When she looked down at the faces of her students, she often saw herself in them. But there is only so much she is able to do because sometimes she doesn't know how to answer those questions for herself either. Dominique shared, "It's exhausting because you don't always have an answer. And it feels so personal to me being a woman and being Black. It's frustrating. I don't have answers for myself. So sometimes, when speaking to them if they're discouraged or they're angry, I don't always have the thing to say to them that would make it better. That feels hard. And I'm a person; I don't take me off when I'm in the classroom. I don't leave my teacher self at school either."

Days after can be particularly "emotionally exhausting" for Dominique because her own feelings and those of her students are heightened in these crisis moments. Dominique sees DAP as a learning process for her students and herself, in that they all develop new skills for having equity-focused dialogues and new skills for socioemotional awareness and development.

Not far away, in another borough of New York City, Adam, a 4th- and 5th-grade teacher, was also reflecting on his identity as Chinese American. In recognizing his identity as a teacher of color, Adam also acknowledged that he is also constantly in a learning process about other communities. This means that his DAP might include some mistakes. Adam said, "I normalize mistakes in my classroom. . . . When I discuss controversial issues, such as the election, the election results, or after the Pulse shootings in Florida, or even the civil rights movement, I might stumble over some language. I have to apologize when my language is not as inclusive as it should be." Adam seeks to model for them how to engage in days after discussions or other justice-centered dialogue, in part by bringing in his own intersectional identities.

Adam recalled one particular day after in which he discussed both his race and sexuality with his students. On the day after the 2016 presidential election, students were "announcing that they were scared they might be deported or scared for their families who were applying for citizenship," and Adam understood the feelings of his immigrant students. It was concerning for another reason, too. "I identify as gay. I have a husband. Our daughter is adopted. I shared that I'm really afraid, too. I now have a president who is not going to support the rights of people who identify as gay or lesbian or bi. I'm very open with my students about my life outside of school in hopes that they would be comfortable sharing who they are. If I don't share who I am or what I'm feeling outside of the classroom, how do I expect my students to be vulnerable with me? Being vulnerable is part of being human, right?"

As both a teacher of color and a gay educator, Adam finds a special connection with his students on days after. This connection builds upon the community he has already established with them, so that they feel comfortable sharing their feelings, complicated as they be, and making mistakes, challenging as it may be to apologize and learn anew. On days after, Adam summarized, "You can't check your feelings at the door. You can't check your identities at the door. You can't check your biases at the door. You always have to constantly be checking them in front of your students, so that they know to do it, as well."

Even though they teach different ages, Kendra's experiences resonate with Dominique and Adam. In the urban school where she teaches, she works with predominantly students of color and other teachers of color. That doesn't mean days after are automatically easier for her, however. Kendra noted that there is an "extra burden of being a woman of color" in leading the conversations because "the reality is that any scrutiny or consequences we face could be harsher." She noted that "as a teacher of color, there's a lot of mask wearing. Because I'm a Black woman, there's already a perception about what I believe, what I think, where I stand on stuff." If she chooses not to discuss certain issues, it is not about "intentionally avoiding them"; rather, it is navigating the difficult terrain of how "processing events in front of others when we're not okay ourselves" could affect her. For example, she experienced "complex emotions" in the spring of 2020 in the wake of Ahmaud Arbery's murder because she felt "glad for not having to physically show up to work and for kids." Kendra shared more about what these emotions look like for her: "It can be a complex mix of not wanting to offer more label options to how students already categorize me as a Black woman, in addition to ensuring a lesson/discussion/space that is a value-add during those times. But the students gain from seeing our humanity and honesty in those moments. And, sadly, it's going to take a while to counteract, via media literacy and academic discourse, the lies and misinformation since it's dominated our culture for 4 to 6 years. If we don't, they ultimately lose by seeing a wider gap of what's offered at school that prepares them for life versus what's overlooked in favor of some 'standardized' curriculum."

White Teachers

As explained earlier, the teaching profession remains overwhelmingly white, and this is not likely to change as preservice teacher preparation programs also serve predominantly white future educators taught by predominantly white faculty, subsumed as they are in the overwhelming presence of whiteness (Sleeter, 2017). Many white teachers are hesitant to engage in justice-oriented pedagogy with white students, particularly if they are in conservative communities where discussions of equity may be frowned upon or directly forbidden. When white teachers do not push back against administrative policies that curtail equitable discussions and DAP in the classroom, or when they adopt this stance themselves, they protect their own whiteness. To say that they want to remain "neutral" or "unbiased" is protecting their own whiteness. Often, to present "both sides" in a discussion or ask students to "debate" some of these days after issues is exercising their privilege. That they can see racism as something ever worthy of debate is evidence that they have never had to live with it. Picower (2021) helps us see the connection between whiteness, white people, and white supremacy:

> Within this system of White supremacy, Whiteness is the ideology and way of being in the world that is used to maintain it. Whiteness is not synonymous with White people; instead, it is the way in which people—generally White people—enact racism in ways that consciously and unconsciously maintain this broader system of

White supremacy. While individual people of color may also enact
Whiteness, they do not benefit from the broader system of White
supremacy in the ways that White people do. White supremacy is
the what, White people are typically the who, and Whiteness is the
how. (pp. 6–7)

Often, when white people are confronted with these ideas about racism and whiteness, they become defensive, hostile, and resistant. This is
evidence of white emotionality (Matias, 2016) that is antithetical to justice and equity-oriented teaching because it centers the needs of white
people rather than the experiences of people of color. White people who
demonstrate this emotionality often co-opt discussions about race and
racism to make it about them and how they are feeling, making it about
their own "white tears." It is deeply important that on days after, when
tensions and emotions may already be heightened, white teachers do not
perpetuate white emotionality. This doesn't mean that white teachers cannot feel emotions, often deeply, about the injustices that are happening,
but rather, they should not let their own defensiveness, confusion, or guilt
get in the way of true student-centered pedagogy.

I talked to many white teachers who said that they believed in justice and equity and yet repeated these inequitable ideas about not taking
a stand on so-called political or controversial issues. These are directly
in contradiction to one another. White teachers cannot support justice
and equity and then refuse to address the most critical issues of our time
in their classrooms in favor of "neutrality." We know that one major
way that white students get socialized into ideas of whiteness and white
supremacy culture is because they are surrounded by white communities
and white educators. Something has to disrupt this cycle of socialization, of hearing the same messages of "normalizing" whiteness. Indeed,
white students' lack of knowledge on many days after is also evidence
of white privilege. That their families don't have to talk to them about,
for example, another killing of an unarmed Black person doesn't mean
that teachers should not talk to them about it either. On the contrary,
it means that teachers have even more responsibility for ensuring that
students' understanding of race and white supremacy are supported in
school, rather than conforming to the call to "protect their innocence."
Such a call protects and perpetuates white supremacy. In the case study
chapters at the end of the book, there will be more stories of white
teachers engaging in DAP with their students, be they white students
or students of color. Here, now, we turn to white teachers discussing
both the importance and the complexity of DAP as a white teacher of
students of color.

Quinn is a first-year teacher, a white woman in her mid-20s teaching
classes of all Black 6th- and 7th-graders in Chicago. Her students have all

been born and raised in the surrounding neighborhood, while Quinn grew up in a suburban town in a neighboring state. Her undergraduate teacher preparation program had a few classes about racial justice and equity, and Quinn is very comfortable talking about her own white identity development. When it comes to teaching her Black students about identity, however, she hesitates with knowing exactly what to do and how to do it. "I'm just a white lady, and I don't want it to come off as a white savior," she stated. "It's always my fear. I don't want to come into a classroom to try to teach them about racism because they know about that already. I don't want to come in and act like it's something I can teach them about." Quinn recalls her student teaching experience where she used the book *The Skin I'm In*, by Sharon Flake. One of the book's themes is colorism, "and colorism is something they can relate to but I never can." She hopes that, with more experience, she will continue to learn and grow in her confidence for how to engage in these discussions on days after especially. When thinking about her unit on the trial of Laquan McDonald (discussed in Chapter 7 in more detail), Quinn admits that "I definitely still have a little anxiety about it. I'm wondering how I will come off and how are students going to interpret what I'm doing." What makes Quinn's story different than other novice teachers who I talked with (and whose stories, ultimately, are not part of this book) is that she did not let this hesitancy stop her from a commitment to DAP. Instead, she used the time to reflect on why she was hesitant, as well as what that meant for her as a person and as a teacher, and pushed forward with her plans. Importantly, she did not uncritically rush into days after discussions without careful attention to how her own positionality would affect if or how her students would trust her in these vulnerable moments. She was attentive to wanting to create space for dialogue but in a way that did not contribute to more harm.

Donna has been teaching high school for 12 years, so she is a bit more familiar with how days after discussions go. With her students, almost all of whom are people of color, she wants to "create a space for them to talk where I'm not the center of the conversation." Donna believes it is important that white teachers recognize that "it's not our job to tell students that they're oppressed" but instead offer the space to students if they want to have a discussion. This was challenging on the day after the 2016 election because Donna believed "the Trump presidency was going to make things worse for people of color or if their families are immigrants." She strove to make sure that what students said was centered and supported. Donna seeks to center not just pain but also joy, and to examine her own whiteness in the process. Donna recognizes that it's "not a clear road" or a straight path to what DAP looks like every time. She tries to balance "listening to students, providing resources that they may not be getting otherwise, and supporting them in developing their thinking."

Leah has a similar approach to Donna in her middle school classroom. Leah takes issue with other white teachers—both at her school and elsewhere—who aren't aware of the implications of equity and justice on days after. "I would like to push back a little on the idea that it's not obvious" to white teachers who don't engage in DAP. "There's no way that it's not obvious, but they probably are not going to ever say it or even admit it to themselves. They're not going to let it come to the surface of their consciousness, but they're definitely aware" of the racial implications of many major events. Through her DAP, Leah hopes to support students in learning "about those injustices at a deeper level, but then also helping them feel empowered and like they have efficacy. Sure, they care about those things," like racial violence, gun control, and climate crises, "but then they also can do things in their lives to change it. They can create a new, different way forward."

Toby is also a white veteran teacher with many memories of days after. He explains, "My privileges and my own sociopolitical identity mean that sometimes it's a choice for me whether or not I want to engage in [DAP], but for other students or teachers, they don't have that choice. I try to navigate how to work through emotional burnout versus wanting to be a consistent critical educator." Like earlier teachers discussed, Toby has "an arsenal of research and a rationale on my side about why we're going to engage in this. Just because you're saying that it's political, does it mean that it's not something that we should be able to approach in English class? And, in fact, here's all the reasons why I think the English class should be the place where we are engaging in all of these things." For Toby, DAP is "something that [he] felt convicted about as an educator," saying that he needs to use his positionality to "push the boundaries because the status quo is harmful and is enacting all of the gaps in education that we see."

Finally, we hear from Carrie, a 14-year veteran social studies educator who teaches predominantly students of color in Atlanta. Carrie knows that teachers often hear that teaching for justice and equity, especially on days after, is biased. Carrie clarifies, "My goal is not to indoctrinate students. My goal is to teach them the history of those [who] history has ignored, the reasons racism and sexism still persist, America's role in maintaining those -isms nationally and internationally, and our responsibilities in making changes to those foul systems." She "[doesn't] have the time or the energy or the interest in debating the need for social justice. I'm too busy teaching my students how to fight for it."

CONCLUSION

The teachers in this chapter revealed the importance of several character-istics that support DAP. First, they were willing to be vulnerable with their students. They understood that days after moments are emotional, and they approached these discussions with open hearts and a willingness to simultaneously engage in the uncertainty. They were also curricular risk takers who engaged in creative insubordination when necessary. As they worked through their own fears and challenges, they were also attuned to how their own positionality affected their choices and what this meant for their students.

Student Spotlights: Days After the Capitol Attack

What did my teacher do after January 6, the day a mob attacked the Capitol? She did absolutely nothing. I was disappointed because I thought that she would say something about the things that had happened, but she acted as if everything was normal, and absolutely nothing had happened the day before. Since we were on Zoom, I used the chat to ask her if she knew what had happened, but she did not respond to my question. I wanted to talk about it with the entire class, but since she didn't respond, I felt as if she didn't want me to bring it up. No other students brought it up either. I know that some people in my class would have been concerned too, because I see Black Lives Matter and other social justice signs in front of their houses, but there are also Trump supporters as well.

I think that my teacher didn't want to cause any arguments about politics between my classmates, and that's why she didn't bring it up. I have a feeling that she supports social justice because every once in a while, she says, "Everyone matters," but she doesn't go out of her way to do the right thing. I was hoping that she would talk about it with the class and inform the students who didn't know about it already, because everyone should know about things that are happening in the news.

At my next book club meeting, where we were reading a book called *White Bird* by R. J. Palacio, I asked what everyone else's teacher had done to talk about the Capitol situation, and lots of people in the meeting said that their teachers had not done anything, but my mom and I decided to do something different. We decided to talk about it. During the book club, because it was our turn to lead the discussion, we showed some videos and pictures of the attack on the Capitol. We talked about bystanders, upstanders, and perpetrators in the book we were reading and during the attack on the Capitol. My teacher should have done this too; she should have educated us about the attack on the Capitol, but because she didn't, some of the people in my class were unaware that this event even happened. The truth is that not enough people are doing what the people in our meeting did: standing up for what is right. We need to come together as a whole, and if we do this, we can defeat the wrong, the hate, and we can make peace.

Author Bio: Corabella Dover is in 6th grade and lives in Orange County, California. She thinks that everyone should practice social justice because you can't do it if you don't practice. She currently loves all animals, especially dogs, cats, and any other fluffy pet. She loves reading, and when she is not in her bed with her nose in a book, she is on the soccer field playing with friends.

* * *

Insurrection day: the day when the Capitol turned into hot flaming garbage.

Out of all three teachers I saw for virtual learning that day, the only person who said anything was this old, probably conservative, white guy teacher. To go along with the mood, he also prepared some half-assed thing for us to listen to. I don't know if he meant it or not, but he was really vague and didn't really tell us anything besides something bad happened at the Capitol. If he said anything else, it was "I think. . . . " "I think . . . " isn't good enough when no one at school is telling us anything and are treating us like 5-year-olds.

If I were them, I would tell the kids the truth because that is what they deserve. The truth is what happened, why they did it, and what people are doing about it. A clean answer with no biases. Sure, I get it if you aren't going to tell preschoolers and younger the news, but some of the older kids should get at least a little bit of info! All in all, it was a very annoying, crappy day when the adults treated us like objects who wouldn't get what is going on and wouldn't feel anything about it. I think I understood what they meant from watching the news. I feel like they should have higher expectations for us, as we do for them.

Author Bio: Marjorie Wiese is a 7th-grade female student from East Lansing, Michigan, who attends Haslett Middle School. She is one of the only Black people in her school. Marjorie gets good grades, is an extrovert, and likes to play video games.

CHAPTER 6

The Intersections of Teaching and Politics on Days After

Now that we have a better sense of the purpose of Days After Pedagogy (DAP), how it focuses on all students, and what teacher skills and dispositions align with DAP, we can turn to some extended examples of what DAP looks like in the classroom. The next two chapters are organized by topic, illustrating how several teachers from different geographic areas, grade levels, and/or content areas approached teaching on similar days after. These cases demonstrate how the tenets of DAP are applicable across contexts *and* how they have to be nuanced through understanding one's students, one's own identity, and the sociopolitical and sociocultural factors inside and outside of one's classroom.

The topics shared here are not the only days after that teachers discussed, nor are they the only events that occurred in the years that the participants have been teaching. All teachers acknowledged that they "can't cover everything that happens in the world," nor is this book a call to do so.

This chapter focuses on the intersections of politics and Days After Pedagogy. What do days after look like in the wake of elections, gun violence, environmental crises, and gender injustice? While "elections" are clearly political, the other topics here may seem farther from that category. Yet, in recent years, as issues of justice and human rights have become politicized (and hyper-partisan), the teachers' memories of these days after are clearly shaped by their understanding of their school community's political beliefs. All these stories will feel incomplete—they may leave you wondering, but then what happened? Or how specifically did the teachers do x or y? The purpose is not to drill down to the minutiae of what happened but rather to explicate how teachers remember it and how and why they made certain choices. The *how* of days after is in both the practice itself and the decisionmaking.

All of the research for this book—and most of the stories that stuck out for teachers the most—happened in the wake of the 2016 presidential election, a time that could easily be classified as one of contention, polarization, partisanship, and general political turmoil. In such times, it becomes both more important and more precarious for teachers to discuss controversial issues in their classrooms (Hess & McAvoy, 2015). As discussed in Chapter 2, "there is substantive debate about which criteria teachers should use to determine an issue's openness" (Geller, 2020a) since some issues that were previously considered "closed," or settled and lacking in legitimate viewpoints, suddenly became "open" again in public discourse (Hess, 2009). In Geller's (2020b) work about teacher political disclosure after the Trump election, teachers "said that the polarization and contentiousness in the political climate made it difficult for them to know the right thing to do in the classroom. While the dynamics they described—bullying, contentiousness, racism, and intolerance—are not unique to the Trump era, most described feeling that they had been heightened or unleashed since the 2016 presidential election and a number of them observed that their students were parroting Trump's language" (p. 38). Thus, Geller (2020b) asks us to refocus the discussion on open/closed issues, neutrality, and disclosure because teachers must recognize that "non-disclosure is a political choice, too." Instead, we should be asking, "How can teachers' political opinions in the classroom be used in ways that are responsible, professional, and help students learn?" (p. 39).

DAYS AFTER ELECTIONS

What do teachers do on the day after a new president is elected? What happens if the staff, students, and families supported the person who won? What if their candidate lost? What if the school community is divided or the teachers supported a different candidate than the majority of the families in the community? On these days that feel hyper-politicized, what types of pedagogical shifts and moves do teachers make in their classrooms? Here are some examples of what teachers remember about their election-related DAP.

2016

When Adam talks about it, he makes sure to say "the day after Hillary Clinton lost the election," as opposed to naming the winner. At his New York City public elementary school, Adam notes that colleagues and "especially students thought that was a pretty devastating day." He started the day by having his students share their feelings about the results. His students were afraid of being deported or harmed by the newly elected President Trump. In a school that "fosters a lot of feminists," the girls "came in just broken." One student said, "During such times, we need to have more courage and share that with the world." Adam and his 4th-grade students decided to change the plans for the day (again) by creating "shields of courage." Throughout the day, they talked about and wrote on their shields: How do we show courage for ourselves? For our family? For our community? It was a way to "recenter ourselves during that moment." At the end of the day, Adam checked in with his students and asked, "How does one become president?" Upon hearing students' answers, "I realized that, 'Oh, wow, my students really don't know the whole electoral college system and even local politics.'" Thus, the *day* after became *days* after.

Pointing to the wall in his classroom, Adam recalls creating a chart that illustrated the three branches of government. In the week after the election, they discussed the Constitution and then created classroom norms and rules together, "but we called it our classroom constitution, and we went through a voting system in which every table became a local county." Adam also led them in a discussion of campaign finance and how that plays a role in elections. Each table, or county, was assigned a socioeconomic status (what Adam called low, middle, and upper class) that dictated the funds they had available for campaigning. Students were, "of course, devastated" when they realized their county might not have enough money to compete with more resource-rich counties. "But," Adam says, his eyes lighting up at the memory, "then they also realized, all right, so we don't have money, what other resources do we have?" In one county, there were some students who were good speakers and writers, and they "realized that they could utilize that to their advantage." Through campaign posters and slogans, "their use of words surpassed a lot of other counties and they ended up winning the overall election!" Adam reflected later that he thinks this form of DAP achieved his goal in helping his students to ease some of their anxieties, as it helped them learn that "there are a lot of factors that go into an election and, by understanding more about how officials get elected, it helped them think more about what can they realistically do about this?" In this one example, we see Adam exemplifying the belief that DAP is appropriate for all ages and all content areas, and that it requires knowing your students and focusing on what they need in the moment. It illustrates how Adam supported students' agency, their socioemotional needs, and their sociopolitical awareness on what they felt were difficult days.

Across the country in suburban Michigan, Oscar was teaching high school history. When I asked him about teaching after the 2016 election, he first harkened back to previous elections. The year 2008 stands out because he "gave away [his] presidential vote to [his] students." He petitioned for an absentee ballot and, after talking about elections and each of the candidates with his U.S. history class, had a secret ballot in class. "Eighty-eight percent went to Obama," Oscar remembered, "and 12% went to McCain." Oscar had "thought it would be a fun thing to do" because he didn't anticipate such a landslide for Obama who, he confides, he was planning on voting for anyway. After the vote, his students watched him fill it in and saw him mail the ballot. "My argument to my colleagues was that we don't vote for the president anyway, unless I'm one of the 538. It was the most educated vote in the state because 80 kids got to participate in one vote." For any students who were of voting age, Oscar said, "They had to vote on their own, they weren't allowed to participate" in his ballot. So, the day after that election, it was a celebration. That was a good day.

In contrast, teaching on the day after the 2016 election was akin to teaching on September 12, 2001. "It was the second hardest day I ever taught," he said. Even several years later, during our discussion, Oscar pauses a lot when he tells this story, clearly still emotional about his memories of the day. "I remember how devastated everybody was," except for the student who wore a Trump shirt to soccer practice. The students were "distraught and hopeless," especially Muslim and immigrant students because of Trump's racist rhetoric and promises of travel and immigration bans (which did come to fruition). The students were "really terrified" about Trump's history of sexual assault and were in a state of "disbelief and shock." Oscar also remembers that he "got a compliment from the principal that I handled it really well," passed on from a parent. Oscar thinks this is because he also focused on the importance of civic action and engagement. In his predominantly white classroom, he has always included government action projects, such as attending school board meetings or canvassing for a candidate of their choice. This came up as part of their discussion on the day after about "how important it is to be civically involved."

And finally, we turn to Melissa in Austin, Texas. In her dual-language elementary classroom, they had been studying voting patterns and electoral maps leading up to the election. In math, they had cocreated a living timeline about when different groups were granted the right to vote. They made comparisons and, alongside reading about voting rights, analyzed the dates mathematically. "We talked a lot about the right to vote and what it meant," Melissa said, "and everybody had some sort of connection to what Donald Trump had been espousing and they had a lot of awareness of it." With the exception of one biracial student, all of Melissa's students were Latinx, and everyone was an immigrant, a child of an immigrant, or a grandchild of an immigrant who lived with them. They talked about Trump's election "a *lot*," Melissa emphasized, "but the kids, all of us really, lived in the bubble that Hillary Clinton was gonna win. It was really hard to process." That morning, Melissa headed to school before dawn, having barely slept, and cried on the drive to school, "just sobbing, thinking about how I was going to face the kids and what I could even do with them that day." It wasn't going to be an ordinary day, anyway, because a special visitor was coming to their classroom.

Prior to their voting rights unit, the students had done a unit on Afro-Latinx identity and anti-Black racism in Mexico. It's important to understand what that unit was and how students engaged in justice-oriented discussions in order to understand what happened the day after the election. Some of the activities that Melissa and a friend, a local professor, did were on the Cuban census and why people could choose to identify as Black or white. They discussed the Transatlantic Slave Trade and engaged in a critical math study of how long it lasted and the locations involved. "We used math really explicitly to have deep conversations about the impact of slavery on Latin America and the United States. Mexico had its first Black president in the 1830s, so we talked about the difference in timing between their first Black president and our first Black president." They did two culminating projects. First, they made dioramas of *palencas*, or communities of formerly enslaved people who created free communities in Mexico. Second, they wrote the stories of Afro-Latinx heroes as dramatic plays. To prepare for writing their plays, they watched a documentary in which a scholar was speaking on the topic. And, it just so happened, she was giving a talk at the local university. She agreed to visit the class, and they eagerly prepared their plays to show her. The catch? The only time she could be there was the morning after the election.

That morning, as they waited for their important visitor, the class "had to deal and reckon with" what had happened. Melissa put up a big piece of chart paper, the usual form her "morning message" would take, a place where they could make a connection to what they were going to learn for the day. In bright turquoise marker, it said, "Welcome friends. Remember that you are always safe here. Use your sticky note. What are you feeling today?" At the bottom, a heart and Melissa's name. Melissa saved a photo of it and, as I look at it now, 4 years and a new president later, their tiny handwriting is still deeply heartbreaking. Words like "mad," "angry," "worried," and "disappointed" fill their sticky notes: "I feel so sad that I want to cry. Because Donald Trump won and he will build the big wall." What Melissa wanted them to know overall was that "they were safe, that I loved them and that, when they were with me, they were okay. 'Cause I would have straight up taken out anybody that came in my classroom to take my kiddos," referencing ICE raids. The messages on their notes truly illustrate what Melissa wondered: "What are we doing to people, to children?"

Their time was cut short though, when another visitor arrived, and one not as welcome as their visiting scholar. A school counselor came to visit the class and did a "targeted intervention that was just the worst example of what adults do to children on the day after." In Melissa's mind, on these traumatic days after, "there's two different things you can do, right? You can wrestle with the reality of what's happening and how it's affecting us, or you can lie to children and tell them that their feelings aren't real." The counselor, unfortunately, did the latter. "People always couch these things in being concerned about children's feelings and [how] they're little and no one should scare them, but they're already scared. So she came in and she told them that nothing was going to happen. Everything will be fine. Nothing bad can happen. [Trump is] just one person. He can't do anything. <u>And, of course, none of the kids believed this.</u>" Melissa's students had family members "in very precarious positions" and Trump's election made their situations even more precarious. As Melissa listened to the counselor talking at (not with) the children, she knew they were going to ask her why the counselor lied to them. "I'm going to have to deal with this," she recalled, because she did not want to dismiss the students' concerns or "pretend like it doesn't exist" as the counselor was doing.

Just as Melissa predicted, when the counselor left, the students were quick to jump back into discussion, not just about the election but about the counselor's comments. They brought up a common topic of discussion in Melissa's class: adultism. Melissa said she had been working on her own adultism, even asking the kids to "call me out when they would see me doing it because it wasn't something I wanted to do, but sometimes it would just come out like a habit." When the counselor left, the students asked, "Was that adultism?" When Melissa asked why they thought so, they responded, "She thinks that we're too young and we can't understand. She's telling us a lie to try and make us feel better, but it's really adultism, 'cause she's lying to us. She thinks it's okay to lie to us." Melissa agreed with them; that was adultism, a common trope on days after. Their conversation then returned to processing the events together: "I talked about how I was afraid. They talked about how they were afraid. They talked about how their families were responding" to the election. Then it was time to make a decision. The visiting scholar was set to be there soon. What did they want to do?

Look no further than another of the sticky notes on their morning message to find the answer: "I hope we do something fun today like math and the play." Upon reflection now, Melissa noted that welcoming their visitor "was the exact thing we all needed because it just took us out of that day. We dealt with the election day a bit, but then we <u>had something uplifting and meaningful that tied to our learning.</u> That helped distract from the routines of school. I think part of what's really important on these days after is that we don't just do the motions, but that you disrupt it in some way."

[handwritten margin note: Want to be treated like adults. students understand]

The Days After the Days After

Of course, just months after the election came the inauguration of Trump in January 2017. Many schools around the country, as they would typically do, watched the inauguration. Other districts and schools gave teachers the choice, and some teachers gave their students the choice. Melissa was one of those teachers. Not only did they not watch the inauguration, but "we didn't do school that day," she said. "We didn't want to pretend it was a normal day." Instead, at the students' request, Melissa created a bunch of *mariposa* (butterfly) cutouts for protest signs. Mariposas are a symbol of immigration, something they had learned about the year before. "They said, mariposas can cross the border. Even if Trump builds his wall, they'd make it across the border." The students decorated their mariposas with slogans and symbols: "No Hate," "We Love Immigrants," and "No Wall." One that said "Immigrants are Welcome Here" had a background that looked like states on a map. Many mariposas included flags, including one whose wings were made to look like the flags of the United States and Mexico.

In many ways, as Melissa remembers it, "that whole year was like the day after." Trump's constant mandates, policy changes, and racist, ethnocentric, and xenophobic rhetoric meant there was no reprieve from the fear and worry that plagued students in November 2016. "We were always processing what was happening and how things were changing," Melissa said. Families were often crying in parent–teacher conferences about what would happen to their children if they were deported. How could they ensure that their children did not end up in the foster care system? "These were real things that families were talking about at home. If we at school said, 'It's okay, none of that's real,' we're not just dismissing the kids and telling them they're too little to understand, we're also saying that their parents don't understand." On days after, too many adults are "very quick to try and find the easy way around things." Connecting to one of her primary content areas, Melissa noted, "I wonder what children learn from that, you know? That's a thing in math too, right? Adults are constantly trying to give kids the easy trick to solve the math problem, but then they don't understand why it works. There's so many deep connections between how we engage in any kind of topic around racial justice and how we engage in mathematics. If I don't think you can handle understanding how our country really works, I probably also don't think you can discover mathematical ideas on your own. If I think you need to be told something's a certain way in math, then I think I need to control what you have access to, what you can see, and what kinds of realities you can imagine."

This, for Melissa, is why it is so important to engage in DAP in math class, even though so many teachers would say that math is not the place for it. Because of their days after discussion about Trump and, specifically, his border wall, "it came up all the time" throughout the year. DAP with a justice-oriented focus meant that "students were able to make these deep historical connections throughout the year. What was really important to make that happen was that we didn't ignore the present. We made sense of the present in light of the past, and we used math to interrogate what the present looked like. All this math is just a tool for reading the world. We read the world through texts, but we also read the world mathematically, and we can use those tools to make sense of things and to understand." A justice-oriented Days After Pedagogy can also do the reverse. Just as math can help students read the world, DAP can help students be more critical about how they engage in subjects like math.

DAYS AFTER GUN VIOLENCE

When Chris saw the news that some Republican lawmakers were pondering whether teachers should carry guns in class to prevent more school shootings, he admits that he thought "it was the stupidest question that has ever been asked." But he also wanted the students in his English as a Second Language class to be able to engage in a substantive discussion and share their perspectives on this plan. Chris arranged for Latinx law students from a local university to join his class for a debate. His students "got to see that they could participate in debate and discussion with law students about something big. . . . They all have the ability to talk about this question of should I have a gun right now in class or not. They can tackle that thoughtfully." This debate, it should be noted, was structured as a policy debate, not one about people's humanity, which, as teachers noted in earlier chapters, is not up for debate at all.

Such a debate, although absurd, doesn't seem surprising these days. The country's lockdown amid the COVID-19 pandemic limited the incidence of mass gun violence in schools, churches, and other public places for nearly a year. What a cruel tragedy that the reason that so many people weren't dying from mass gun violence is because so many were dying from COVID-19 and the related issues of inequity that a pandemic context made visible and exacerbated.

Some might think that gun violence is an event that teachers may be less hesitant to talk about than other events. After all, isn't everyone devastated on those days? Isn't everyone worried about what has happened and wouldn't everyone support teachers checking in on their students on the day after? Yet, because of the connection between gun violence and (a lack of) gun control in the United States, even discussions of school shootings have become politicized in the news media and, thus, in class-rooms. There are even sitting U.S. senators at present (2021) who be-lieve that the shooting in Parkland, Florida, was fake and have hurled insults at youth survivors. This extends to other instances of mass gun violence in churches, malls, concerts, movie theaters, and clubs. The ab-horrent politics of elected officials aside, teachers still have to find ways to engage in DAP in these moments. Although many teachers might avoid these topics, as they do others, because they fear partisan views on gun control, the teachers portrayed in this book feel and act differ-ently. "Of course" that is something they talk about, many remarked. Below, teachers share how they discussed gun violence—and, in par-ticular, those examples that had been politicized in the news for various reasons—on days after.

One Teacher, Multiple Discussions

Yolanda, you will recall from earlier chapters, is the only Black teacher in her school and district. As a high school special education teacher, some of the classes she teaches are self-contained, in which she is the only teacher. Other classes are inclusion classes, where she works with a co-teacher who specializes in a particular content area. In her time as a teacher in this rural, predominantly white district, Yolanda recalls three different ex-amples of gun violence that she discussed with her students on days after.

In June 2016, 49 people were killed and 53 more were injured in one of the deadliest mass shootings in U.S. history. Pulse Nightclub was a well-known gay club in Orlando, Florida, and news of this devastating tragedy spread quickly around the world, including to the rural town where Yolanda taught. "On multiple levels, [it] was close to home for me," she recalled. "It was something that I paid attention to and knew a lot about and I wanted my students to be aware." As a gay woman, Yolanda felt it was important to talk about not just gun violence itself but the identities of the victims. It felt like a natural fit because the school was an International Baccalaureate school with an emphasis on real-world connections and engagement. "I mean, we flash the news across TVs all along in the hallway. So let's talk about it in the classroom, too," Yolanda recalls saying to her co-teacher. Her administrator was also "completely on board" and told her to "take whatever approach you would like." They planned to use NewsELA to differentiate articles from the *New York Times*, making them more accessible for the learners in their classroom. After students read the articles, they discussed what gun safety and gun control meant, as well as how to be "more accepting of all people." It did not go exactly as planned, however. While some teachers worry about parental pushback, in this case, it came from the students. Yolanda, sigh-ing as she told this part of her story, remembered that students "didn't see why we need[ed] to talk about it. They were like, 'Oh, that's a gay club? Why do y'all care?'" This was difficult for Yolanda to hear. "It's a lot of lumping people together, just a lack of knowledge." So, even though the day was meant to be about gun violence, it ended up being about identities: "It took a while to backtrack and even get them to understand [the importance of honoring] different people and cultures. A lot of teaching came into that, as well."

Another discussion happened a year later, with a different group of students, in October 2017, after 58 people were killed and over 850 injured after a mass shooting at a country music concert in Las Vegas, Nevada. This then became one of the deadliest mass shootings in U.S. history. Unlike after the Pulse shooting, when Yolanda waited several days to determine if and how she should approach it with her students, this was one that she felt would resonate more with them because of their love of country music. And, after the discussion a year prior, she was ready. This time, "the very next day, I changed what I was talking about. I felt like this instance was more relatable to my students," Yolanda said, "I even had a student whose sister was at that concert." Her students, overall, "believe in the right to bear arms. The gun talk is every day. It's a hunting culture." As they processed this moment, Yolanda wanted them to reckon with what it meant to "support gun culture" at the same time as condemning this particular tragedy. "I'm that person where lesson plans get scratched every day," Yolanda said.

Then, 4 months later, it happened again. This time, it was a school shooting in Parkland, Florida. And this time, it was the students—the same group who Yolanda was teaching at the time of the Las Vegas shooting—who brought it up. "I was one hundred percent in support of the walkout," Yolanda remembered, "but [I told them] I want to know why you're doing it." She was concerned that her students did not fully understand their peers' rationales for walking out, and she wanted to ensure they did. Indeed, after the walkout, they told her, "We really didn't know why we were walking out. We were just doing it because everybody else was doing it. So what's something else we can do?" Thus began the "What's Your 17?" campaign. In honor of the 17 victims, they developed a challenge for each other and their classmates: "What 17 positive things or 17 positive impacts you can make, whether it's in your school or in your community, something to honor each and every victim?" They raised money by selling T-shirts and donated to charities run by Parkland survivors. They petitioned the principal for his support (and got it) and then arranged for individual classrooms to "get together and come up with 17 different things they personally would do to make a change or prevent school shootings from happening." What is most amazing to Yolanda is that "it's been a campaign that continued. It was a major impact there." Yolanda is hopeful that the way the students leaned into activism after this gun tragedy (as compared to the others where they did not want to discuss and where she is the one who brought it up) will shape how they think about gun violence moving forward.

Other Insights on the Days After Parkland

Very similar to Yolanda, Penelope, a high school social studies teacher in Michigan, did not want her students to walk out after Parkland if they had not developed a clear rationale for it. She, too, was in full support of the walkout, but she wanted her students to be able to articulate their choices and plans. Penelope's students had big plans. Three young women called her over the weekend ("Yes, they have my phone number.") and said, "We know this is our movement and it is our responsibility and we have to own it. And if we do all the work to organize it, will you go on the bus with us to Washington, D.C.?" Recalling this memory, Penelope's voice gets a bit wistful and she looks down, smiling. "How do you say no to being a part of history? Can you think of a greater honor than my kids inviting me on their movement?" Other students were organizing a walkout at their school. Penelope recalled a lengthy back-and-forth conversation, interspersed with research to solidify their goals and objectives. "Every time they would say something to me, I was like, 'Why? Why?' Just walking them through that process, so that they were fine-tuning their own plans and their own reasons. For example, the administration asked them to walk out into the courtyard [instead of outside the school building] because they felt it would be safer." Penelope was not a fan of this suggestion, and her students were wrestling with it, too.

> *Penelope:* Who do you want to see you walking out?
> *Students:* We don't know.
> *Penelope:* Why would you walk out if you don't know who you want to see you?
> *Students:* I guess we want the school board to see us.
> *Penelope:* So it's the school board that passes rules about gun laws?

When the students weren't sure who made these rules, Penelope worked to "support them step-by-step" in research to figure it out. Eventually:

> *Students:* It's legislators who make the rules about gun laws.
> *Penelope:* And will there be legislators in the courtyard? How do you make them see what you are doing?

In the end, some students went to D.C. (with Penelope tagging along) and other students walked out . . . in front of the school.

After Pittsburgh: Teaching About Gun Violence and Anti-Semitism

Isabelle watched in horror as reports came in about a shooting at a synagogue in Pittsburgh, Pennsylvania. Isabelle teaches at a private Jewish school and is Jewish herself. At the time it happened, many of her students were together at a synagogue, celebrating a classmate's bar mitzvah. Families began taking their kids out of services when news spread, and "there was a lot of chaos and fear," Isabelle remembers. As she learned more about what happened, Isabelle knew she wanted to do something when her students returned to school, especially because of the unit they had just finished. They had read *The Devil's Arithmetic* by Jane Yolen, which talked about the history of anti-Semitism, the Nuremberg laws, Jewish immigration, and the Holocaust. They discussed how "generational racism ultimately led to genocide." She wasn't supposed to contact her principal "because Saturday is Shabbat, and you're not supposed to work, but I knew she'd be on email and she wouldn't mind." Isabelle told her principal that she wanted to address the event on Monday "because it would be irresponsible not to." While the principal was supportive of discussing it, she cautioned that the students might need "some space in between" the event and the lesson because "we didn't want to overwhelm them all day with picturing and imagining this violence." A directive came from the Head of School for all teachers. On Monday afternoon, 2 days after the shooting, there was a special faculty meeting "to discuss how to coordinate responses to Pittsburgh." Some teachers wanted to do smaller activities, like taking pictures of signs that said the community supported Jewish families and neighbors, and to share those signs with the students. For Isabelle, while "that was nice," she wanted to do something that involved more student-centered dialogue. She discussed it with her principal and planned something for the following week.

They started with "The Greenies," a short story by William Goodykoontz. Isabelle chose this short story "about how racism and bigotry is passed down generationally because it's a really good source that could apply to any time and in any place." In connection with their previous unit on the Holocaust, Isabelle hoped that her students would discuss how "hatred is learned, it's not natural. People are taught to hate." Her goal was both personal and pedagogical: "I wanted them to know why it's important to have a strong sense of where you come from and strong knowledge of how to feel comfortable to teach others about Judaism and who we are. And with that knowledge comes the history of anti-Semitism. It's important." Isabelle thought "The Greenies" was a useful way into a conversation about how "if we want people to know and understand us, we have to want to know and understand other people. That's our responsibility. How we combat hatred is through understanding. How can we help make this a two-way street?" She also used the pyramid of hate graphic from the Anti-Defamation League to inquire about "what do we see on this pyramid that is happening today?"

While Isabelle's students had a strong understanding of the Holocaust, both because of their religious and cultural identities and because of what they learned in school, that wasn't the case in every classroom on the days after the synagogue shooting. And yet, other teachers also wanted to link the current anti-Semitic tragedy to a history of anti-Semitism. Just a half-hour drive away, Ann wanted to talk about the shooting with her 6th-grade English class. At first, the students did not understand the significance of the event. "Eleven people were shot, it's not that big of a deal," she remembers someone saying, illustrating just how desensitized youth have become to mass gun violence. "And I said, 'No, this is a really big deal.' But when I brought in an article from NewsELA [about the history of anti-Semitism], as I was starting to teach it, I realized something," Ann recalled. "Only about three of my students knew what the Holocaust was. So I said, 'Well okay, we have to fix this.'" Ann found an infographic online about the Holocaust, because she had to use "a secondary nonfiction text" as part of her lessons. She found an excerpt from *Night*, by Elie Weisel, "so they had stronger background information." During their discussions of the Holocaust, including when she showed photographs of the historical atrocities of gas chambers and concentration camps, which she felt were appropriate to "show them the scale of hatred," the students finally began to understand how a contemporary attack on a synagogue "perpetuated a prejudice" that had existed for decades.

Many teachers would not have introduced the Pittsburgh shooting unless their students brought it up. But, for Ann, there was no question that this was the right thing to do because the shooting perpetuated injustice. And it was her job to talk about and combat injustice in her classroom. The plans for that week didn't matter anymore. According to their district-mandated curriculum map, the class was supposed to be talking about a short text on "the creation of the Ferris wheel," hence the need for a secondary nonfiction text in her replacement lesson. "But why? Why did that matter in the first place?" Ann contends, "And why did it matter after a deadly attack on the Jewish community? Quite simply, it didn't matter then, and it doesn't matter now. The way we did the day after was much more important for their learning and their compassion."

DAYS AFTER ENVIRONMENTAL CRISES

Spike Lee's *When the Levees Broke* (2006) is a stark, unflinching look at a so-called natural disaster that wasn't so "natural" at all. Instead, as news coverage revealed in the wake of Hurricane Katrina and as Lee's film further exposes and interrogates, much of what happened in New

Orleans was a result of human error, neglect, greed, and racism. When I showed this film to my 11th-grade English class, 3 years after Katrina, it was in the wake of two recent hurricanes (Gustav in August 2008 and Ike in September 2008). Hurricane Gustav had led to the first evacuation of New Orleans since Katrina, and much of the media was focused on replaying that coverage, including the language of "Katrina refugees." Given this, I put the planned curriculum on hold and instead turned to Lee's documentary and related articles and artifacts. Many of my students were international refugees, and we problematized the language of refugees in the instance of Katrina, as we simultaneously worked to understand the government's racist actions that led the levees to break 3 years earlier. I remember distinctly that one of my students was quiet for several days. Finally, she raised her hand after we finished the documentary. "I am a refugee because my family was not safe from our government," she said, "and even though I know you can't be a refugee in your own country, the people in New Orleans are also not safe from their own government. I wish they had a way out."

Many other examples of environmental crises are, in fact, less about the environment and more about how governments, policies, and practices contribute to environmental racism and injustice. One example of how a discussion can connect policies and environmental issues is in Leah's social studies classroom. Leah's students cared deeply about water. The year before they were in her class, they did a series of units on the Flint water crisis and the water shutoffs in their hometown of Detroit. They had worked in pairs to create informational videos about the water shutoffs in Detroit, and they were passionate about access to clean water as a social justice issue. When they arrived to her class, "they were all pretty well informed" about water access in the United States. Leah wanted to "expand the conversation beyond just the local" and build on their interest and commitment. In a cross-content collaboration, while Leah taught about different water crises around the world, their English teacher led them in discussions of Linda Sue Park's *A Long Walk to Water* about two young children in Sudan.

In the days after these and other environmental crises and climate disasters, how are teachers to respond? Below are some examples of how teachers took up the charge of teaching for environmental justice on days after.

Days After "Natural" Disasters

Ursula's 3rd-graders had seen the news about Hurricane Katrina. It felt both far away from their lives in Michigan and yet also remarkably close, as they consumed news coverage that included tragic images of children their own age being evacuated from flooded areas, huddled in the New

Orleans Superdome, and bussed to other cities and states away from the devastation of both the hurricane and the levee break. Her students, Ursula remembers, were "very concerned and had lots of questions." They wondered how this could happen. What was happening to children their age? What was happening to their schools and homes? And, most significantly, "what can we do from here?" Although they were thousands of miles away, the students wanted to learn more so that they could do more. The students divided themselves into small groups depending on what they wanted to learn more about. Some groups wanted to do research on hurricanes and learn more about the science of the disaster. Others wanted to learn "about the ways we could help and who we can reach out to." They researched what goods would be most useful to collect and how to get those goods to the people who needed it the most. Learning about the environmental crisis itself, as academic knowledge, was important, but it was also much more than that. Indeed, the process of collecting and sending supplies "made them feel empowered and helped them to see that, even though they're kids, they can still help."

In Rocio's classroom in the Northeast, on the days after another hurricane, relating to the situation wasn't a concern. In fact, the students were deeply and personally affected even though the actual devastation was thousands of miles away. Hurricane Maria devastated Puerto Rico and the Dominican Republic in September 2017. Many of Rocio's students were from those islands and "had to leave the island to come to the States because their homes were completely destroyed." Others who had been in the Northeast for a while still had family on the islands. For Rocio, there was no question that she and her students had to process together. "I had to really take a step back and put some of the work that we were doing to the side because that was relevant to what was going on in their lives. I didn't want to disregard or not take into consideration what they were feeling," Rocio recalled. "Some of my students would come in and they would be devastated every day. They had no way to communicate with people back home. They didn't even know if their family was still alive. It was a very emotional time for them and for myself. So I really had to take a step back and sort of pause the curriculum to support them and their emotional needs." Rocio supported her middle school students in processing their fears and anxiety on the days after through both curricular changes and action-oriented efforts. Curricularly, Rocio felt like "I was still expected to connect to the standards, and I just thought about how I could connect this to Earth Science. We didn't work on just hurricanes, but we learned about tornadoes, tsunamis. We saw other natural disasters that had occurred across the world." They watched videos on YouTube and Rocio prepared activities and handouts related to vocabulary of climate disasters, since one of her school's focal areas is working with English language learners on content-area vocabulary. They found the locations of different disasters on maps, as well, connecting to social studies standards. One of the locations they focused on was New Orleans: "We talked about when that happened, how that happened, how different communities came together to help rebuild after Katrina." They focused, too, on "the steps and struggles" that came along with rebuilding. Although this was an "academic" focus of DAP, the impact was also relational and emotional. As Rocio tells it, "They were really touched by it. I think once they saw other natural disasters around the world, they felt like they weren't the only ones to have gone through something like that."

Beyond the curricular changes, Rocio also supported her students in taking action to assist the affected families in Puerto Rico. A large part of their unit on natural disasters was "how to prepare for them and what we can do to help families that have gone through a natural disaster." First, on one of the school-sponsored "dress-down" days, for which students donated a dollar to wear more casual clothes than the school dress code, her students collected all their funds and gave them to the school counselor "who had connections with a foundation that was working on reuniting families after Hurricane Maria." The school community was "was very receptive to what was going on. They took part and stepped up to try to help families, not only the ones that were coming from the island here, but also the ones that are back in Puerto Rico." Next, students collected food to donate to new arrivals to the area. They also held a fundraiser where they served homemade Puerto Rican food and collected funds through raffles, gift baskets, and a silent auction. "There was a lot going on to try to help," Rocio explains as she tells the story of how so many families united in this common goal, "I have never seen the cafeteria fill up the way it did for the community. Everyone was just 'all hands on deck,' cooking, working, cleaning."

Days After and Amid an Ongoing Climate Crisis

In Maya's high school journalism class, controversial topics weren't necessarily avoided, but they had to be contextualized. "I worked the whole year to establish a relationship with them that's like, 'You can really trust me that I'm not going to just tell you that something is true and it's not." For a year, every day could have been considered a day after an environmental disaster, as the news was replete with stories of flooding, wildfires, droughts, extreme temperatures, and hurricanes. Maya believes it worked out well that they addressed climate change at the end of the school year because students would have pushed back more at the beginning of the year. Many of them had initially said "climate change isn't real." But, thanks in part to the ongoing news coverage of natural disasters, there were many opportunities for Maya to say, "Well, why don't we research that?" She challenged them to find reputable and reliable sources that said climate change isn't real. These days after were interspersed with more "traditional" journalism curriculum about finding sources, verifying that the sources are reliable, and "thinking and processing through other topics that were less controversial."

So, when another environmental crisis happened in the last month of school, Maya used the opportunity for students to take what they had learned from their research on prior days after to enter the Bow Seat Ocean Awareness Contest, "a platform for young people to learn about environmental issues through art-making and creative communication, explore their relationship to a changing world, and become advocates for positive change" (www.bowseat.com). The goal of the contest was for youth to inform others about climate change (hence, the connection to journalism) and its impacts on oceans and wildlife, using five different mediums: artwork, music, video, prose, or poetry. Her students, she remembered, "created some really interesting pieces" that they entered into the contest and turned in as their final assignment for the year. In the end, a year of days after discussions supported one final days after project.

Like Maya, Harper also teaches about climate change. It is typically part of her yearly curriculum as a middle school science teacher. But, one particular day after, the discussion about climate change became even more complicated. Typically, when she is introducing the topic of climate change, because she knows that it is a controversial topic for the families in her district (and thus for her students), she is very clear to say, "We're not talking about global warming. We're talking about climate change because you can't deny that the climate is changing." She knows the term "global warming" has angered students in the past. So, instead, Harper starts off the year by explaining to her students, "In a few years, you're going to be out on your own and I'm not going to be there to tell you how to think and how to feel. Instead, you just have to look at the information, look at the data, and make your own choices." The students focus on examining natural patterns and changes that occur in climate over time, as compared to how things are changing now. The students notice and inquire into why the rate of change now doesn't align with the rate of change in the past, why it doesn't fit the pattern. When they are asked for their own conclusions at the end of the unit, Harper explains, "They say, 'Why does anyone believe other than this?' And I'm like, 'Because they're not looking at the information the way you are looking at the information.'"

In the middle of their unit, suddenly, one of the main sources for their information about climate change disappeared. All of the information about climate change had been wiped from the website of the federal Environmental Protection Agency (EPA). Harper had known this might be coming when the Trump administration removed the information about climate change from the White House website on his Inauguration

Day in January 2017. Slowly, other references to climate change disappeared from other federal websites. The most drastic change—and the one her students noticed—was the EPA. Barron (2018) summarized what happened in that year: "The EPA's site is now riddled with missing links, redirecting pages and buried information. Over the past year, terms like 'fossil fuels,' 'greenhouse gases,' and 'global warming' have been excised. Even the term 'science' is no longer safe. Christine Todd Whitman, the EPA Administrator under George W. Bush, says the overhaul is 'to such an extreme degree that [it] undermines the credibility of the site.'"

The day after the website was altered, when news was spreading about the censorship and how EPA employees and scientists more broadly were reacting, Harper's students were back in class. "All the information was just taken away," Harper remembered, "and that really opened the kids' eyes up to things. They were like, 'Why can't we at least get the information we need?'" Harper was concerned about "how political" to be in their discussion. Their discussion turned to issues of equitable access to information. Harper recalls telling her students that "it's my belief that we should have this information. No matter who the president is, we need information." As part of their discussion, Harper reminded them that the research and information from the EPA website "was still out there. We have to find it another way. Sometimes people only want to put information out there that makes it easier for you to believe what they believe. So you have to make sure that you're really looking at the correct information."

DAYS AFTER GENDER INJUSTICE

Even before the #MeToo movement, stories of sexual assault and gender discrimination frequently made the news and spread on social media. While some teachers I interviewed talked in generalities about how they addressed gender injustice in their classrooms, several remembered a particular moment of injustice that compelled them to engage in DAP: the nomination of Brett Kavanaugh to the U.S. Supreme Court. Donna recalls that, during the hearings, she "had no choice" but to share her opinion with her high school social studies classes, even if, in years past, she may have refrained from doing so. "During the Kavanaugh hearings, I had to do it. I felt I had to say that when people report sexual violence, I believe them." Donna elaborated that she understood the "talking points" of those who supported Kavanaugh and his nomination well enough "to be able to explain why they thought it." Yet she also "is more willing now than ever before to be explicit about my own political beliefs. So I hold up a flag when it's me, clearly label it as my opinion. I'll say 'many people believe this or this.'" In the case of Kavanaugh, sharing her opinion meant explicitly stating that she believed and supported Dr. Christine Blasey Ford's testimony. In the process, even though she didn't know if any of her own students had been assaulted, she affirmed that she believed them also.

Several states away, Gemma was used to having "big conversations" in her 6th-grade English classroom. They talked about Trump's Muslim ban and the shooting at the Pittsburgh synagogue. Sometimes these conversations were confined to the classroom, and other times they were taken schoolwide, like when Gemma and her colleague asked their principal to write a letter to school families "reiterating our support for Muslim students and neighbors" in a nearby refugee resettlement community after the travel ban. Gemma is always pleased when this happens, when issues can be more widespread: "[My principal] word-for-word used the language that we had suggested [for the family letter], which was good. It's taken some nudging. But I think we're slowly getting there to a point where it's becoming more systemic and less isolated to classrooms." Even so, when some incidents arise in the world, it's not always easy to know what to do or how to do it. The appointment of Brett Kavanaugh to the Supreme Court was one such incident. During the hearings preceding his appointment, Gemma and her students had many conversations about what was happening: "We spent a lot of time talking about consent, about what it means to continually give consent. There were some great videos that were produced and circulated that we could snag easily for our classroom. But I remember, right before the hearing and when it became clear that he was likely going to be appointed, we had a circle in our classroom and talked pretty openly about consent, and specifically about Brett Kavanaugh and also brought in Anita Hill and other kinds of historical perspectives as to how this isn't new." When I asked her directly about how she'd respond to those who said that you shouldn't talk about this with 6th graders, Gemma specifically referenced the article by Liz Kleinrock (discussed in Chapter 4) about teaching consent in elementary classrooms. "That helped me be like, 'Oh yeah, okay. That wasn't ridiculous that I just did that.' There's definitely a certain level of internal gaslighting that happens when I do this." Gemma's concerns are not unlike other teachers' concerns; she, too, is worried about what is "okay" and what isn't. What makes Gemma's story different from other stories is that she persisted and was confident in both her ability to facilitate the conversation and her students' need to have the conversation. After discussing Kavanaugh himself, as well as the historical factors that influenced the hearings and people's reactions to it, Gemma extended the discussion to the lives of her students in their present moment.

Gemma recalled that "what was really significant and important for me was thinking about it as it relates to touch and as it relates to social media. Our students are on platforms like Snapchat and others. Consent has this really interesting role in social media right now with young female-identified students being asked to send photos you might not feel comfortable with." Gemma and her students had explicit conversations about difficult questions like, "What does it look like when your friend is asking you to do something that you don't want to do? How many of you are in situations with relatives where you're leaving a dinner or you're going home and your family says, 'Go hug your so-and-so, you must do it.'" They spent time "thinking through what does consent in families look like when we might feel that instinct of 'I'm not so comfortable with this.'" Noting that the concept of affirmative consent is also related to classroom greetings, Gemma mused, "What does it look like to say [to students]: 'Do you want to high five? Do you want a fist bump? Do you want a hug? Do you want no physical touch?' Just recognizing that students have a choice." Overall, Gemma argues, "We wait far too long to tell young people that they have agency over their bodies. And I think the messages that are sent both at home and by their teachers can be really harmful."

Xavier was teaching in a very different context: an all-boys private Catholic boarding/day school in the D.C. metropolitan area. Xavier is a theology teacher and has a spirit of rebellion that, he acknowledges, readers may be surprised to find in a religion teacher at a religious school. "We're the rebels around here," Xavier laughs. This means, in practice, that Xavier started the 2018 school year by talking about the Pennsylvania grand jury report on clerical sex abuse, "because who thought we'd be doing *that* again 15 years after we had to do it the first time?" Just weeks later, the confirmation hearings began. Everything about the context of Xavier's school could have made teachers hesitant to talk about it. And, in fact, it did. As far as he knows from discussions with colleagues and students, Xavier was the only teacher to address Dr. Ford's testimony the day after. Xavier first framed the discussion with clear boundaries about what was and was not debatable. They were not going to engage in a debate of "he said, she said," as much of the media were doing. Instead, he started the conversation:

> *Xavier:* Okay. Raise your hands if any of you here are sitting U.S.
>   senators.
> *No hands.*
> *Xavier:* Okay, so we don't have to worry about confirmation, right?
>   We're not addressing the issue of whether Kavanaugh should be
>   confirmed.
> *Nods.*
> *Xavier:* Raise your hands if any of you here are Montgomery County
>   law enforcement officials.
> *No hands.*

Xavier: Okay, so we don't have to concern ourselves with guilt or innocence in terms of evaluating Dr. Christine Blasey Ford's testimony.

Nods.

Xavier: Raise your hand if any of you here have an experience of Jesuit education.

All hands up.

Xavier: Okay, so what we can do is we can have a conversation about Jesuit values. What we can do is we can have a conversation about what it looks like to live these values out loud.

Xavier made these intentional framing choices as a "sort of guard-rail to prevent it from devolving into a polarized 'he said, she said'" and turned it instead into an exercise "where they could be more evaluative as opposed to partisan." Xavier gave the students two texts. First, there was a news article that connected to Kavanaugh's upbringing in a private Catholic school in the D.C. area, which had been referenced in his testimony and in the subsequent media coverage. "The *Washington Post* had run a piece on the party culture of the Catholic schools in the D.C. area in the 1980s," including their school. He paired this with an essay called "Men and Women for Others," by Jesuit priest Fr. Pedro Arrupe. This address, originally given in 1973, is now taken up in many Jesuit schools as a core text for understanding the Jesuits' commitment to social justice. After Xavier's students discussed the texts, his final question that day after was, "Who did you see being a 'man for others' in the *Washington Post* story?" Xavier smiles as he tells this part of the story, remembering "this one kid! This kid!" I, too, can tell the response is going to be powerful. Xavier continues, "This one kid chimed in and said, 'Well, the only person I saw being a man for others wasn't any of the [men who were students]. It was this one girl who stayed at a party, trying to extricate her girlfriend from the party because her girlfriend was too drunk to know what was happening to her and advocate for herself. She was being a 'man' for others.'" Now I see why Xavier remembered "this kid" so clearly. He continues, "And I thought, 'Wow! Okay, there we go!' So that felt really natural. It felt like the kids were able to make something of that. They were able to commit themselves to the message of Arrupe. Even in that context where it was getting a little close to home."

Sometimes things that are "close to home" can make Days After Pedagogy easier, in that students relate deeply to the moments of injustice and feel compelled to dialogue and learn more, to be in community with one another as they process what has happened. Other times, "close to home" can mean that students might resist discussing or analyzing moments that seem to threaten their own understandings of the world, that challenge their privilege, or that push the boundaries of what they feel comfortable talking about. This case could have gone either way, in Xavier's mind. This time it worked, in a sense: "We had some institutional failings in terms of messaging more broadly, but at least in the context of that lesson plan, I felt like they were able to use the event to think through this significantly important piece of our mission and identity, of being men and women in service to others."

On March 13, 2020, Breonna Taylor was killed in her own home while she was sleeping. Louisville police officers forcibly entered Ms. Taylor's home and shot her. One of the officers had been hurt as well, and in their haste to help him, they completely disregarded Ms. Taylor, who was fatally injured. The officer was not.

I only heard about the tragedy of Ms. Taylor's death in May after George Floyd was killed, when the Black Lives Matter (BLM) movement really took off. I had heard of BLM before, but I didn't know much about it until last summer. It was never mentioned in school, nor was the killing of Ahmaud Arbery, Tamir Rice, or Trayvon Martin. I remember learning about BLM through Instagram and reposting a lot of things regarding it. "Justice for George Floyd" was one of the first posts I remember seeing, along with the video. His death was not mentioned at school either. While we were never told not to talk about their deaths, we were never invited to talk about them either.

I think part of the reason teachers don't teach us about these things is that they think we're not ready. But what I don't understand is what we aren't ready for. My teachers allowed us to watch the raid on Capitol Hill, live, but we never have discussions about the killings of Black people. Why were we able to watch the storming of the U.S. Capitol and talk about it later in classes, but we never talk about racially charged issues? We speak more about social issues this year than we did last, so I do think age and "maturity" have a lot to do with exposing us to these topics in a teacher's eyes. Or maybe now BLM is more widely accepted and teachers—white teachers—are more comfortable teaching about it. Either way, I think educating children earlier about the injustices in the world would prepare us for when we come in contact with them and help us learn to reject them.

Learning about racism, homophobia, and other related issues solely through social media can also be dangerous; the sources may be spreading false information, and the content itself may be harmful. Take the video of Mr. Floyd's killing—it's quite graphic, and stumbling across something like that as a child can be scarring. It is still important to know it happened, but within certain parameters. Teachers can provide the proper context and teach kids in a safe, positive way, while social media can't. Teachers can also steer children away from the harmful side of social media while teaching them about these issues and how to prevent them.

I don't think most teachers understand that, if they don't teach their students about these things, students will find out on their own. Their exposure could be good, or it could veer on the side of detrimental. But to minimize students' bad experiences, why not just teach them yourself? It is the best thing for them and for everyone else.

Author Bio: Camille Dotson is a 9th-grader in Atlanta, Georgia. Growing up as a Black girl with a Black activist as a mother, she has always been aware of the injustices she faced every day. Camille loves to draw and has recently started learning digital art. She is also a dancer and has danced now for 3 years. She is also very interested in marine life, mammals and octopuses, in particular.

* * *

My teachers didn't say anything or teach anything about the events that were happening in the summer, like George Floyd's death and Breonna Taylor's death. They didn't hold discussions in Zoom when we came back. I don't know how my classmates reacted or if they did react because we were on Zoom. I feel sad that they didn't discuss it, and I feel that they should've discussed it because it's an important topic that we need to talk about in school. If I was a teacher, I would've talked about and discussed it because it's important.

The same thing happened for Black History Month. Two out of six of my teachers did something for Black History Month. First, my orchestra teacher did something and my English teacher assigned us to write about one Black person that we chose to do. He assigned this on February 25, 2021. He also said we would be working on it for the next month. I am thinking in my head, "If this is a Black History Month assignment, why aren't we doing it in the actual month?" We were also working on commercials in February. I think that we could've waited on commercials to do a Black History Month assignment in Black History Month instead of in the next month. I think that it made it seem like commercials mattered more to him than Black History Month.

My orchestra teacher had us watch a video about the history of the song "We Shall Overcome" and had us tell what we learned about it. I think that was a nice assignment, because it was about how a song that was made in 1790 became a song that Black people would sing in the Civil War and in slavery. It was nice to see how it evolved over time into different songs. I also like it because it combined music and Black History Month, which was what we were supposed to be learning.

Even though my social studies teacher is supposed to teach us about history, he didn't do anything. He didn't have us discuss Black History Month, do a project, or even read about Black History Month. I think that if I was the social studies/history teacher, for the whole month starting from February 1 to February 28, I would've assigned a project. He should've at least talked to us about Black History Month. It is important for me and my classmates to learn about this because it's an important part of history.

Author Bio: Taliyah V. Andrews is in 6th grade in East Lansing, Michigan. She is a middle school student and likes to do gymnastics and play the piano and violin.

* * *

I do not think Black History should only be for a month. I wish my teachers would have said something in the middle of February instead of at the end of February. They should have stopped what they were doing and actually thought about what to do for Black History Month. Black History Month should focus on what we are now. My band teacher was the only person that said something about Black history. They only taught us about one Black person and that was it, and it was more like a lesson rather than a discussion.

We only have 1 month to celebrate our history. Mostly, they only focus on slavery and segregation. They think that is all to our history. They want to make us think that we were just slaves, but we were conquerors, too. I think there should be more months of Black history for all the pain, tears, and blood that were shed on the ground. We were not just slaves. We were protestors, musicians, dancers, athletes, dentists, doctors, nurses, scientists, and other things.

Author Bio: Maya Andrews is in 6th grade, and she lives in East Lansing, Michigan. She is an African American 12-year-old who believes in justice. She likes reading, playing video games, journaling, and playing the flute.

CHAPTER 7

The Intersections of Teaching, Racism, and White Supremacy on Days After

> If now isn't a good time for the truth, I don't see when we'll get to it.
>
> —Nikki Giovanni

The teacher testimonies in this chapter deal with what happens on days after incidents of racism and white supremacy. This is not to say that racism and white supremacy are not everyday events. Indeed, they are so imbued into our society, schooling, and selves that there is no day without them. The days after that are discussed here, however, are the moments when racism and white supremacy come to the forefront of national or local consciousness and demand attention, both to that particular event and to ongoing systemic oppression. There are so many more moments that *should* demand attention, that *should* define national consciousness, and that *should* be talked about with students.

For teachers of color, I hope that you have time and space to care for yourselves, as you support your students. I hope that you have white colleagues who are engaging in Days After Pedagogy in the wake of racial violence and injustice, so you do not have to be the only one. I hope that you can find co-conspirators in your schools.

For white teachers of white students, your students may see these moments as unrelated to their lives, and it is up to you to make them see otherwise. You *have* to learn how to talk about what is happening. As a fellow white educator, this is on us, every time and all the time. We cannot pretend to be surprised anymore. We have to do what we said we were going to do when we were reading those antiracist books and completing those antiracism checklists. Our white students are not "too young" or "too naive" to learn about this, as earlier stories in the book demonstrate.

Finally, for white teachers of students of color, make sure you know how to support your students of color if you try to have these conversations. This is a time to ensure you know what you are doing before you do it. It's important to not do more harm by entering into these conversations without careful thought and planning. Yet this fear also cannot hold you back; this book is one way to start or continue your careful thought and planning. Consider Carrie's comments about being a white educator who engages in DAP in the wake of racial injustice: "To borrow from the Abolitionist Teaching Network, 'Don't be basic. We must embody the spirit of Black Lives Mattering, not just say Black Lives Matter.' What we do as educators should be revolutionary. Students need to know that not all opinions deserve to be heard and respected and they need to be taught how to speak up against those opinions. If we avoid discomfort, that assertiveness will be lost and those opinions will continue to fester. . . . This *is* political. There are particular times, lessons, events that we have to be unequivocal in what is at the root of the problem. At the root of the problem is racism. To shy away from that is also racism." Carrie echoes what it means for Black lives to matter at school, as Watson, Hagopian, and Au (2018) explain:

> Educators can and should make their classrooms and schools sites of resistance to white supremacy and anti-Blackness, as well as sites for knowing the hope and beauty in Blackness. The ferocity of racism in the United States against Black minds and Black bodies demands that teachers fight back. We must organize against anti-Blackness amongst our colleagues and in our communities; we must march against police brutality in the streets; and we must teach for Black lives in our classrooms. (p. 13)

This chapter is divided into sections that are, in many ways, artificial divisions. There is a section on racial violence and another on white supremacist events, yet racial violence is also a white supremacist event. For the purposes of organization, the sections here then represent how educators talked about the events, how they are often covered in the (admittedly problematic) news media, and how readers may encounter future days after for which they are looking to adapt their pedagogy: days after global terrorism, racial violence and police brutality, white supremacist events, immigration injustice, and school-based racist events.

DAYS AFTER GLOBAL TERRORISM IN A U.S. CONTEXT

Ursula was teaching her second year of 2nd grade on September 11, 2001. The attacks were far away from Ursula's small conservative town in Michigan, but the effects were felt there and throughout the world. "The next day, kids came to school and they were sharing their parents' words as if it was their own words," she remembered. "It was as if they had already internalized it all." There was a large military presence in the town, so many of the students were concerned "and crying because their parents were talking about signing up to join the National Guard or being deployed to get the people who did this to us." This language of "us" and "them" was apparent even on the day after when still little was known about the perpetrators. Students' emotions were raw, and Ursula "realized these are 7- and 8-year-old kids who have big things on their minds. They are more in tune with the world around them than we give them credit for."

Even though they always started their day with a "morning meeting," on 9/12, she broadened the prompt. She asked them, "What's on your mind today?" It "brought out all kinds of things, and it was just a conversation in a very matter-of-fact, honest way. It was an age-appropriate space for them to share their thoughts and feelings about what happened." While she doesn't remember the specifics, Ursula does know that her DAP became her daily pedagogy after that because, ever since then, she has started the morning meeting with some open-ended question. Ursula did not "direct" the meetings after that either, "because kids would start to respond to one another and practice their dialogic talk."

As much as 9/11 was "an eye-opener" for students, it also was for teachers. Oscar, a white man who grew up in a small town in Michigan, was teaching in a similar small town, although not the same one he grew up in. He recalled, "I had no interactions with anyone who practiced Islam," which became important when he realized how his students were talking about what happened on 9/11. Oscar was teaching world history at the time. "It was the Greeks and Romans test day," he said, "I didn't know what to do. I had to get my test done. The students were finding out throughout the morning, and they asked to turn on the TV. I said we're not watching it. I was 25 years old, trying to hold my position of authority. There were no cell phones then, but there was a TV in every classroom, and some teachers turned it on, so students saw what happened in real time. I elected not to, mainly because I was so tunnel visioned on doing what I thought was my job, to give that test. Part of me is thankful for that." Oscar still didn't realize the magnitude of the event until he left school for the day.

Now, every time he meets a new social studies teacher, Oscar talks with them about what it was like to teach on 9/12. "We didn't know what 9/12 was going to be like, because we didn't understand 9/11 *was* 9/11 as it was happening. It was all so confusing, and I didn't know what I was going to do the next day." He decided that he would "take a cue from my education classes" in his teacher preparation program: "When you're not sure about something, turn the questions to the students." He wasn't sure how long the discussion was going to take, so he recorded a long segment about the Taliban that he saw on TV that evening. "I wanted to make sure I had something ready to go depending on how long the discussion took. Well, it ended up taking the whole class. I put a free write on the board.

We didn't call it 9/11 on 9/12, so I didn't use that term yet. I just wrote, 'What do you know about what happened yesterday? What do you think about it? What should we do?'"

Although he taught several groups of students that day, it was his 9th-grade U.S. history class that stands out in his memory, now decades later. There were many angry responses that were concerning for Oscar to read and to hear. He tried to explain "this isn't Pearl Harbor," but it was difficult to contextualize the discussion, even for him. "I was just trying to stay 10 pages ahead of the kids in the history book at this point, to even get through the year. And then this happened, and it meant a lot of new learning for me and for them." Part of that learning meant not just learning the answers to their questions but also about how to facilitate difficult discussions in the classroom. They had internalized, in just 24 hours, the nationalizing rhetoric of "us" versus "them," as Ursula's younger students had, and they had the words to express it. Then one student shared, "I just wish they'd quit being so mean." She was the one Muslim student in the class. She wore a hijab. She shared with the class that, in just 24 hours, people had attacked a local Islamic center. Oscar knew he "had to do something" to make her feel not so alone in his class. He didn't want it to seem like it was "one opinion over here, 29 opinions over here," and he needed a way to "eliminate this tension." In talking with his assigned mentor who knew more about Islam in world history, Oscar developed a plan for addressing students' misperceptions about the connection between 9/11 and Islam. He hoped this would feel supportive for his Muslim student, but "I still didn't know if it was the best thing to do." He came back the next day, now 2 days after, with more information, that recorded documentary, and one goal for the day: "I want you to understand that the Taliban is a terrorist organization. It is an extremist group. I want to make sure you separate Islam as a religious faith and this extremist group of people who also practice Islam." He started then with one key question: "We do the same thing with Christianity, separating the faith and extremist groups who use the faith to justify their extremism. Can you give me an example of how this happens in Christianity?" A moment passed. And then another. And then: "One bright kid in the back of the room said, 'The KKK.'" Oscar remembers this as "my first lightbulb teaching moment," the moment that he had heard other teachers talk about, when "all the lightbulbs popped on at once," or when students all seemed to make a connection and he could see the learning and processing happening in the moment.

In his role as a social studies teacher on 9/12 and other days after, "I never want any student to assume that their first opinion about something is what they should always have. I don't expect kids to memorize the Bill of Rights. That's not important to me. I want to create discussion opportunities for them so that when they get to making big life decisions and democratic choices, they can say, 'I've thought about this before.' I want them to try to understand other people. And there are some sides we don't argue. We don't argue on the side of white supremacists." In the days after 9/11, Oscar said he learned an important pedagogical lesson that he has carried with him in the years since. Stated in his characteristic direct way: "You're doing a shitty job if you don't talk about politics."

Beyond 9/11

In Eliana's social studies class the day after Osama bin Laden was killed by U.S. Navy Seals, the rhetoric of global terror was seemingly at an all-time high. His killing "fit into the narrative of the U.S. 'bringing its enemies to justice,' and Bin Laden represented the quintessential enemy of the early 21st century," Eliana recalled. "One memory that stands out to me most is a kind, soft-spoken student, A., revisiting what he remembered about September 11, 2001. I couldn't possibly recall details, but I do know that this stands out to me because it dawned on me that Bin Laden was 'The Boogeyman' to some of my students." Her students had been 7 or 8 years old on 9/11, and "they had experienced a sort of trauma that was exacerbated by the utter confusion of the day and of not understanding what the World Trade Center was or why anyone would do something like that."

There was an "interesting mix" of students in her class that semester. When she posed the question, "What impact will this really have on global terrorism?" for example, the students were divided as they were on many social issues: "This is only going to make things worse," "Nothing is going to change," and "This *is* a big deal." Looking back, Eliana recalls that, in the media at the time, there was "something so unsettling about people celebrating this moment, and the value of Osama bin Laden's life— because I was a devout Christian at the time—seemed entangled in this sense of vindication or comeuppance. It was as though the almost 10 years between the 9/11 attacks and bin Laden's assassination were obsessively vengeful, and this was the 'inevitable' moment of victory. What I wish I had been prepared to discuss was, one, why we weren't similarly obsessed with the perpetrators of other kinds of violence and, two, whether this would stem the tide of Islamophobia in the U.S. and worldwide."

During their days after lesson, they watched a news report about the raid on the bin Laden compound, and one of her students "jokingly said, 'Why don't you pick on someone your own size?' Other students chuckled, but it's possible there was a grain of sincerity in that comment. I know that two girls in the class, A. and Y., were consistently vocal about their disgust and disapproval of the military industrial complex." Eliana wishes now that she had delved deeper into her students' comments, but instead, she directed the conversation to be more policy focused, about the Geneva Conventions and a consideration of international law. Reflecting on her DAP, Eliana noted, "I have deep regret about not knowing how to capitalize on these thoughts and feelings to raise students' consciousness about the complexities of the entire situation."

DAYS AFTER RACIAL VIOLENCE

In the wake of Trayvon Martin's murder, Gemma was thinking about her students, the few Black and Brown youth in her school at the time. "My gut reaction was 'Oh my gosh, this could have been one of our students.' My friend really checked that instinct and said it was far more likely that we were teaching future Zimmermans in our predominantly white classrooms." This comment made Gemma think more about what her role could be as a co-conspirator for racial justice, particularly in critical moments like days after. "What would it look like to work with white children who, like me, were growing up in this predominantly white [northeastern town]?" In her school, 5 miles from her childhood home, Gemma wanted to challenge the fact that "we were not engaging in conversations about race and identity and had the potential to do some great harm without that information."

In the stories below, we see echoes of what Gemma describes here: a commitment to working for racial justice in predominantly white spaces, recognizing that days after racial violence should not only be discussed in spaces that serve predominantly students of color. We also see teachers who teach primarily youth of color reckoning with what these types of days after mean for their students.

The Emergence of Black Lives Matter

Kelly was up all night, again, watching the footage on CNN as they covered the protests in Ferguson. "I just couldn't go to sleep," she told me. "My plan the next day was just first to say, 'Hey, have you heard this is going on?'" And the answer would be "either no or 'I kind of think I heard a little something.' So the starting point is just me telling them, 'Well, your country is in turmoil right now and here's why.'"

After Ferguson, a lot of students did not know what she was talking about. Unfortunately, she sighs, this is typical for the student population in her rural school that serves predominantly white, middle-class, conservative families. For those who did, "there was so much misinformation because they just heard a snippet of it [the news] or maybe their parents told them something." Even though Kelly had learned about Black Lives Matter as an organization and as a call to protest in the wake of the murder of Trayvon Martin 2 years prior, after Ferguson was the first time she heard her students parroting the "All Lives Matter" discourse. She wanted to connect the day after to what they were reading at the time, *To Kill a Mockingbird*. (Kelly is quick to clarify that this is her district's choice for reading, not her own.) She also wanted to historicize the call for racial justice in the wake of racial violence. To do so, she found a video on YouTube about the Scottsboro Boys, which she used to discuss the concerns about how Michael Brown's murderer would be tried. Would it be similar to the all-white juries in the Scottsboro trials? Would it result in a similar miscarriage of justice? She wanted her students to understand that the protests in Ferguson were part of a longstanding struggle for justice and equity, a public call to resist anti-Blackness, and the hope for a racial reckoning that was too long in coming.

Since that time, Kelly addresses every instance of police brutality and racial violence that makes national news, which is "far too many, far too often." She is deeply committed to ensuring that her white students don't ignore what is happening, taking advantage of their privilege not to have to know or understand. This extends to other days after, as well. Kelly shared one example of how she had to convince another teacher that addressing issues of racial justice was important on days after. "I co-teach with another white teacher and once, when the Syrian crisis was going on, I talked in class about Syrian refugees. I used some photos in class and she was like, 'How do you keep track of all this news? How do you do this in front of the whole class?' And I just looked at her like, 'Dear God, woman, how do you not?!'"

Zara's school is similar to Kelly's in that her predominantly white students "don't have a lot of experience with oppression." This is why she thinks it's deeply important to engage in DAP on issues of racial violence and police brutality. After Trump was elected, she changed her high school English curriculum. They normally read *Romeo and Juliet* in freshman English, but Zara opted for *Othello* to open a conversation "about manipulation and unchecked power, about believing things without questioning them. 'Fake news.' Let's talk about victims and how race plays a role in how people are perceived, or rather misperceived and manipulated."

Zara said it is challenging to have discussions about racial justice. Students repeat what they hear from their families about Black Lives Matter, and Zara responds, "We're not saying all lives don't matter, but we're saying that these lives, Black lives, are often disregarded. So why is their life less valuable?" She uses news reports, scholarly journal articles, and other supplemental texts to show students that BLM is not a response to an isolated incident, that it extends from a legacy of racism and white supremacy. On one day after, Zara used charts and maps about hate groups around the country, including in their state. She wanted students to examine the increase in hate groups over time, so they looked at data from 2014, 2016, and 2018. The students were surprised to see the uptick in hate groups, and Zara challenged them to think about the causes of that uptick. "It didn't take a lot of guessing" to get to the root, she remembered. Zara wanted her students to see that, "while they don't have experience with oppression, we can still work hard to identify that there is indeed a problem. Part of the problem is that we think it's not our problem, but if you're going to be a global citizen, every problem is our problem."

There are many reasons that DAP is challenging work. In this case, Zara's context could make some teachers concerned about pushback. This would explain why many of her colleagues do not engage in similar days after discussions. She doesn't see remaining silent as an option, though, as evidenced in this excerpt from our interview:

> *Zara:* We may not have a whole lot of people who can *empathize*, but getting to the point where they can *sympathize* or at least recognize that there is a problem and ideally recognize that they are part of the problem, then when we've gotten somewhere.
> *Alyssa:* That's a huge undertaking.
> *Zara:* Yeah. That's what education is about though, right?
> *Alyssa:* Yes, I think so. But a lot of people would say that teachers have to be neutral and that what you're doing is the opposite of that. What would you say to them?
> *Zara:* I would say that my job is to challenge their thinking. That person and I would disagree on what neutral means. Sitting there silently and just nodding, that's not educating. There's nothing active about that. That's passively informing. Informing is different from educating. . . . So my idea of neutral is to stir the pot until something boils, and their idea is to not have a pot at all.

National Headlines in a Local Context: Teaching About Laquan McDonald in Chicago

On the night of October 20, 2014, 17-year-old Laquan McDonald was shot 16 times and killed by Chicago police officer Jason Van Dyke as he was walking away from the officer. After more than a year, Van Dyke was charged with murder, and in 2018, he was found guilty of 2nd-degree murder and sentenced to almost 7 years in prison. An inspector's report issued in 2019 found that Van Dyke and 15 other officers and supervisors had engaged in "an elaborate coverup," including exaggerating the threat posed by McDonald, not turning on their recording devices, and destroying records of witness interviews.

Quinn was still in college, far away from Chicago, when McDonald was killed. By the time she started teaching at a K–8 public school, very close to where McDonald had been killed, it was the year of Van Dyke's trial. All of her 6th- and 7th-graders identified as Black or African American, and Quinn is a white woman. As the trial was unfolding, Quinn knew that "the community was very, very impacted by it" and that Chicago Public School administrators were also concerned. They sent letters and emails home to families about talking with their children about the trial.

As a first-year English teacher, Quinn wasn't sure what the balance was between making space in the classroom to talk about the trial and Black Lives Matter more broadly and staying "on track" with her lesson plans and standards alignment. "I wanted to talk to my students about it, especially because I know they are so passionate about it. For another assignment, they asked me if they could write their papers about Colin Kaepernick and police brutality, so I knew that this was clearly something that they wanted and needed to talk about." In the moment, then, because she was "caught up already in teaching other things that I didn't feel prepared to" change her entire unit plan, Quinn opted for several shorter student-led discussions as the trial came to a close. Then, the day after Van Dyke was found guilty, she asked her students, "Does anyone know what is going on? Does anyone want to say or share anything?" In her 6th-grade class, even though they previously had seemed "to be itching to talk about it," not many students responded. They did not seem to want to engage in the discussion, and some students appeared to be still processing. In her 7th-grade class, it was a different story. They were very engaged in a conversation, "a lot of talking, energy at a hundred percent," to discuss the trial and what the outcome had been. The outcome had been a surprise for many, including Quinn's students. In fact, the school had previously sent home a letter before the verdict was released, saying that all after-school activities were going to be canceled on the afternoon of the verdict and families were cautioned to stay inside because "they were anticipating protests." On the day after the verdict was released, when the students were in fact back in school even though there had been rumors that the school was going to close if there were protests, Quinn pulled up a live stream from Twitter that showed activists speaking about the verdict and the BLM movement. "I gave the little preface like, 'If you feel uncomfortable or you don't want to have this conversation, you can step out to another classroom.'" None of her 7th graders chose to leave, although Quinn acknowledges that "that could just be because maybe some of them didn't feel comfortable excusing themselves because everyone else was so into it."

Quinn did not want the day after to end there, however. She knew her students wanted to talk more about racial (in)justice, and while she had already been planning to introduce a unit on BLM at some point in the year, the local context compelled her to develop this unit sooner than anticipated. Three weeks later, when it was time to begin their second ELA unit, Quinn introduced their new essential question: "How can we respond to injustice in our community?" The plan was that "students will be able to use a variety of texts (podcasts, videos, novels, news articles) to gain understanding of injustice in their community, and how they can respond to it. They will be able to participate in, execute, and facilitate productive conversations about topics that may be emotional or controversial." They then wrote original realistic fiction stories about (in)justice and activism. Reading through Quinn's unit plan, what stands out is the careful planning that went into ensuring that the students' criticality and discussion skills were well supported. It is an 11-week unit, which to many teachers feels like a lot of time. But the time that Quinn gave to this topic about which her students cared deeply reflected her care for them and their humanity. Quinn and her students read articles on activism and Black Lives Matter, including "Letter From a Birmingham Jail" and "Five Years On: Recalling Trayvon Martin and the Birth of Black Lives Matter." They read excerpts from Angie Thomas's *The Hate U Give* and then watched the film. Finally, they engaged with multimodal texts by listening to an NPR story "Civil Rights Activism, From Martin Luther King to Black Lives Matter" and episodes from a podcast called "16 Shots" about "how Van Dyke and McDonald intersected that night, the alleged cover-up, and the long history of friction between African-Americans and the Chicago Police Department" (WBEZ Chicago, 2018).

DAYS AFTER WHITE SUPREMACIST EVENTS

Violet's colleagues told her she should not talk about Charlottesville on the day after. "Oohh, you better be prepared for some backlash," one told her. An administrator also told her it wasn't a good idea. Violet was exasperated: "Are you kidding me? This is a current event. We need to talk about this! So the hell with that. I'm doing it anyway."

In Charlottesville, Virginia, in August 2017, right-wing, racist, anti-Semitic, and neo-Nazi groups converged on Charlottesville, Virginia, in what they called the "Unite the Right" rally. The rally, which included a torch-lit march and racist chants, was spurred by local government's decision to change the name of Robert E. Lee Park to Emancipation Park and to remove a statue of the Confederate general. Violent clashes ensued between protestors and counterprotestors. Soon after, the rally was declared unlawful and the governor of Virginia declared a state of emergency. In the early afternoon, one of the Unite the Right protestors drove his car into a group of counterprotestors, killing Heather Heyer and injuring over a dozen others (Facing History and Ourselves, 2017). Later that afternoon, President Trump made a national address about the "egregious display of hatred, bigotry, and violence on *many* sides" (emphasis added), willfully ignoring the white supremacists' responsibility. As this was happening, Violet watched the news and read updates on social media, knowing she would change her plans for the next day.

Because she works in a predominantly white, conservative community, Violet considers herself an ideological outsider. She likes her job as a high school English teacher, but there is often a gulf between her and her students' political beliefs. She had made the choice not to engage in DAP on one of the most difficult days after that she can remember: the day after the 2016 presidential election. She has regretted it since. "This is what I should have done after the election," Violet said, acknowledging that her own white privilege had allowed her to not engage. "I knew I should have done something, but I didn't. And now something else had happened, and I couldn't just ignore it again."

While reading the news online, Violet came across a photograph of a Black police officer standing in front of white men wearing Confederate flag shirts. He was protecting them and defending their right to protest. "I'll never forget that picture. I saw it and knew I wanted to use it as a journal prompt. I wanted my students to write about it. I wanted to hear their thoughts." Violet admits that she steeled herself for their responses, but she was pleasantly surprised. "The conversations we had!" Violet exclaimed, clearly moved at the memory. "They were so powerful! I had formed my own opinions of what I thought students would say. I just had this idea like, 'Oh, I can only imagine what so and so's gonna say. And I hate that I feel that way because I'm doing the same thing that irritates me about other people. I am human." Instead, Violet was glad to hear that her students found the white supremacist activities wrong. "I was glad it was such a learning experience for me, probably even more so than for my students. It was a clarification that there are those difficult conversations needed. They need to start as early as they can in the classroom. It was such a good thing."

From Charlottesville to Capitol Hill

Xavier's private Catholic school in D.C. was not in session when Charlottesville happened, but they started a new school year soon thereafter. Their first day of school, then, became a day after. Xavier had already been learning more about discussion-based pedagogy, and this moment was a way to put those new beliefs into action: "I knew that we had to sit with and talk about this." The plan was to show a documentary from Vice News, have the students complete viewing guides while they watched, and then discuss what they saw and learned. Xavier saw it as "a chance to show these kids, on day one, we're not going to duck the big issues. We have to be able to talk about these things together out loud, and that's how we were going to operate in this class. We weren't going to shrink from those kinds of moments, and we were going to use this discussion-based learning as a 'democracy prep.' In a democracy, you have to have the tough conversations and engage with the issues of the day, so that's what we're going to do."

Xavier is thoughtful and measured in how he described students' responses. "I think it was a lot for them to digest. But at the very least, they were able to see the reality." Of course, as teachers are wont to do, Xavier remembers one student who responded in a way he did not expect or understand. "One kid, I remember. The question on the worksheet was, 'What was one thing you noticed in the documentary?' And the kid responded 'how biased the media was,' and I was floored. I mean, you've got Nazis marching through the street with torches and the thing you're noticing is that the media is trying to knock these guys down a couple of pegs?" Overall, however, Xavier thinks that "they were able to find something in the video to make a note of. It was hard. It wasn't like it filled me with a rosy sunshiny feeling, but I felt it was productive."

Xavier's DAP affected his practice long term, as he considered what it meant to establish a classroom community first before introducing a critical incident like Charlottesville. "I've moved away from dropping that heavy a weight on them right away. I did that same model for 2 or 3 years. On the first day, we sort of drop a giant bomb in the middle of the classroom and try to defuse it," Xavier shared, "but I moved away from that. I'd rather build a collaborative culture first."

Opportunities for Xavier to engage in DAP continued to arise in the years to come, including after another dangerous "rally." After the 2020 election victory of Biden over Trump, Trump and his supporters began making a baseless public case that the election had been stolen by means of widespread voting fraud, especially in Democratic urban strongholds. After more than a month of pressure on local and state election officials not to certify the results, the attention of the then-president and his most diehard supporters turned to the final tallying of votes by the vice president, House of Representatives, and Senate on January 6, 2021. After a morning rally in which President Trump repeated many of his claims of electoral fraud and encouraged rallygoers to march to the Capitol and to "fight like hell," a crowd of the rallygoers (now at the Capitol) attacked the building, breaking through barricades and into the Capitol building itself. The crowd erected a gallows outside the building and could be heard shouting "Hang Mike Pence!" As the insurrectionists moved through the building—including the congressional chambers and offices—government officials were moved to secure locations. After a police officer and a protester were killed, the Capitol was retaken from the attackers, and in the early hours of the next morning, the Electoral College vote count was completed.

From across the city, Xavier watched as this all unfolded. "Our first day back from winter break was January 7. I mean, I had a game plan. I had gotten my work done early to make sure that I wasn't scrambling at the last minute to come up with a lesson plan, and then. . . ." Xavier laughs ruefully, "Then, you know, the Republic is at risk. So I changed it." He preplanned what he was going to say to introduce the conversation:

> My lesson plan radically changed at 2:30 P.M. yesterday. So here's
> what we're going to do, because I just don't feel right. You know,
> I grew up in D.C. I'm a lifelong Washingtonian. I grew up on
> Capitol Hill, 5 blocks from the Capitol building, so I have all these
> formative experiences, like when I was 4 chasing squirrels on the
> Capitol grounds. I have experience of walking to and from my high
> school and cutting across the Capitol grounds to do it. And I've had
> experiences with the Capitol police department, not anything super
> contentious but, like, you put a foot wrong and they give you some
> blowback and then you put your foot right. For me the context of
> that event was so strange. It is not surprising because I've been alive
> and paying attention for the last 20 years, but it's really jarring.
> My personal associations with this place and with the people who
> are in charge of protecting it made it such that I would never have
> anticipated that something like this could happen.

Thus, for Xavier, his Days After Pedagogy was both personal and professional. "Part of it was my own personal stake in wanting to underline for the kids this is super remarkable. This is not the kind of thing that happens all the time," Xavier explained, "I didn't feel right just doing a couple of Kahoot quizzes to remember characters from the Book of Genesis." Because they were learning virtually, Xavier decided it was appropriate to offer students "an opt out if they were not ready for this conversation." In the four classes he taught that day, three classes had 90% of the students stay, and in one class, most of the students left, "which was weird," Xavier acknowledged.

For those who stayed, "I just sort of opened the floor. I had a series of questions up for them to journal about what they noticed. The questions I used were: What are you thinking and feeling right now? What are your questions and concerns? How do you understand or explain this phenomenon/where did this come from? And then, what's the response?" Xavier's last question was a big one and connected to the school's mission and vision. As a Jesuit school, their goal is for graduating students to be "loving, religious, open to growth, committed to doing justice, and intellectually competent. So I said, 'Okay, this is a big question, but what would our response look like if it came out of those values? What should people do now, those who are loving, religious, intellectually competent, open to growth, and committed to doing justice?'" Xavier had his own goals for the class beyond the school's overarching ones. He wasn't trying to achieve some sort of political end, but rather wanted to create a space without concern for academic content or standards that gave them room to process and "mark this as a really unusual experience. Again, especially in the pandemic, I'm really concerned about their well-being, so this was to create space for them to feel okay."

Upon reflection, Xavier thinks those goals for student support and thoughtful engagement were both met. As in his memories of the day after Charlottesville, Xavier still thinks about those whose responses were not what he hoped: "I do have some concerns that some of the kids who opted out did so because their sympathies were elsewhere and they kind of read the room and recognized that they didn't want to sit through and be exposed to that." However, "almost without exception, they said that this was really wrong. The president bears a lot of responsibility for it. It was personally jarring. They talked about it in terms of something you wouldn't expect. There wasn't a lot of virulent pushback. Taken together as a whole, they were able to appropriately digest the magnitude and origins of the event. They could see it was the kind of thing we need to respond to."

Most important for Xavier, his students were able to "see the racial component of it. I have some really courageous students of color who were able to say that the way that these particular protesters were treated felt really different." This time, the white students were able to see and validate their peers' experiences. For Xavier, this was a welcome change—and a noticeable one. "I might be naive in this, but I really do think that the summer [2020] protests really marked a change. I came into those conversations expecting that I was going to get the 'whataboutisms' and dismissiveness. I was going to get the 'Yeah, but things are much better than they were.' I was ready for those conversations, and I didn't get them. From my white students, I got a lot more super genuine concern, recognition, and empathy. I think they were able to see both the specific, unique horrors of the George Floyd killing. But then, because it was being amplified almost weekly, they were able to see for the first time, 'Oh my gosh, there is a pattern. These things are happening a lot.' So they're coming into these conversations now, as opposed to my previous experience, less defensive and more willing to explore reality as opposed to feeling like they have to explain it away."

DAYS AFTER IMMIGRATION INJUSTICE

"There's no way to avoid talking about it," a former student told me. "It's constant and every day now." She was doing her student teaching in a school that served predominantly immigrant and refugee families. For years, there was constant media coverage of Trump's speeches, proposals, and policies. Every day was a new day after, all revolving around immigration injustice. Her students would come in each morning and ask the same question, "Did you see what happened? Do you think something else will happen today?"

As the stories below illustrate, while issues of immigration injustice did not begin in Trump's presidency, his rhetoric and policies caused irreparable harm. Especially for teachers who were working in communities with immigrant youth, immigration-related days after took on new meaning during his presidency. The stories below focus on Latinx immigrants, although of course not all immigrants are Latinx and not all Latinx people are immigrants.

In Colorado, Toby's high school students were reeling from the news. Trump had just made a nationally televised speech about "what he was calling the crisis at the border and providing justification for why he felt a border wall should be built." As Toby was watching the speech and simultaneously monitoring his social media timelines, he knew he was going to have to change his plans for the next day. Toby found a resource guide from the *L.A. Times*. Toby was hopeful that a days after conversation could focus on comparing the truths with the lies that were the basis of Trump's claims about a border crisis and need for a border wall.

Over the next 2 days, students poured through the resources and talked about what they were seeing. For example, using visual aids, the students compared what the border looks like between the United States and Mexico and between the United States and Canada. Toby posed the question, "What are some differences that we see? Why might these differences exist?" The following day, students participated in a Socratic Seminar where they had an opportunity to talk about what they felt was important, what they found to be true, or what was misinformation. Toby remembered, "There were a lot of Latinx students who appreciated having that space to be able to talk, to have their peers see how the situation at the border has been politicized. Some of them actually expressed feeling freed by having those truths shared. For others who were not Latinx, their standpoint was more like, 'Wow, I didn't know this. I'm glad to see actual facts about what the situation at the border is like.'"

Protests on Days After

It was her "favorite day of teaching of all time," and there is still a spark in her voice when she talks about it, even years later. In her bilingual elementary school classroom in Texas, Melissa and her students—all but one of whom were Latinx—had spent a lot of time talking about immigration policies under the Obama administration. In 2014, they "sent letters to Obama about stopping deportations and about how deportation processes and fears of deportation impacted their daily lives," Melissa explained. Then came an upsetting day: the Obama administration had deported two million people. "We talked about the significance of that, and how two million is more than a number. Two million is really people's lives and their family members' lives." The day after, they found out about a protest at the University of Texas–Austin campus, which was close to their elementary school. Campus organizers had planned a protest while President Obama was there for an invited speech. Melissa's students were eager to go. Especially after learning about the deportation process in their lessons and being personally impacted, "for them, going and advocating against deportation was really of the highest priority." Melissa called families and all gave permission for their children to attend. Then she went to her principal and asked if she could take the students, adding quickly that "the parents already agreed!"

So, the next day, off they went. "The kids were so excited. The thing that made it such a powerful moment was that it was so natural to schooling, the way the whole thing went. We just walked down the street to a public bus." Melissa had enlisted a few chaperones to go with her, including a special education teacher, her then-boyfriend-now-husband, who was a student at the university, plus a couple of other university students. They each picked up a brown-bag lunch to take with them to eat on campus. "They all got on the bus, and the bus was full with college kids on their way to class, right? College kids, but then also all these little kids. The kids were asking them questions about college. The shuttle bus dropped off in one place and we had to walk through campus. And many of them had not been to campus before. I always think about how these campuses that are technically public aren't really open spaces that people can just go. They were looking at these iconic landmarks—the giant football stadium, the tower—and seeing them in front of them. They were also getting a sense of what college is like and the movement of people." They brought their own signs, too: "I am human." "Stop tearing families apart." "Keep families together."

Melissa and her students eventually reached the protest area where campus organizers had been chained to a statue of Martin Luther King Jr. since the night before. "When we got there, the organizers of the protest didn't know that we were going to show up with a bunch of kids, so that was really exciting for them. This was a big group of kids whose parents were immigrants and who felt very powerfully and intensely about what they were arguing for, why they were there, and what they were doing. One girl [decided to speak] and cried while speaking. And the whole crowd of people were just in tears. Then she was invited to unlock one of the activists and she was excited to do so. They ended up putting our group of kids at the front and let them lead the march. That [led to] a really powerful cry. There was a lot of crying."

After the students arrived at the library, Melissa remembers an older professor coming up to the students and telling them how great it was to see them there. He gave each of them his business card and told them to stay in touch. "They were thrilled, saying, 'We have to save this! This is a real college professor!' I think it gave them confidence. I loved that they had a sense of ownership of the college space, too. These are Latinx kids, the children of immigrants. They are underrepresented at that university, and they were part of shutting it down for a day."

Melissa ran into her principal at the end of the day, who told her about being at the dentist's office and seeing the protest covered on the local news on the TV in the waiting room. She said he laughed as he told her, "You told me you were going to protest. You didn't tell me you were going to march!" "Look," Melissa replied, "no one goes to protest to sit on the sidelines." Her principal understood and said, "I hope the district doesn't notice." Whether the district noticed or not, the families "were really happy about the whole thing, 'cause they were like, 'My kid came home excited and felt powerful.'"

As for the students, they reported, "It was the coolest day ever." Part of what Melissa sees as the power of this day after is that it was "the total disruption of a school day," but their new experience built on the things they cared about and made them feel powerful in a moment of injustice. "And they were made into stars, being allowed to lead the protest! [They got to participate in] all the things about a protest that make it a powerful experience: the chanting, the movement, the sense of people together doing something, how loud it is, how forceful, and how it occupies space. They got to experience that and not just read about it. That's what they kept talking about. They were like, 'We read about Martin Luther King Jr. marching, but we didn't know what it sounded like. Now we know what it sounds like.' It was such a good day."

This is powerful DAP that lasts. What students learned in Melissa's class has stayed with them. Reflecting on what they meant to her and where they are now, Melissa said, "They were the best. They are graduating from high school next year. And they're still great. I did hear from parents after Parkland, when the students were organizing walkouts and protests, some of the kids from that group were organizing those things at their schools. They had a model, and they kept that spirit moving."

DAYS AFTER LOCAL RACIAL INJUSTICE

The earlier stories from teachers point to how they engaged in DAP when racial violence and white supremacy made national news. Teachers also found themselves using DAP in moments when injustice came home, so to speak: when there were examples of racism and white supremacy in their individual schools. Of course, we know that racism and white supremacy are inherent in the fabric of schooling. There is never a day in which racism isn't part of schools. The days teachers talked about here, however, were days after critical incidents that led to increased attention from the community and/or the local news.

When Students Wore Symbols of White Supremacy

In rural Michigan, one of Kelly's white students had worn a Confederate flag T-shirt and then, a week later, came to school with his head shaved. She had two Black students in her class, and they asked her to bring it up.

Kelly gathered research on the history of the Confederate flag and began class by explaining "its history and why people are offended by it." The white student then explained "why he didn't think it was offensive. He claims that the head shaving was unrelated to any of it. He was like, 'Does it make you think I'm a Nazi?' And we were like, 'Yeah, we kind of do.'" Kelly remembers that it was a "weird discussion" at points because of awkward laughter and pauses that she attributes to her students' maturity (or lack thereof) and experience having difficult conversations. When the Black students were ready to speak, Kelly was grateful for their contributions because she wanted the white student to "hear right from their mouths" about the impact of the student's choices. Importantly, Kelly did not spotlight her Black students in an effort to teach her white student, and she did not make them speak on behalf of their entire racial group. In the end, things turned out as well as they could have in that moment. "I don't know that anybody's minds were blown," she shared, reflectively, "but at least they got to share." The white student ended the conversation by saying, "I could just not wear it. I'm not wearing it to piss anybody off." While the larger goal would have been for the student to understand the significance of the shirt and understand the difference between intent and impact, the short-term goals of having him not wear the shirt to school and allowing the Black students a space and time to speak up were accomplished.

When Students Made Symbols of White Supremacy

Just an hour away from Kelly's classroom, something similar happened in Leah's school. The context was very different, however, as the school served predominantly students of color and the school was intentionally committed to "real-world" and "place-based" learning. Leah remembered one year when two of their students were stopped by police while they walked home from school. Although thankfully nothing tragic happened, "it was a scary moment for them, and their parents reached out to the school. In their homeroom, they had a circle [discussion] where the boys got to share their story and talk about what happened with the whole class. They all got to process it together."

Then, one day on a class field trip, a photograph was taken that showed a white student making a hand gesture while standing behind students of color. In Leah's words, "He's white and he was doing the 'okay' symbol behind them and he had a kind of glare on his face. I can't really describe it, just kind of a creepy stare." A parent saw the photo, was disturbed, and brought it to Leah's attention. "She told me, 'He's doing the white power sign. This is really scary and traumatic.' And that was when I learned about what the white power sign was."

The day after, Leah discussed the photo and the symbol with her entire class. "It was not necessarily about that boy in that picture, but just about the symbol and what it meant. [We talked about] how it was being used and the expectation we had with our middle schoolers going forward." It was important to Leah to talk about the power of symbols, including how they could be appropriated for different purposes. This is an important lesson beyond days after: Words and symbols have multiple meanings, and these meanings can change over time. "It's a really tricky thing to talk to middle schoolers about. A white power symbol is also an okay sign, which is something that little kids or even adults use all the time," Leah explained. "They were getting caught up in how ambiguous it was and how it doesn't always mean that. I didn't want it to become a thing where they were reacting against the people who were telling them they couldn't do this. It was more presented to them as an explanation of what this symbol is now being used as. It's being co-opted. No one's telling you that you can't use it. We're just letting you know that if you do, this is how it might be taken." To Leah, this felt like a good balance of discussing symbolism and individual choices without explicitly spotlighting the one student who made the gesture in the photo. Her DAP appeared to work as intended.

Until a year later, that is, when the "the same thing happened again, and it was the same boy and it was the same setup of a picture. It was him in the background of three boys of color and he had a creepy look on his face." I'm sure Leah can see the shock on my face when she tells me this. "Yeah, I know," she continues. "This time, the principal addressed it and talked to him." While it appeared that the student thought he was "experimenting with middle school humor," he said he did not realize that "it doesn't matter that he's not intending it" to cause harm. The principal, a Black woman, focused on this idea of intent versus impact: "She addressed the issue that he wasn't seeming to get, which is that, even if you're not intending it to be that way, this is how people are reading it." This incident happened to connect with what Leah was teaching at the time. "We were doing a unit about Reconstruction, and it fit right into a lesson we were doing about symbology of hate then and now."

To Leah, this isolated incident isn't so isolated. It is part of a wider racist system and one that they work to address in their school often. To not address an incident like this on the day after would feel disingenuous. Leah continues:

> I feel really glad that they're a part of our school and they get to make these mistakes and be in a community that will support them and help them figure out how to navigate these sorts of things. It is so complicated and it's not something just parents can give to their kids. Adults in our world right now can't figure it out! It is something where we need all hands-on-deck to figure it out. We knew we needed to address it in a way that's going to support the student being a caring member of this world and not just someone who adds to the hate.

When a Community Clings to White Supremacy

Gemma tells me about an incident when a white student spray-painted racist graffiti on the school's football field. "It's kind of a long story, but it feels important," Gemma told me, "because it started back in the heart of the Civil Rights Movement." The graffiti was not an isolated incident but part of a legacy of racism and white supremacy in a district that had once viewed its creation as an independent district as "seceding from the union, so they took on the iconography of the Confederacy as their mascot." That meant that Gemma's DAP needed to contextualize this current incident within a broader history.

"They used the Confederate colors, gray and blue, took on a Confederate soldier as mascot, and flew the Confederate flag. In the heart of the Civil Rights Movement! Across the country, folks were erecting statues to General Lee and others as pushback. This mascot was what the pushback looked like where I teach." Almost from the beginning of this change, Gemma said that there have been people in the community who challenged the mascot and flag, including a former teacher. Until the early 1990s, there were small images of Confederate flags on the school busses. The school eventually got rid of the mascot imagery, but they kept the team name, the Rebels. Then, during Gemma's first year in the district, students went to the school board and said, "We really have to look at the legacy of our school." They were unsuccessful, however, and the board said that the Rebels name would stay. Despite this "win," some white students and families were upset that it had even been challenged. They "started wearing Confederate flag gear to the high school, saying, 'yes, we are the Rebels.'"

Next came the formation of a social justice union, led primarily by students of color, to "take a critical look at what's happening in our own school community and surface the fact that this is not a safe space for a lot of students." This time, when the students started the movement to change the Rebels name, they were ultimately successful. "Soon after the school board made the decision to change it—without a new one in place yet—there was a major uproar from white members of our community. It was mostly adults who had attended the high school and they started what they called the 'Rebel Alliance.' They were successfully able to vote down our budget twice consecutively in a district that never ever votes down a school budget." The division and violence continued: A white male adult in the community was later found guilty for stalking the adolescent leader of the social justice union. A 7th grader was assaulted by another white male adult. Then an 18-year-old white student spray-painted the football field with racist graffiti against the Black male student who had initiated the name change. He painted, "[student's name] is a dumb n-word" across the field. The white student was initially going to be charged with a hate crime, but, Gemma said, the anger in her voice reverberating, "that charge got dropped because it would have 'ruined the student's life' who had done it. [No one cared about] the student who the crime was committed against."

This whole time, of course, Gemma was teaching. There were a series of days after amid this ongoing struggle for justice that Gemma attended to. One was the morning after the school board finally agreed to change the Rebels' name. When students arrived, they were not happy. "Honestly, most of my sixth graders, especially my white students but also some of my sixth graders of color, were devastated at the change. They could not understand it, could not contextualize it." Gemma's DAP included examining texts and dialoguing with peers. First, she "read the statement that student leaders had given at the school board meeting." Then, she paired the petition to change the name with "images from the yearbook that had been circulating that clearly demonstrated the connections to Confederacy." Finally, they talked about hate symbols. Armed with this additional knowledge, they moved into restorative circles to have conversations about how they felt about the change.

It wasn't long before another day after arose. This time, a few months later, it was after the racist graffiti on the football field. The night it happened, Gemma was out for the evening and ran into a former student's mother, the mother of the Black student whose name was spray-painted as part of the graffiti. "That was how I learned what happened. I was pretty shaken. Having had a relationship with that family and knowing that student deeply, I was pretty wrecked." But she knew she would have to address it on the day after. Gemma "went into action mode" and reached out for help from a trusted colleague. They planned what Gemma would do in her classroom the next day.

Gemma introduced a text-based protocol to look at two news articles. First, they examined a local newspaper article about the hate crime on the football field. Then they compared it to a piece about a similar hate crime against LeBron James. They discussed how "folks are not protected against hate [and] how this is impacting Black folks across the country." After the students did a gallery walk and wrote their responses around the room, they ended the period with a restorative circle to respond to the question, "What do you want to do about it?" Gemma told her students, "This is *our* community and I want to talk about it, but I don't want to stay in the intellectualization of it. I want to actually move it through to an action step."

Gemma left it up to her 6th graders to decide what they wanted to do next: "Our students decided that they would cover the field with messages of love to cover over the hate messages." When they discovered that no one was allowed on the field, they quickly changed plans by hanging posters all over the gates to the field. It was a beautiful gesture and a beautiful sight: their colorful posters blowing in the breeze, greeting students, families, and staff who walked by with words of hope and love.

"One of the things that floored me was their ability for empathy," Gemma commented. "A few of my students' posters said things like, 'Are you okay?' I realized that the 'you' was actually about the person who had committed the crime, with students thinking 'this person has to be harboring a lot of hate, and they need help.' To see the way in which my students were able to grapple with the deeper levels of what causes a person to go to this place of hatred was pretty remarkable." Importantly, Gemma realizes—and supports her students in realizing—that white supremacy is both about individuals and institutions, about specific moments like this and about systems that enable such moments to happen.

The students had come a long way on these days after. Just months before, they had been "so shaken by the change of the name, to the point where some people were crying and painting their faces and creating T-shirts and the whole mess. And now these same exact students were able to cover the field with these messages, have deep understanding that this wasn't okay, and trace that back to what happened earlier in the year."

CONCLUSION

In the last two chapters, teachers' experiences when days after intersected with politics, racism, and white supremacy illustrate both the complexity of DAP and the importance of it. In each of the stories included here, we see teachers striving for conversations that work to dismantle oppression and respond to students' trauma. In the process, they work to support students' agency through student-centered lessons that humanize people of color and challenge systems of whiteness and white supremacy. Importantly, they do not see days after as "teachable moments" to be hastily taken up devoid of criticality and nuance. Instead, they carefully consider their own and students' identities and positionalities. These cases also illustrate that DAP focused on racial justice can be accomplished with all ages and all content areas.

Student Spotlight: Looking Back on Days After

I don't think I ever had an honest conversation about major injustices in society before this year. At my school, we always had the typical moments of silence and education on 9/11, but really nothing else. If something big happened the day before or was on the news, it was known about as we went throughout our day but never addressed. That changed in my senior year, though, and I think it really has to do with the program I'm in and the large media coverage of injustices all spring and summer before school started. This year, I'm in a smaller class that is specialized for students who want to go into the health care field. Although my current teachers never specifically labeled their political affiliations, their open-mindedness and the conversations we have had led me to believe that they are Democrats. My teachers are more outspoken on social justice than any teacher I have had before, and part of our curriculum is government/current events re-lated. One of our many assignments is doing current event writeups where we select an article from the news to dissect.

This has led to productive conversations so far in our year, with topics surrounding the 2020 U.S. presidential election, the death of Ruth Bader Ginsburg, the Black Lives Matter movement, and other specific social in-justices surrounding LGBTQ+ and Asian communities. Right around the time when Ruth Bader Ginsburg passed away, I had to present one of our current event writeups to the class. As an individual who looked up to Ruth Bader Ginsburg and saw the impact she left on society, I did my presentation on an article related to her death. I really valued that my teachers allowed room for me to share my thoughts and feelings regarding her death, and they prompted our whole class to spend time on this topic to make me feel heard.

I feel let down that classes in my past years never had these hard con-versations about injustice and tragedies. I think that if more individuals had these conversations at younger ages when our minds are more im-pressionable, then ignorance and racism wouldn't be as common among individuals in society. Also, when social injustices and horrific tragedies do occur, it wouldn't be as difficult to start conversations related to these events and what is wrong with our society. I shouldn't have to seek out individuals to have these conversations with. They should be freely had to discuss and improve our society.

Author Bio: Paige Carletta is a freshman at Northeastern University, major-ing in nursing. She wrote this piece as a high school senior in Hamlin, New York. As a young white woman, Paige thinks it is especially important to work for racial justice. Some of her favorite things to do are reading her favorite books, playing with her two puppies, and trying new food!

CHAPTER 8

Conclusion

PART 1: INSTITUTIONALIZING A SPACE FOR DAYS AFTER PEDAGOGY

It's really important that there are open spaces in schools that are already ready and poised to do this work.

—Eric, middle school music educator, New York City

Many of the teachers in this book are finding ways to engage in DAP in spaces that might not feel supportive for justice-oriented, student-centered pedagogies in general, let alone in the tense and potentially traumatic moments after major events. They are doing this with a commitment to taking risks, to being creatively insubordinate, and to working through their own fears and challenges. But what would it look like if educators didn't have to do that? What would it look like if there were schools that, institutionally, supported Days After Pedagogy in multiple ways? Do schools like that exist? Can they?

It turns out, after talking to Eric, I am convinced that not only *can* they exist, but they *do* exist. Eric is a music teacher and cofounder of a public school in New York City, Metropolitan Expeditionary Learning School (MELS). Eric is a 6th- to 8th-grade instrumental music teacher and leader of the school's community meeting spaces and their schoolwide equity team. In his 18th year of teaching, Eric describes himself as a gay Chinese American cisgender male. If you have ever doubted the possibilities of public education, talking to Eric would restore your faith—and then some.

As Eric tells it, when there was an opportunity for groups to "bid" on founding a new public school in the New York City schools system, "we want[ed] to do something very experimental and see how far we could push a progressive model within a public school." And push it they did. The administrators and teachers created and nurtured a space where DAP is not just allowed but encouraged and expected.

A few structures make the school uniquely suited to DAP. First, there are no textbooks. "Everything is what we call a living curriculum," Eric explained. "The curriculum is entirely collaborative, where teachers work together to generate the curriculum and it revolves around large-scale interdisciplinary projects that often involve partnerships with community organizations. The heart of the curricular work is that every student is involved in some kind of social action project in every grade, and they generally span classes." In addition to a focus on teacher collaboration, there is also a focus on teacher leadership. Eric shared that "more than half the teachers are teacher leaders. When you talk about school ownership, this is one of those schools that just has distributed leadership off the deep end!" There are teachers who lead grade-level teams, department teams, crew teams, community meeting teams, equity teams, and other committees. To be sure, it sounds like a lot of work. But it is work that matters to the teachers because they feel a sense of agency and empowerment that we see far too little of in most public schools with top-down, hierarchical, bureaucratic structures. As Eric noted, "When you have the majority of teachers that are participating in the core work of building the school, then something very different emerges in the way teachers interact with the school." This dramatically affects teacher retention in a system where it's difficult to keep teachers for longer than 3 years: "We have one of the best retention rates in the city, above 90%. It's a place where teachers feel a lot of ownership over the curriculum, they can be creative, and feel like they're really connected to the work of social justice."

The students' schedule at MELS also supports DAP. According to Eric, there are at least two "very clear spaces where students are going to talk about and respond to" any major events in the news. First, there is a class called Crew. One teacher meets with 15 students during first period every day to have opportunities for group and community leadership. "On a normal day—and there's never really a normal day—there is a set structure for Crew. There's some kind of check-in, like 'roses and thorns,' and then there's a quotation for kids to respond to." After that, students will work together to complete a challenge as part of an outdoor education initiative. (An example of these challenges that readers might recognize is the human knot.) "They might succeed or fail. But the important thing is the debrief: What did you do well? What did you learn? Students call it their family space." Each teacher determines a social action project that aligns with an overarching Crew theme for the year, such as racial bias. Teachers work collaboratively to design lessons and activities in 2-week units, but they also know that, as Eric described it, "Your Crew is your own. One of the fantastic things is every teacher brings their own personality and love to the projects. There's something very unique about kids and teachers doing that work, bringing their own selves to the space and being encouraged to do so. Crew is very much a shared space with students and teachers." It is the first place where DAP emerges, Eric explained: "We know that when Donald Trump is elected, when any number of shootings happen, when Black men and women are murdered by police, we know they will discuss it in Crew." These days after moments can also inspire longer inquiry, deeper learning, and social action.

A second space for DAP is Community Meeting. Every week, each grade meets as a collective. While there can be many different purposes of the meeting, including some logistical ones, the meeting "always begins with an open space where any student can grab the mic and speak. Whatever teacher is leading it, often myself, we'll say, 'We're open for announcements, appreciations, apologies, and activism.' So students can give announcements, they can apologize to the community for something, they can appreciate someone in the community, or they can describe activism they've taken, because it's a core part of our school." The day after the school shooting in Parkland, Florida, is one day after that "stands out the most to me," Eric remembered. "It was incredibly impactful for any school community," including MELS. Eric was leading Community Meeting that day and, as soon as he put down the mic and opened the floor, "there's about 120, 130 kids in each grade, and they didn't stop talking. The flood gates opened and they didn't stop." When Eric talked about this moment, his eyes lit up and he sat forward in his chair. He was still, years later, so excited at the memory—not excited about the event that caused such a meeting, but so proud of what his students had done. "It was kind of like the holy grail of community meeting in which the kids move into some kind of action and organize themselves. And I think that's why Parkland really stands out to me. It wasn't just one day after. It was multiple days after." The students asked for additional Community Meetings so they could plan their walkout and what their signs would look like.

Eric also recalled a comment from a student who spoke about how another school needed support. MELS is colocated with two other schools, meaning that there are three separate schools that share one physical building, a common practice in New York City (and one that is often ripe for inequities). They also share a campuswide athletics team. A student noted that she wanted to include one of the colocated schools in MELS' plans. "They don't know what they're doing because they don't have Community Meetings," she said, "so how do we get them involved?" Eric laughs at this part of the memory: "I remember thinking, 'Kids are so wacky. They have no idea how weird our school actually is'" to have a Community Meeting space. The moment also stands out for another reason: "It became clear in that moment that that was the space in which they were going to organize. Teachers were going to sit back, make sure that no one got themselves into trouble, and just let the kids take it away. That's how kids talk about it, too, how incredible that moment of Community Meeting was where they organized themselves into a protest."

Another moment where the Community Meeting supported days after dialogue was in the wake of the murder of George Floyd in May 2020. George Floyd was detained by police officers in Minneapolis and, just 17 minutes after police first arrived, had died after being pinned to the ground by three police officers. One of the officers, Derek Chauvin, was charged—and later convicted—of 2nd-degree unintentional murder, 3rd-degree murder, and 2nd-degree manslaughter. Witness videos, which quickly went viral, showed the white officer kneeling on Floyd's neck for more than 9 minutes, despite protests by Floyd and bystanders that he could not breathe, and even after Floyd had lost consciousness and paramedics were at the scene. Prosecutors later added more serious charges to those against Chauvin and charged three of the other officers, as well. Floyd's murder, and his pleas captured on video, rekindled Black Lives Matter protests and uprisings around the country and abroad.

The day after Floyd's murder, students were learning virtually. Eric had not checked the news before he started the 10th-grade Community Meeting on Zoom. As soon as Eric finished welcoming everyone, one student unmuted himself, and said, "Guys, Minneapolis is burning." Neither Eric nor the other students knew what the student was talking about. But, even if he didn't know what happened, Eric did know one thing: "Whatever I had planned to do was clearly not being done. Kids are going to figure it out and educate each other." While that Community Meeting did not lead to a major action, it did provide a much-needed space for students' socioemotional processing and support. "I was grateful that that space was there and kids were able to talk and process, just trying to figure out what they could do."

In the Crew classes and the Community Meetings, Eric knows that it might be the first place that students encounter DAP, but it won't be the only place. As a music educator, he is also committed to providing space in his classroom. It doesn't take much for him to know if an event is worth discussing: "If it's major enough for kids to talk about [on their own], then that's what we're talking about today."

On any type of day after—be it an election, an instance of racial violence, a school shooting—Eric said that he will start his classes "by asking if there's something students still want to talk about, not knowing if they've finished talking in Crew or whether there's something that came out of Crew that a kid wants to announce to the class." One example of "the day after mattering in a musical way" was after the case against Eric Garner's killer was dismissed by a New York City grand jury. In July 2014, Eric Garner, a 43-year-old father of six, lost consciousness and died as a result of a chokehold used by an NYPD officer in Staten Island. Garner was being arrested for allegedly selling loose cigarettes when NYPD officer Daniel Pantaleo forced him to the ground and put him in a chokehold, a practice that was banned by the police department.

Bystander video captured Garner repeatedly telling the officer, "I can't breathe." Those final words have since become a rallying cry for protests against police brutality. In the wake of his death, New York City settled with Garner's family in a wrongful death suit, but a grand jury and federal prosecutors refused to press charges. When he heard the news about the grand jury one evening, Eric "knew my students were going to be incredibly incensed the next day. I remember thinking to myself, 'If not now, then when? When am I going to do something about this musically in my career?'" They were in the middle of a unit on jazz music. Eric described the day after to me, a longer version of which is published in his article (Shieh, 2016).

"I put in front of them John Coltrane's song, "Alabama," which he had written for the bombing of the church in Birmingham. It's an incredibly moving piece of music. We sight read it. I remember feeling really charged to understand and interrogate with students the linkages between music and social change. And, if there really weren't any, then what the hell are we doing? What are we supposed to do as musicians? That conversation opened me up to and made me veer toward a very different several weeks of curriculum than I had planned."

As other teachers shared, often the day after turns into *days* after. The same was true for Eric and his students. "We started looking at theories of jazz that were inspired by the Black Power Movement and the idea that particular kinds of music could change the way you think. We started doing these projects in which kids were trying to play songs in a way to change people's minds and to try to interrogate the power of music." Importantly, Eric noted, he also wanted students to examine how "music doesn't work and where it kind of falls short."

Eric discussed another example of DAP. As I write in the next section, the COVID-19 pandemic felt, to many, like one never-ending day after. Amid this ongoing trauma were multiple examples of racial violence and white supremacy. At the end of the 2020 school year, after they had been learning virtually for months, "students were desperate to feel like they could do something because the sense of helplessness was real, as was the trauma that comes from that." In the virtual environment, many of their major projects had been pushed aside to deal with more day-to-day emergencies of the pandemic, but Eric and colleagues "decided we're going to conclude every class with some kind of project that was agency generating. I think I would have done it anyway, but it was certainly heightened by the fact that I was meeting with other colleagues. We were all worried about the same thing, which is how do we get these kids to feel that their voices matter." Eric was teaching a music production unit at the time where "our final project was going to be making remixes to speak toward what was going on in the pandemic or a social issue they cared about. Seventy-five percent of them chose to do their remix on Black Lives

Matter." Their projects were about music, to be sure, but Eric's 7th-graders also valued that their projects were "about making a difference, responding to this present moment." Eric then compiled all of their remixes onto a webpage, and students shared their projects during a presentation of learning to the entire 7th-grade and family community.

The students were glad to have this as their final project. "This is a school where kids are used to the curriculum feeling real all the time," Eric mused, but then the pandemic hit and this was finally "the first thing that felt real to them all year. Some kids that we had lost came back on board. It went over really well with our students, and it was a great way for us to end the year."

After talking with Eric, it is clear that he is the type of educator who would engage in DAP no matter where he was teaching. But what makes his DAP so robust—and what makes MELS students' days after experiences so rich, supportive, and meaningful—is that the school community is fully engaged and committed to this work. Although writing about a model of human rights education as opposed to a model for schoolwide support for DAP, Hantzopoulos's (2016) work is relevant here, as she explains that the most humanizing schools are those that center a culture of care, respect, critical questioning, and participation. These spaces "center the dignity of students and teachers" (p. 16), much in the way that Eric's school does.

As I wrote at the beginning of the book, teaching on days after is not just a *time* when you teach; it is a *way* that you teach. In Eric's story, we see that way so clearly and powerfully. It is a story of possibility, a story that allows us as educators to imagine and reimagine how we make space for days after moments in our own spaces. And how, above all, we must work with our colleagues and our students to do it.

PART 2: WHERE DO WE GO FROM HERE?
SOME FINAL ADVICE FOR TEACHING ON DAYS AFTER

Interviewing the teachers whose stories grace these pages was truly a privilege. Their testimonies about the importance of DAP and what it has meant for them and their students is why this work is so important. Like the asset-based pedagogies discussed in Chapter 2, DAP is not "easy" to do. Indeed, it is exhausting and challenging. It, in the words of one educator, "takes teaching up a notch because you need to be so flexible." Karissa expands on this idea, arguing that adaptability on days after is necessary because "it's really important to see our students as whole people and not just vessels for our lesson plans for that day. . . . It's the only way to teach. If students are spending so much of their lives here, the system needs to serve them and model what we hope eventually will trickle out into the rest of the world. I can't control the world, but I can control my classroom. That's our little corner of the world where I can bring my hopes for the broader world and the things that I hope that they take with them." Adam's dedication to DAP is similarly informed by an overarching commitment to justice and equity: "I think creating a better tomorrow is another reason why this work is crucial. It's about humanity. One thing that I stress in all of our discussions is that you don't have to agree with my perspective, but, in disagreeing with my perspective, you shouldn't disagree with my humanity. I think that's the most important thing for students to understand is that you can disagree with someone's ideas, but you can't disagree with who they are as a human being."

Yet there are so many other educators I hear from who share these commitments but have a difficult time turning their intentions into actions. Some of this concern and hesitancy may be due to the complexities highlighted in Chapter 5; they may be worried about parental or administrative pushback, may work in contexts where there have been explicit or implicit statements to not discuss certain topics or events, or may experience discomfort or fear about leading a discussion that they don't have clearly planned.

Others may never have learned about how to facilitate these moments. Fiona, in her third year of teaching, felt like days after incidents were happening more and more, but she still wasn't prepared for how to ensure they were supportive, productive, and meaningful: "Honestly in this political climate, especially as a science teacher, more controversial topics" keep arising, when students are "repeating what they hear in the media or repeating what they hear from their parents. I feel like I'm having to navigate these conversations more. I'm not saying it's all negative, but it's really pushed me to think" about DAP. Maya expressed similar concerns about a lack of preparation in teacher education *and* a lack of professional development as a teacher. She elaborated,

> Students are so accustomed to things like shootings or other world events that happen often. They are like, "Oh yeah, that happened, moving on," which is highly problematic. I'm not entirely sure how to address that. We have not been prepared to any degree. How do you address that with your students in a way that's productive? That makes them not numb or deadened to the recurrence of the events and makes a positive impact?

My hope is that the teachers' stories in this text answer those questions and more. My hope is that educators who have concerns about their ability to engage in this work see that they can still do this work. This doesn't mean to engage in DAP uncritically or without regard for our students' identities and what they need in the moment. It means that knowing those things will support our DAP, and our DAP will support knowing those things. I wanted to center teachers' experiences in this book because, too often, their voices are left out of decisions about policies and curriculum. Through Student Spotlights, youth also shared what happened—and, in most cases, what did *not* happen—on days after in their own schooling. Their narratives point out not just the danger of silence that people will remember "one day," but that the silence is deeply affecting our students *right now*.

The following is a brief, by no means exhaustive, summary of some final advice for teaching on days after.

1. ***Reject a call to "neutrality":*** As we have seen throughout, DAP is not a neutral endeavor. Neutrality protects and advances privilege, white supremacy, and oppression. Even to claim neutrality is a privilege. Especially on days after, attempting to teach "both sides" in the wake of injustice is deeply problematic. Some may claim that you are "just teaching your opinion." In fact, I always tell my students, yes, actually, it is my opinion, *but* it is my opinion because I have read and learned over the years from decades of evidence that [fill in the blank with the issue you're discussing].

2. ***Remember students' humanity:*** At the heart of our DAP must be our students' humanity. This is something we should consider and focus on *every* day, especially in the days after injustice. Reflecting on the Student Spotlights, consider how different their stories could be if their humanity had been centered on days after. Instead of stories of missed opportunities and silence, they could have been writing stories of transformation and possibility.

3. ***Remember that positionally and identity matter greatly:*** If we identify as white, or cisgender, or as a man, or in any other dominant identity category, we cannot rely on our colleagues who occupy more marginalized identities to be the only ones teaching about these issues and moments as they happen. For example, it should not and *cannot* be only teachers of color who address ongoing instances of racial violence and white supremacy. We don't know when these instances will happen, but we know they will, sadly and inevitably. White educators, we cannot pretend to be surprised anymore. One way to start developing an antiracist stance needed to engage in quality DAP would be to learn more about and work to develop racial literacy. Using Sealy-Ruiz's (2021) concepts of critical love, critical humility, critical reflection, historical literacy, archaeology of self, and interruption, you can begin your "journey to becoming racially literate and eventually taking action to interrupt racism when [you] see it happen in their schools and classrooms" (p. 5).

4. *Establish community dialogue norms and agreements and reinforce these
   on days after:* No matter the age of one's students, it is important to
   model for students what social justice and equitable dialogue look
   like. These norms can be developed in collaboration with students
   and colleagues and can be adapted based on students' age. Whether
   students are 5 or 15, dialogue norms can reinforce that, for those
   occupying dominant identities, intent does not mitigate impact. It
   doesn't matter what you intend to do. If the impact is harmful, you
   have still caused harm.

   By way of example, in my own classes and in the work I do with
   practicing educators and PK–12 students, I use suggested norms from
   Sensoy and DiAngelo (2014) as a starting point. For example, "Strive
   for intellectual humility. . . . Notice your own defensive reactions,
   and attempt to use these reactions as entry points for gaining deeper
   self-knowledge. . . . Differentiate between safety and comfort. Accept
   discomfort as necessary for social justice growth. . . . Identify where
   your learning edge is and push it."

   After I introduce these as a way to help students see the
   difference between what might be "typical" classroom rules or
   guidelines and more equity-focused agreements, I prompt students to
   self-reflectively rank these in a few different orders, based on those
   that they have the most practice with doing, are most worried about
   doing, are most bothered by when *other people* don't do it, and are
   most bothered by when they catch themselves not doing it. We return
   to these ideas often, especially on days after.

   However, as thoughtful and helpful as Sensoy and DiAngelo's
   norms may be, they also leave room for centering of whiteness and
   the white gaze. Their norms cannot apply to all groups in the same
   way. For example, "accept discomfort" is something I want my
   white students to practice, but I do not want their discomfort (or
   comfort) to lead to discomfort for students of color. Thus, I also
   include other nonnegotiable norms that emphasize that it is not up
   to those from marginalized groups to

   - be "nice," "civil," or "calm" in the face of dehumanization or
     discussions about this oppression;
   - educate others about their experiences;
   - speak for their particular marginalized group(s);
   - "debate" or prove the existence of oppression or marginalization;
   - make others feel comfortable; and
   - give others' "opinions" equal weight to their experiences.

   To expect those individuals to do so is to engage in continued
   oppression and dehumanization.

5. **Collaborate:** DAP is best when not done in isolation, just as justice-oriented work more broadly is best when done as a collective. Remember, "you can do this, but not alone. Build community, find mentors, and keep your job" (Agarwal-Rangnath, Dover, & Henning, 2016, p. 95). Consider which colleagues in your school have similar commitments to justice and equity. Who can you be in dialogue with about what you are doing and how you are doing it? How can you share resources and lesson ideas? Identify these colleagues in advance. It would be helpful to set up a system for communication in the wake of such events. For example, you might have a social media group or a shared virtual folder where people post materials. Also, turn to colleagues to offer and receive emotional support, to process together what has happened. If you anticipate pushback from the community, you may also seek proactive support letters. Administrators can issue statements or reminders that it is important to address justice and equity on days after. Importantly, the idea of collaboration is not building dependent. That is, if you feel like an ideological outsider in your department or school, remember that you are not doing this work alone. There are educators at other schools in your community and around the country who are engaging in this work. Perhaps they are not down the hall, but they are there, and the virtual world— be it social media groups, webinars or professional development workshops, or virtual inquiry groups or book clubs—can offer a space for connection and collaboration.

6. **Prepare for pushback:** There are ways to proactively ensure that you are ready if families or administrators attempt to curtail your DAP. Gutiérrez's (2016) strategies for creative insubordination also work for DAP if you are faced with pushback:

> » Press for explanation
> » Counter with evidence
> » Use the master's tools
> » Seek allies
> » Turn a rational issue into a moral one
> » Fly under the radar

You might also consider the following proactive efforts and skill building:

a. **Prepare a rationale statement:** This document explains your reasoning for why you are teaching about a particular topic and/or engaging in a particular type of pedagogy, such as DAP. Preparing it ahead of time does not mean you need to send it in advance. Rather, consider how you might feel when a parent calls to complain that you talked about an election, for example. In that moment, you may feel upset, concerned, or defensive. If you have a proactive rationale already written (that you can use in multiple situations), then you do not have to write a new email, write a new justification for this work, and gather your sources in an already stressful moment. Instead, you can quickly open up the document you have previously written, adapt it for the particular situation, and email it back to your principal or parent.

b. ***Remember your district's mission and vision:*** Statements about diversity and citizenship are especially relevant for engaging in DAP. Even if you are not in a content area that seems to be related to a particular event, districts' and schools' overarching learning goals apply to all subjects and grade levels, and you can use them as needed. In addition, many districts and schools have recently been issuing more public statements and/or forming "diversity, equity, and inclusion" committees. While we know that these statements often do not live up to their expectations (Andrews & Harper, 2020), you can remind administrators or families about the importance of translating visions into actions.

c. ***Consider how you will practice your DAP:*** How will you introduce the topic? How will you engage in a conversation if there are students who are pushing back? Practice what you will say and how you will say it. We have nothing to defend when we teach about these moments; we do not have to ask for either permission or forgiveness. We are not indoctrinating students, and we are not politicking. We are teaching *for* justice and equity. We are not teaching to be partisan; we are teaching to address human rights. So, when we respond to students, we can practice doing so in a straightforward manner.

You can also practice mindful communication and interruptor phrases, or common communication moves you can do to make it clear to students that you cannot tolerate what they are saying or that you need them to expand more so you can respond more clearly. Mindful communication strategies are longer sentence prompts and habits of communication that you can adopt. Here are some examples adapted from Lee Mun Wah's *The Art of Facilitation* (2004).

> » "What I think I heard you say was. . . . "
> » "When you said _____, it made me feel _____."
> » "I think we may have different ideas about _____ because _____."
> » "Can you help me understand what you meant by _____?"

> » "I need your help understanding _____."
> » "Your comment stuck with me because _____."
> » "Can you tell us why you believe _____ is true/not true?"

Interruptor phrases are shorter responses to in-the-moment student comments. However, whereas mindful communication strategies invite more discussion, interruptor phrases address harmful or questionable comments in a different way—by stopping them from becoming more harmful immediately. Here are some examples adapted from "From Privilege to Progress" (2020):

> » Please consider the impact of what you are saying.
> » That's not funny.
> » That is not okay with me.
> » I didn't realize you think that.
> » I'm going to stop you there.
> » Hold on. I need to process what you just said.
> » What you just said is harmful.
> » We don't say things like that here.

The idea here is not necessarily to create a "safe" space, as "safe" space language is complicated when it comes to classroom community. First, we can never guarantee a completely "safe" space in our classrooms because we don't know what students are going to say to and about each other and each other's communities. And even if I could guarantee what happens in my small classroom space, we are working in, as bell hooks (1984) says, an "imperialist capitalist patriarchal society" (p. 92) that is also cisheteronormative and white supremacist. Many of our schools are on stolen land. I can absolutely do my best to ensure, for example, that no one makes explicit racist, homophobic, sexist, transphobic, xenophobic, or otherwise discriminatory statements. But truly the most I can do is engage in what scholars like Subini Annamma call harm reduction—address it when it happens and be swift and decisive and clear in how I do so. I cannot do *no* harm, but I can work to do *less* harm. Further, I don't actually think the classroom *should* be safe for all viewpoints. I am not going to debate another person's right to exist. These phrases can support strategies for harm reduction even in the absence of a completely "safe" space.

Epilogue: January 2021

It is time we "brave up," and take the risks inherent in creating educational spaces that disrupt, defy, and reimagine what it means to teach, and learn, in increasingly diverse worlds.

—Dover and Rodriguez-Valls (2018, p. 17)

The hardest part about writing this book was knowing when to stop. Because there *is* no way to stop because the events keep happening. This book should have been finished 6 months ago. And yet, here we are, still in the midst of a global pandemic, and I am typing away in my "home office" (read: basement corner, surrounded by my children's toys, the sound of my dog snoring on the floor, and my husband typing at the other corner desk behind me). We are in the midst of what feels like one never-ending day after. In the last 6 months since I started writing this Epilogue, the world has continued spinning, but along with it has come ongoing anti-Black racism and anti-Asian violence, national protests and uprisings for racial justice and abolition, wildfires consuming the Pacific Northwest, virtual learning for many children around the country, and a childcare crisis. Beyond the colonized borders in the United States, so many other marginalized groups in other nations have struggled for their existence and humanity.

I feel as Vellanki (2020) writes, "My words and my work seem futile in this moment, they feel small and inconsequential when measured against all the pain, suffering, and upheaval we are experiencing, individually and collectively. And all the courage, compassion, and conviction we are surrounded by."

According to the news media, these events are "unprecedented," yet as sociologists and historians are rightfully quick to point out, these events are part of a pattern, a legacy of white supremacy, settler colonialism, and oppressive policies and practices that perpetuate injustice. All of these things continue to be a stark reminder that every day, to some*one*, some*where*, is a day after some*thing*.

I have started and stopped writing this Epilogue four different times: in April after the start of the COVID-19 pandemic, in June after the murders of George Floyd and Ahmaud Arbery and coverage of Breonna

Taylor's murder (although she had been killed months before with little attention paid), in November after the U.S. presidential election, and January 7, 2021, the day after a domestic terror attack by white supremacists on the U.S. Capitol as Congress was attempting to certify the election results for Joe Biden and Kamala Harris. It is also the day after two Democratic senators from Georgia, Raphael Warnock (the first Black senator elected in the state) and Jon Ossoff, won a runoff election and "flipped" the Senate majority to the Democratic Party. As I write, there are thousands of teachers from across the United States entering their (mostly virtual) classrooms and trying to figure out what to say to their students, what to *do* in this moment of not knowing what to do. I know this because I run a Facebook group about teaching for justice on days after, and when someone shared the group more widely, it went from 2,000 members to over 14,000 on the day after the Capitol attack. It is now at almost 20,000 educators. I am simultaneously glad that the group exists for those looking for support and wish that it did not have to exist in the first place.

This ongoing need to rewrite the Epilogue is also a reminder that DAP is relevant no matter the year, no matter the event. Almost all of the research included in this book was done before the COVID-19 pandemic, and indeed, an entire book could be written about days after in 2020 and 2021 alone. In lieu of that, Neville (2021) writes in the Prologue to her beautiful dissertation:

> There was a story of a middle school teacher in South Dakota who stood outside the smudged screen door of one of his students. There, he taught her algebra, Expo marker scratching graphs across the large whiteboard in his hand. There was a story of a shopper at a grocery store who noticed that an elderly woman hadn't found the toilet paper she needed. The man gave her his, stating "I can't get the look on her face out of my mind." There was a story of the school board president in the East Lansing [Michigan] school district raising $12,000 and hundreds of donations in a matter of days to send to preK–12 kids and the elderly. Many months later, in the magazine Vanity Fair, there would be a story of grief from author Jesmyn Ward so profound and so awfully beautiful that its mere mention would cause a reader's knees to tremble. There were many stories of a jazz musician, a pianist, a drummer, a vocalist standing on balconies and leading renditions of Italian or Chinese or Spanish folk songs with hundreds of their apartment-mates. There were stories of humans leaning out their windows, clapping in disjointed unison, forming a cacophony of raucous applause to envelop these humans as they walked home in their scrubs from hospitals, their feet dragging, their heads bowed, their hearts and bodies weary. There were many stories.
>
> Coronavirus-19 caused the global pandemic that is threatening our lives and daily routines. It did not cause the innumerable inequities laid bare across

our society. The most vulnerable are now made even more susceptible to disease: the homeless, the elderly, the poor, those without health care, humans who are not provided a bailout while the non-human are. The disease has vastly and disproportionately affected Black and Brown communities, with responses from government officials that reinforce and reflect the racism and anti-Blackness already rampant in society. The children in our U.S. K–12 public school system are experiencing disruption in their education and in their daily lives and well-being, and are often forced to sit in front of computer screens for hours a day, taking in content. Our teachers are fighting to provide a quality education for their students in the midst of these enormous curricular and emotional challenges and are also standing up to a system that seeks to sacrifice their and their students' safety. Some schools do not have the means to provide adequate digital technologies to students. These schools do not have the resources that they need because of a long and tired history of racism, classism, colonization, and oppression. The disease has made visible the many inequitable fissures that constitute our society; it has not created the gaps in income, health care, education, and well-being, but it has elucidated the need to protect the most vulnerable. It has also made abundantly clear how connected each of us are to one another, how obvious that it is each other that we need. (pp. 2–5)

And, in the middle of the pandemic, there was another presidential election in November 2020. The day after turned into days after as the country waited for a final confirmation. In the interim, incumbents Trump and Pence cried "election fraud" and forced states into recounts. Poll workers counted and recounted at all hours of the day, especially since there were so many mail-in votes because of the pandemic.

"WHAT WILL WE TELL THE CHILDREN?"

This is a question that many teachers asked in the wake of the riot that brought white supremacists storming into the U.S. Capitol as Congress sought to certify the recent U.S. presidential election results on January 6, 2021. It is a question asked on many days after, to be sure. But, as Ladson-Billings (2021) pointed out, in a blog post titled "But what will we tell the children," "there is only one thing to tell them: the truth."

Rann Miller is a former history teacher turned journalist in New Jersey. On January 7, the day after the Capitol attack, he wrote a blog post titled, "Had we had class today . . .": "Sharing a classroom with you was one of the great joys of my life. Truly, my time with you shaped me; as a professional, as a father, and as a human being. So on days like today, it is no shock that I think of you. On days like today, the day after a seminal moment in modern history, we'd sit down and spend the next 45 minutes or so talking about it. For the class of 2013, they knew it as 'circle time.' On those days, whatever the lesson plan was, I'd scrap it. I have no doubt that today would be any different, were I still in the classroom" (Miller, 2021).

Unlike Rann, Robert was still teaching high school history on the day after the Capitol attack, one of many days after he had experienced across his long career. Robert shared a written reflection with me about these moments:

> I have been a classroom teacher for 37 years, and, naturally, a lot has happened. It wasn't until very recently—COVID, in fact—that I really began to reflect on the history I have experienced with my students.
>
> When I was younger, my parents were able to tell me where they were when they found out John Kennedy had been assassinated. Every American could. I wonder what it was like to be a classroom teacher in 1963? I took some time to reflect as to what a similar watershed moment would be during my long teaching career. As a history teacher, this was a welcome challenge. These days, particularly after 9/11, illustrate the importance of "being with" your students during days after. I had students write immediately after 9/11 and after the Obama presidential election, and I have these short essays bound and I continue to use them in my teaching.
>
> The number of these events is staggering, and I'll just name a few. I can tell you where I was and how I responded personally and as a teacher to these events all of which took place during my teaching career: the fall of the Berlin wall; the genocide in Rwanda; 9/11; Obama's election; Nazi and confederate flags being waved in American streets and capital buildings; the murder of George Floyd; and the siege on the U.S. Capitol.
>
> What did my diverse groups of students need from me during these times? What did I do for them? What could I have done?
>
> I can identify many times during my teaching tenure that I felt this country was at a critical moment. However, the current time feels more critical than ever. I do remain very optimistic. That optimism is fueled by my daily experience with my students who see the world through a different lens than previous generations.

On January 7, like Robert and Rann, Lauren knew she wanted to tell her students the truth. But what did that look like for 5- and 6-year-olds, especially in a virtual learning environment? Lauren, a Black woman, is a fourth-year kindergarten teacher at a public school in Atlanta, Georgia. Her students are racially and socioeconomically diverse, and Lauren says that she "finds parts of her identity in each of her students by making meaningful connections with her students and their caregivers." Lauren's educational philosophy is that "academics are a piece of the puzzle of education. It is equally, if not more, important to teach compassion, social justice, and critical thinking." The day after the attack on the Capitol, Lauren knew she had to let this philosophy of justice guide her.

"I started by telling my students about how scared I felt during the terrorist attack on 9/11/2001 when I was 6 years old . . . only a few months older than they are now. I expressed that it is okay to feel scared, sad, and/or confused, in addition to any other emotions they may be feeling. I defined terrorism for my students, and then we discussed why rules and laws exist. This was a review of a lesson we did months ago, but many students remembered the overarching idea that they are in place to keep people safe (physically and mentally/emotionally)," Lauren explained.

Then Lauren showed several photographs that had been shared in the news. Some responses included: "I see someone carrying a desk." "I think that person is not supposed to be climbing on the building." "I wonder why the people are hiding." Three students "gave me a thumbs up through the computer screen that they had seen/heard about the events of the day before." Lauren said that her "intent was to give space to see, think, wonder, and process, thus my only response was 'thank you for sharing.' Afterwards, I went through the pictures and told them what was happening in the pictures. We finished the discussion by talking about the importance of leadership, which we talked about a few weeks ago when we talked about character traits that we want to see in ourselves, friends, and leaders. In closing, we held space for any final questions, comments, and feelings. Some other final thoughts from students were: 'Are they still climbing on the building?' 'I saw this on my mom's TV.' 'Were the people [hiding] scared?'"

Lauren responded to the last question by saying, "They may have been scared. Do you think they were scared?" Of course, while she was saying this, Lauren was answering the question for herself in her head: "I couldn't help but think about my least favorite moments being a kindergarten teacher: having to explain and practice active shooter/intruder drills and tell my students that we must take this extremely seriously because it is a possibility that someone may come in this building with weapons and try to harm us. I wanted to say that it was likely one of the scariest moments of their lives."

And then what happened? It is still kindergarten, after all, so "we took a wiggle break and began our phonics lesson for the day."

Overall, this portion of Lauren's lesson took no more than 25 minutes, but it was meaningful for her and for her students. Her students "were sincere and thoughtful. They had impactful questions." On a day when many teachers weren't sure what to do or how to do it—or even *if* they should do something—Lauren was steadfast in her convictions. The reason for her conviction is the perfect summary for Days After Pedagogy: "I told them that they are likely to learn more specifics about January 6, 2021, as they get older, but I wanted them to know what happened while they are in kindergarten. I owe them the opportunity to be informed about the world in which they will grow. History is happening around us, here and now. Kindergarteners are insightful and critical thinkers when given the chance. We must give them the chance."

A Letter to Educators and Children

To current and future teachers,

Someday, perhaps soon or perhaps in the distant future, you will be teaching the children who were kindergarteners in 2020 and 2021, the children who started school in the years when school looked very different. These were also the years when your own profession changed seemingly overnight. The letter below is for these children and, even though they can't read it now, I hope that it inspires you to think about your future students and what days after could mean for them.

* * *

To the kindergarteners of 2020 and 2021,

What will you remember about these years? These years when you stayed indoors, left preschool one day never to return to the same classroom or teacher, saw friends and family only on the other side of a screen? What will you remember of the world outside the walls of your home? I think a lot about those who graduated from high school or college in this period, whose years were supposed to be the most special, the rite of passage, the culmination of everything, cut so short, as the world seemed to crumble around us. But I also think of you, dear children, whose years were filled with drive-by birthday parties and virtual yoga or gym class in your living room. You may have learned to cook, to be there for one another, to resolve conflict within your home, to be creative and build makeshift homemade concerts and movie theaters. You may have listened and watched as people around the country stood up against racial violence and sought to enact change. Your years may have been filled with learning about loss at the same time that many people who don't understand education worried about "learning loss."

This is my wish for you. That even if you did not know it at the time, that you learn someday what happened in these years, when you learned to write, spell, and read on a computer screen; when you learned to wear masks for hours of the day and, in many cases, did so better than adults; and when you were constantly told to wait. Wait for birthday parties, wait for family reunions, wait for play dates and hugs and the feeling of a backpack on your shoulders as you walked into a new school building for the first time.

My wish for you is that you have teachers who tell you the truth about what happened, even if it's hard to hear or doesn't seem to make sense at the time. Because you are the best of us, and surely it doesn't make sense why so many people were hurting each other and endangering each other and our planet. But you have to know this and wrestle with this because it's much easier to learn early than to unlearn late.

My wish for you is that you have teachers like those in this book. That your teachers are filled with the courage and the conviction to support you in the ways that you deserve. That you have teachers who have been prepared to take on these moments, who feel supported by administrators and families, and who can work together to be ready for the days to come. This is no small task for them, but I know they are up to it. Sometimes you get lucky; sometimes you get a teacher like the ones in this book. Your teacher is reading this book because they want to learn how to teach you not just how to read and write and do math, but how to navigate, and eventually change, this world.

My wish for you is that, on the days after that inevitably come in your future, the classrooms where you find yourself are ones of compassion, care, and commitment. That they are spaces for you to process what you are feeling, ask questions, and find ways to make the world a better place. That what you remember is not silence, as so many grown adults remember about these days, but conversation. Not ignorance, but love. And not denial, but action.

My wish for you is that your days after are less ones of tragedy and more of triumph. That there are fewer days of injustice and more of justice. That the moments we remember are ones not of trauma, but of joy and healing and hope. Because this is what I see in your faces and hear in your voices. My wish is that your future days after remind you of the wonder you feel at the world now, that they are examples of the possibility and promise that I see in you every day.

Methods

What started as a small sample of five teachers morphed into a much larger project when teachers shared the call for participants on social media. Interviews with the 50 teachers profiled for this project, including the 40 featured in this book, took place primarily from 2018 to 2019, although some extended into 2020. Teachers completed a brief demographic questionnaire and then participated in a 60- to 120-minute virtual interview. Two participants shared their perspectives in writing as opposed to an interview; we corresponded via email or a collaborative document, with me asking questions and them responding asynchronously.

For virtual interviews, we used the Zoom platform. As a critical qualitative researcher, I admit that I was worried about establishing rapport and building trust in a virtual interview, especially since the interviews happened years before the world turned to Zoom in the pandemic. I was asking about difficult moments, both personally and pedagogically. While I knew some of the participants prior to the study, or they were friends of friends of friends, this was not the case for everyone. Yet what I found to be true was that teachers who signed up were eager to talk. They wanted to talk about days after because (1) these were some of the most memorable days of their careers, (2) they thought about them a lot but rarely talked with colleagues about them, and (3) no one had prepared them for these days, and they hoped their stories would help support the next generation of teachers to face these moments in more thoughtful and proactive ways. And finally, they wanted to talk about days after because they saw justice and equity as core to their praxis and believed that DAP was integral to living out this purpose.

Participants generously shared their perspectives and memories in virtual interviews with me and/or a graduate research assistant. During the conversation, we talked about their general philosophy of teaching, what days after they remembered, what they did or didn't do, and how they felt about it. We talked about the challenges and possibilities of DAP and if and how they felt prepared and supported to take on this work. There were many tears (mine and theirs), even with people I had just met. There was also much laughter.

Interviews were recorded and transcribed verbatim, and then sent to participants for their review. They had opportunities to add, amend, or delete what they had shared. While some participants added more information to their transcripts, no one deleted anything. Participants also shared artifacts, documents, and multimedia that they had used in their days after lessons. Participants were given a chance to use a pseudonym and choose it if they wished. Several participants preferred to use their real name, as listed in the participant table.

Over the course of many hours, cups of chai, large and small Post-it Notes, and graduate students who pestered me to learn qualitative analysis software (which, I admit, I foolishly refused), I reviewed interviews, coded for themes, and came away with the central arguments in this book. I knew immediately that I wanted to write a book as opposed to articles because there was so much richness to the teachers' stories that I did not want to cut short because of a journal-required word count. Their stories, I think, and I hope you agree, deserve more than 10,000 words.

STUDENT SPOTLIGHTS

A key component of Days After Pedagogy is not just what is *taught*, of course, but also what is *learned*. Educators know there is always a difference between the intended curriculum, the implemented curriculum, and the received curriculum. While this research did not involve students as participants, this is a task I hope to take on in the future. Instead, there are Student Spotlights interspersed throughout the book. These are written from the perspective of either current or former students about what they remember happening (or not happening) on days after in their own schooling experiences. Some participants write about one event; others write about multiple events. Some write about the silence; others write about the dialogue. All are deeply thoughtful, engaged, critically minded, and justice-oriented youth who inspire me. It is an honor to include their words here.

APPENDIX C: Participant Profiles

Name (pseudonym unless otherwise noted)	Grade and Content	School Type and Demographics	School Location	Years of Experience	Participant Self-Described Demographics
Adam	Elementary (Grades 4–5)	Urban public, predominantly students of color	New York City	8	Chinese American gay man, mid-30s
Ann	Middle school English language arts	Suburban public, predominantly students of color	Southeast	5	White woman, mid-30s
Bethany	Secondary English as a Second Language	Urban public, predominantly students of color and immigrant students	Midwest	1	White woman, early 20s
Brittney	Secondary Spanish	Suburban public, predominantly white students	Midwest	2	Biracial Black and white woman, mid-20s
Carrie (real name)	Secondary social studies	Urban public, predominantly students of color	Atlanta	14	White woman, early 40s
Chance (real name)	Middle school English language arts	Urban public, predominantly students of color	Atlanta	8	Black man, early 30s
Chris	Elementary (Grades 5–6), bilingual school	Urban public bilingual, predominantly students of color and immigrant students	Northeast	4	White man, early 30s
Dominique	Middle school English language arts (previously K–2)	Urban public charter, predominantly students of color	New York City	5	Black woman, late 20s

(continued)

Appendix C: Participant Profiles (continued)

Name (pseudonym unless otherwise noted)	Grade and Content	School Type and Demographics	School Location	Years of Experience	Participant Self-Described Demographics
Donna	Secondary social studies	Urban public magnet, predominantly students of color	Northeast	12	White woman, late 40s
Eliana (real name)	Secondary social studies	Suburban public, predominantly students of color	Northeast	11	Afro-Latina woman, early 30s
Emily	Secondary mathematics	Rural public, predominantly white students	Midwest	20	White woman, early 40s
Eric (real name)	Middle and secondary music	Urban public, predominantly students of color	New York City	18	Asian gay man, late 30s
Fiona	Middle school (Grade 7) science and "STEAM"	Suburban public, predominantly white students	Midwest	3	White woman, mid-20s
Gemma	Middle school (Grade 6) English language arts	Suburban public, predominantly white students	Northeast	9	White woman, mid-30s
Greta	Middle school world languages (German) and computers	Suburban public, predominantly white students	Midwest	1	White woman, early 20s
Harper	Middle school (Grade 8) science	Rural public, predominantly white students	Midwest	16	White woman, late 40s

Name	Subject/Grade	School type	Location	Years	Demographics
Isabelle	Middle school English language arts (Grades 6–8) and world cultures (Grade 8)	Suburban private Jewish, predominantly white students	Southeast	7	White Jewish woman, early 30s
Jacob	Secondary English language arts	Urban public, predominantly students of color	New York City	3	White gay man, mid-30s
June	Secondary special education: English language arts and social studies	Urban private for students with special needs, predominantly students of color	New York City	14	White woman, late 30s
Karissa (real name)	Elementary music	Urban public, predominantly students of color	Seattle	4	White woman, mid-20s
Kelly	Secondary English language	Rural public, predominantly white students	Midwest	15	White woman, mid-40s
Kendra (real name)	Secondary English language arts	Urban public, predominantly students of color	Atlanta	15	Black woman, mid-40s
Lauren (real name)	Kindergarten	Urban public, predominantly students of color	Atlanta	1	Black woman, mid-20s
Leah	Elementary social studies	Urban charter, predominantly students of color	Detroit	3	White woman, early 30s
Lisa	Secondary mathematics	Suburban public, 50% students of color, 50% white	Southwest	22	White woman, late 40s
Mackenzie	Secondary English language arts	Suburban public, predominantly white students	Midwest	13	White woman, mid-40s

(*continued*)

Appendix C: Participant Profiles (continued)

Name (pseudonym unless otherwise noted)	Grade and Content	School Type and Demographics	School Location	Years of Experience	Participant Self-Described Demographics
Maya	Secondary journalism and yearbook	Rural public, predominantly white students	Midwest	10	White woman, mid-30s
Melissa (real name)	Elementary (Grade 3), bilingual	Urban public bilingual, predominantly students of color and immigrant students	Austin	7	Latina woman, early 30s
Natalia	Elementary (K–1) dual-language program	Urban public, predominantly students of color	New York City	18	Latinx woman, late 40s
Oscar	Secondary social studies	Suburban public, predominantly white students	Midwest	20	White man, early 40s
Penelope	Secondary world languages (Mandarin) and social studies	Suburban public, predominantly white students	Midwest	19	White Jewish woman, mid-40s
Quinn	Grade 6/7 English language arts in K–8 school	Urban public, predominantly students of color	Chicago	1	White woman, early 20s
Rocio (real name)	Middle school science and leadership	Suburban public, predominantly students of color and immigrant students	Northeast	2	Latina woman, early 20s
Scarlet	Elementary (Grade 5)	Urban public, predominantly students of color	New York City	9	White woman, early 30s

Name	Teaching assignment	School context	Region	Years	Demographics
Sophia	Elementary (Grades 4–5), all subjects	Urban public, predominantly students of color	New York City	22	Puerto Rican/American woman with indigenous roots, mid-40s
Toby	Secondary English language arts	Urban public, predominantly students of color	West	14	White man, early 40s
Ursula	Elementary literacy coach (kindergarten and Grade 1 for all five elementaries in district)	Suburban public, predominantly white students	Midwest	19	White woman, early 40s
Violet	Middle school English language arts	Suburban/rural school, predominantly white students	Southeast	13	White woman, late 40s
William	Grade 2	Suburban public, predominantly white students	Midwest	8	Black man, late 30s
Xavier	Secondary theology	Urban private Catholic, predominantly white students	Metropolitan D.C.	17	White man, mid-30s
Yolanda	Secondary special education	Rural public, predominantly white students	Midwest	7	Black lesbian woman, late 20s
Zara	Secondary English language arts and drama	Rural public, predominantly white students	Midwest	15	White woman, early 40s

APPENDIX D: Social Media Resources for Supporting Days After Pedagogy, *Curated by Ellie Friedman, Briana Markoff, and Renée Wilmot*

Author or Group Name and Website	Account Name	Account Type	Description
Abolitionist Teaching Network https://abolitionistteachingnetwork.org/	@atn_1863	Twitter and Instagram	Nonprofit founded by Dr. Bettina Love that aims to connect and cultivate abolitionist educators nationwide.
Ace Schwarz	@teachingoutsidethebinary	Instagram	A middle school teacher whose content focuses on LGBTQ+ issues in the field of education. In 2019, they received national recognition from GLSEN for their work in LGBTQ+ advocacy.
African American Policy Forum	@aapolicyforum	Instagram	Intersectional Think Tank cofounded and led by Dr. Kimberle Crenshaw.
Alfred Shivy Brooks	@callmeshivy	Instagram	High school teacher and activist in Atlanta. He creates content about racial and educational justice and founded Teachers for Good Trouble.
Black Education Matters https://blackeducationmattersresources.com/resources	@black_education_matters	Instagram	Resources designed to affirm and inspire Black youth, diversify curriculum, and educate educators.
Black Lives Matter at School https://www.blacklivesmatteratschool.com/	@blmatschool	Instagram	A national coalition organizing for racial justice in education, including annual week of action in February.
Blair Imani http://blairimani.com/	@blairimani	Instagram	Creator of the series "Smarter in Seconds," breaks down social justice issues in 30-second videos.
Bree Newsome https://www.breenewsome.com/	@breenewsome	Twitter	Artist, activist, and political thought leader. She famously climbed the flagpole in front of the South Carolina Capitol and removed the Confederate flag in 2015.

(continued)

Appendix D: Social Media Resources for Supporting Days After Pedagogy, Curated by Ellie Friedman, Briana Markoff, and Renée Wilmot (continued)

Author or Group Name and Website	Account Name	Account Type	Description
Brittny Sinitch	@fivefootoneteacher	Instagram and YouTube	Secondary English teacher and survivor of the Marjory Stoneman Douglas High School shooting.
Dear PWI https://www.dearpwi.com/	@dearpwi	Instagram	Testimonies and calls to action testimonies from students of color at predominantly white institutions.
Decenter the Teacher	@decentertheteacher	Instagram	Resources for white teachers to center the emotional well-being of students and challenge white supremacy in education.
Diane Ravitch https://dianeravitch.com/	@dianeravitch (T)	Twitter	Research Professor of Education at New York University and a historian of education. She is the founder and president of the Network for Public Education (NPE).
Diversify Our Narrative www.diversifyournarrative.com/	@diversifyournarrative (Instagram)		Grassroots organization of high school/college students advocating for more diverse narratives in books, curriculum, and teaching practices.
Dwayne Reed	@teachmrreed @teachermrreed	Instagram Twitter	Teacher and educational activist focused on equity.
Educators for Justice https://educatorsforjustice.org/	@educatorsforjustice	Instagram	An organization committed to creating a positive, inclusive, and empowering educational experience for students of all individual intersections, ethnic backgrounds, and socioeconomic statuses.

Name/URL	Handle	Platform	Description
Facing History and Ourselves https://www.facinghistory.org/	@facinghistory	Instagram	Nonprofit that creates curriculum and resources to address racism, anti-Semitism, and prejudice at pivotal moments in history.
Ijeoma Oluo https://www.ijeomaoluo.com/	@ijeomaoluo	Instagram and Twitter	Author of *New York Times* best-selling *So You Want to Talk About Race* (2018) and *Mediocre* (2020). Intersectional antiracist.
Indigenous Peoples Movement	@indigenouspeoplesmovement	Instagram	A global coalition bringing awareness of issues affecting Indigenous people around the world.
Jesse Hagopian https://iamaneducator.com/	@jessedhagopian	Twitter	Author, *Rethinking Schools* editor, and teacher of ethnic studies at Garfield High School—the site of a standardized test boycott.
Jorge Santos https://www.jorgesantos.site/	@restoringracialjustice @j_nyc_s	Instagram Twitter	NYC educator, restorative justice coordinator, and a special education teacher.
Joseph Capehart https://www.josephcapehart.com/	@okjsph @mistercapehart	Instagram TikTok	Liberian American poet, organizer, and 7th-grade reading teacher in NYC.
Ki Gross/Woke Kindergarten	@akieag (woke kindergarten Twitter) and @wokekindergarten (Instagram)		Akiea "Ki" Gross is an abolitionist educator and creator of Woke Kindergarten and many other educational resources. They focus on creating and sharing liberating pedagogy, particularly for young learners.
Kids 4 Antiracism	@kids4antiracism	Instagram	Brittany and Melanie, educators focused on antiracism and social justice for kids and their adults.

(continued)

Appendix D: Social Media Resources for Supporting Days After Pedagogy, Curated by Ellie Friedman, Briana Markoff, and Renée Wilmot (continued)

Author or Group Name and Website	Account Name	Account Type	Description
Learning for Justice (formerly Teaching Tolerance) https://www.learningforjustice.org	@learningforjustice @ learnforjustice	Instagram Twitter	Educational nonprofit arm of the Southern Poverty Law Center that provides free resources for teachers.
Lit C.I.R.C.L.E. (Curriculum for the Inclusion and Representation of Communities of Color in Literacy Education) https://www.litcircle.org/	@lit_c.i.r.c.l.e	Instagram	Organization that provides free curriculum resources that center the voices and experiences of those who have been traditionally silenced and erased in classrooms.
Liz Kleinrock	@teachandtransform (Instagram) and @ teachntransform (T)	Instagram and Twitter	An antibias, antiracist middle school educator. Her resources are helpful for teachers looking for resources and classroom activities.
Monique Melton www. moniquemelton.com	@moemotivate	Instagram	Antiracism educator, published author, international speaker, and host of the Shine Brighter Together podcast. She is also the founder of Shine Brighter Together, which is a community dedicated to Black liberation.
Movement for Black Lives https:// m4bl.org	@mvmnt4blklives	Instagram	A national network of organizations and individuals creating a broad political home for Black people to learn, organize, and take action.

Name	Platform	Description
No White Saviors @nowhitesaviors	Instagram	Community organization in Uganda whose content focuses on the global harms of white supremacy.
Paige Layle @paigelayle	TikTok and Instagram	An autistic woman who has used her platform to discuss the reality of disability and its intersections with other social identities.
Rebecca Nagle @rebeccanagle	Twitter and Instagram	Cherokee queer/two spirit writer and activist, the host of "This Land" podcast, and the codirector of the National Indigenous Women's Resource Center.
Social Studies for Social Justice @socialstudies4socialjustice	Instagram	Compilation of resources for progressive/radical teachers of social studies.
Steven Benson @detroitteacher	TikTok	Literacy coordinator and former high school English teacher in Detroit public schools.
Teachers for Black Lives @teachersforblacklives	Instagram	A California high school English teacher who hosts an account for white and non-Black educators to hold each other accountable to teaching for Black lives.
Teaching for Change https://www.teachingforchange.org/ @teachingchange	Twitter	Nonprofit organization that creates professional development, publications, and resources for educators and families.
the conscious kid https://www.theconsciouskid.org/ @theconsciouskid	Instagram	An education, research, and policy organization dedicated to equity and promoting healthy racial identity development in youth. Supports organizations, families, and educators in taking action to disrupt racism in young children.

(continued)

Appendix D: Social Media Resources for Supporting Days After Pedagogy, Curated by Ellie Friedman, Briana Markoff, and Renée Wilmot (continued)

Author or Group Name and Website	Account Name	Account Type	Description
ThePeahceProject https://www. thepeahceproject.com	@thepeahceproject	Instagram	Focuses on celebrating Asian identity through media.
Woke Teachers	@woketeachers	Instagram	Compilation of resources for teachers to educate themselves about inequality.
Zinn Education Project	@zinnedproject @zinneducationproject	Twitter Instagram	Founded and inspired by historian Howard Zinn, a nonprofit that provides resources for teachers looking to teach history "outside of the textbook."

References

Agarwal-Rangnath, R. (2020). *Planting the seeds of equity: Ethnic studies and social justice in the K–2 classroom.* Teachers College Press.

Agarwal-Rangnath, R., Dover, A. G., & Henning, N. (2016). *Preparing to teach social studies for social justice: Becoming a renegade.* Teachers College Press.

Andrews, D. C., & Harper, S. (2020, June 2). *6 Considerations for school leaders making a statement about George Floyd.* www.edweek.org

Au, W. (2007). High-stakes testing and curricular control: A qualitative meta synthesis. *Educational Researcher, 36*(5), 258–267.

Au, W. (2020). *High-stakes testing, standardization, and inequality in the United States.* Oxford Research Encyclopedia of Education.

Ayers, R. (2015). *An empty seat in class: Teaching and learning after the death of a student.* Teachers College Press.

Ayers, W. (2005). *Teaching toward freedom: Moral commitment and ethical action in the classroom.* Beacon.

Baldwin, J. (1963, December 21). A talk to teachers. *Saturday Review.*

Bandura, A. (2001). Social cognitive theory: An agentic perspective. *Annual Review of Psychology, 52*(1), 1–26.

Banks, J. A., & Banks, C. M. (2001). *Multicultural education.* Routledge.

Barron, L. (2018, March 1). Here's what the EPA's website looks like after a year of climate change censorship. *Time Magazine.*

Blitz, L. V., Anderson, E. M., & Saastamoinen, M. (2016). Assessing perceptions of culture and trauma in an elementary school: Informing a model for culturally responsive trauma-informed schools. *Urban Review, 48*(4), 520–542.

Bloom, S. L. (2010). Trauma-organized systems and parallel process. In N. Tehrani (Ed.), *Managing trauma in the workplace—Supporting workers and the organisation* (pp. 139–153). Routledge.

Boutte, G. S. (2008). Beyond the illusion of diversity: How early childhood teachers can promote social justice. *The Social Studies, 99*(4), 165–173.

Brito, C. (2018, October 12). *Teacher started lessons about consent to third-grader class after Kavanaugh hearings.* CBS News. https://www.cbsnews.com/news/liz-kleinrock-brett-kavanaugh-los-angeles-california-consent/

Chao, T., & Jones, D. (2016). That's not fair and why: Developing social justice mathematics activists in pre-K. *Teaching for Excellence and Equity in Mathematics, 7*(1), 16–21.

Chomsky, N. (1999). *Profit over people: Neoliberalism and global order*. Seven Stories Press.

Cole, A. (2016). All of us are vulnerable, but some are more vulnerable than others: The political ambiguity of vulnerability studies, an ambivalent critique. *Critical Horizons, 17*(2), 260–277.

Cook-Cottone, C. (2004). Childhood posttraumatic stress disorder: Diagnosis, treatment, and school reintegration. *School Psychology Review, 33*(1), 127–139.

Delpit, L. (Ed.). (2018). *Teaching when the world is on fire: Authentic classroom advice, from climate justice to Black Lives Matter.* New Press.

Dover, A. G., & Rodriguez-Valls, F. (2018). Learning to "brave up": Collaboration, agency, and authority in multicultural, multilingual, and radically inclusive classrooms. *International Journal of Multicultural Education, 20*(3), 59–79.

Dunn, A. H. (2015). The courage to leave: Wrestling with the decision to leave teaching in uncertain times. *Urban Review, 47*(1), 84–103.

Dunn, A. H. (2018). Leaving a profession after it's left you: Teachers' public resignation letters as resistance amidst neoliberalism. *Teachers College Record, 120*(9), pp. 1–34.

Dunn, A. H. (2020). "A vicious cycle of disempowerment": The relationship between teacher morale, pedagogy, and agency in an urban high school. *Teachers College Record*. Advance online publication.

Dunn, A. H. & Certo, J. (2016). Tested students to testing teachers. *English Journal, 105*(4), 104–107.

Dunn, A. H., & Downey, C. A. (2017). Betting the house: Teacher investment and teacher attrition in urban schools. *Education and Urban Society*. Advance online publication.

Dunn, A. H., & Durrance, S. B. (2014). Preparing [or prepared] to leave? A professor-student dialogue about the realities of urban teaching. *Teachers College Record*. www.tcrecord.org

Dunn, A. H., Sondel, B., & Baggett, H. C. (2019). "I don't want to come off as pushing an agenda": How contexts shaped teachers' pedagogy in the days after the 2016 US presidential election. *American Educational Research Journal, 56*(2), 444–476.

Facing History and Ourselves. (2017). *Resources for teaching after Charlottesville.* www.facinghistory.org

Freire, P. (1972). *Pedagogy of the oppressed*. Bloomsbury.

Freire, P. (1984). Education, liberation, and the church. *Religious Education, 79*(4), pp. 524–545.

From Privilege to Progress [@privtoprog]. [Instagram photograph].

Gay, G. (2002). *Culturally responsive teaching: Theory, research, and practice*. Teachers College Press.

Geller, R. C. (2020a). Teacher political disclosure in contentious times: A "responsibility to speak up" or "fair and balanced"? *Theory & Research in Social Education, 48*(2), 182–210.

Geller, R. C. (2020b). Teacher political disclosure in the Trump era. *Annals of Social Studies Education Research for Teachers, 1*(1), 37–41.

Gilson, E. (2011). Vulnerability, ignorance, and oppression. *Hypatia, 26*(2), 308–332.

Giroux, H. A. (2010). Rethinking education as the practice of freedom: Paulo Freire and the promise of critical pedagogy. *Policy Futures in Education, 8*(6), 715–721.

Gorski, P. (2019, April). Avoiding racial equity detours. *Educational Leadership*, pp. 56–61.

Gorski, P. (2020). *Equity literacy: Definitions and abilities.* www.equityliteracy.org

Gutiérrez, R. (2009). *Framing equity: Helping students "play the game" and "change the game."* https://www.todos-math.org/assets/documents/TEEMv1n1excerpt.pdf

Gutiérrez, R. (2013). The sociopolitical turn in mathematics education. *Journal for Research in Mathematics Education, 44,* 37–68.

Gutiérrez, R. (2015). Risky business: Mathematics teachers using creative insubordination. In *Proceedings of the 37th Annual Meeting of the North American Chapter of the International Group for the Psychology of Mathematics Education* (pp. 679–686).

Gutiérrez, R. (2016). Strategies for creative insubordination in mathematics teaching. *Teaching for Excellence and Equity in Mathematics, 7*(1), 52–60.

Haas, M. E., & Laughlin, M. A. (2000, April). Teaching current events: Its status in social studies today. Paper presented at the annual meeting of the American Education Research Association, New Orleans, LA.

Hagopian, J. (2020). Making Black Lives Matter at school. In D. Jones & J. Hagopian (Eds.), *Black Lives Matter at school: An uprising for educational justice.* Haymarket Books.

Hantzopoulos, M. (2016). *Restoring dignity in public schools: Human rights education in action.* Teachers College Press.

Hawkins, K. (2014). Looking forward, looking back: Framing the future for teaching for social justice in early childhood education. *Australasian Journal of Early Childhood, 39*(3), 121–128.

Hess, D. (2002). Discussing controversial public issues in secondary social studies classrooms: Learning from skilled teachers. *Theory & Research in Social Education, 30*(1), 10–41.

Hess, D. (2004). Controversies about controversial issues in democratic education. *PS: Political Science & Politics, 37*(2), 257–261.

Hess, D. (2009). *Controversy in the classroom: The democratic power of discussion.* Routledge.

Hess, D. E., & McAvoy, P. (2014). *The political classroom: Evidence and ethics in democratic education.* Routledge.

hooks, b. (1984). *Feminist theory: From margin to center.* South End Press.

hooks, b. (2000). *All about love: New visions.* HarperCollins.

Jones, T. (2018, October 25). There's nothing virtuous about finding common ground. *Time Magazine.*

Journell, W. (2010). The influence of high-stakes testing on high school teachers' willingness to incorporate current political events into the curriculum. *The High School Journal, 93*(3), 111–125.

Journell, W. (2011). Teachers' controversial issue decisions related to race, gender, and religion during the 2008 presidential election. *Theory & Research in Social Education, 39*(3), 348–392.

Journell, W. (2013). What preservice social studies teachers (don't) know about politics and current events—And why it matters. *Theory and Research in Social Education, 41*(3), 316–351.

Journell, W. (2017). Framing controversial identity issues in schools: The case of HB2, bathroom equity, and transgender students. *Equity & Excellence in Education, 50*(4), 339–354.

Kendi, I. X. (2019). *How to be an anti-racist*. Random House.

Kohli, R. (2021). *Teachers of color: Resisting racism and reclaiming education*. Harvard Education Press.

Kumashiro, K. (2015). *Against common sense* (3rd ed.). Teachers College Press.

Ladson-Billings, G. (1994). *The dreamkeepers: Successful teachers of African American children*. John Wiley & Sons.

Ladson-Billings, G. (2006). From the achievement gap to the education debt: Understanding achievement in US schools. *Educational Researcher, 35*(7), 3–12.

Ladson-Billings, G. (2014). Culturally relevant pedagogy 2.0: aka the remix. *Harvard educational review, 84*(1), 74–84.

Ladson-Billings, G. (2021, January 7). *But what will we tell the children?* https://blackandsmart.wordpress.com

LeCompte, K., Blevins, B., & Ray, B. (2017). Teaching current events and media literacy: Critical thinking, effective communication, and active citizenship. *Social Studies and the Young Learner, 29*(3), 17–20.

Lee, M. W. (2004). *The art of mindful facilitation*. StirFry Seminars & Consulting.

Lo, J. C. (2019). The role of civic debt in democratic education. *Multicultural Perspectives, 21*(2), 112–118.

Love, B. L. (2019). *We want to do more than survive: Abolitionist teaching and the pursuit of educational freedom*. Beacon.

Lyiscott, J. (2019). *Black appetite. White food. Issues of race, voice, and justice within and beyond the classroom*. Routledge.

Matias, C. E. (2016). *Feeling white: Whiteness, emotionality, and education*. Sense.

Mezirow, J. (1997). Transformative learning: Theory to practice. *New Directions for Adult and Continuing Education, 1997*(74), 5–12.

Mezirow, J. (2000). *Learning as transformation: Critical perspectives on a theory in progress*. Jossey-Bass.

Mezirow, J. (2008). An overview on transformative learning. In J. Crowther & P. Sutherland (Eds), *Lifelong learning: Concepts and contexts*, pp. 40–54, Routledge.

Michael, A. (2015). *Raising race questions: Whiteness and inquiry in education*. Teachers College Press.

Miller, R. (2021, January 7). *Had we had class today. . . .* https://medium.com/chocolate-nuisance/had-we-had-class-today-c61270ca6a88

Moore, A. (2020). *Antiracist teacher education and whiteness: Towards a collective humanization* [Unpublished doctoral dissertation]. Michigan State University.

Moses, L., Rylak, D., Reader, T., Hertz, C., & Ogden, M. (2020). Educators' perspectives on supporting student agency. *Theory Into Practice, 59*(2), 213–222.

Muhammad, G. (2020). *Cultivating genius: An equity framework for culturally and historically responsive literacy.* Scholastic.

Neville, M. (2021). Prologue to a dissertation: March 2020. *Journal of Curriculum and Pedagogy.* Advance online publication.

New York State Education Department. (2020). *Culturally responsive-sustaining education framework.* www.nysed.gov

Nieto, S., & Bode, P. (1998). *Affirming diversity.* Pearson.

Paris, D., & Alim, H. S. (2014). What are we seeking to sustain through culturally sustaining pedagogy? A loving critique forward. *Harvard Educational Review, 84*(1), 85–100.

Paris, D., & Alim, H. S. (2017). *Culturally sustaining pedagogies: Teaching and learning for justice in a changing world.* Teachers College Press.

Patel, L. (2016). The irrationality of anti-racist empathy. *The English Journal, 106*(2), 81–84.

Patel, L. (2019). Fugitive practices: Learning in a settler colony. *Educational Studies, 55*(3), 253–261.

Payne, K. A., & Journell, W. (2019). "We have those kinds of conversations here . . .": Addressing contentious politics with elementary students. *Teaching and Teacher Education, 79,* 73–82.

Picower, B. (2021). *Reading, writing, and racism: Disrupting whiteness in teacher education and in the classroom.* Beacon Press.

Rethinking Schools. (2008). *A time to end the silences.* https://rethinkingschools.org/articles/a-time-to-end-the-silences/

Robertson, D. A., Padesky, L. B., & Brock, C. H. (2020). Cultivating student agency through teachers' professional learning. *Theory Into Practice, 59*(2), 192–201.

Sealy-Ruiz, Y. (2021). *Racial literacy: A policy brief.* National Council for Teachers of English.

Seider, S., & Graves, D. (2020). *Schooling for critical consciousness: Engaging Black and Latinx youth in analyzing, navigating, and challenging racial injustice.* Harvard Education Press.

Sensoy, Ö., & DiAngelo, R. (2009). Developing social justice literacy an open letter to our faculty colleagues. *Phi Delta Kappan, 90*(5), 345–352.

Sensoy, Ö., & DiAngelo, R. (2017). *Is everyone really equal? An introduction to key concepts in social justice education.* Teachers College Press.

Shalaby, C. (2017). *Troublemakers: Lessons in freedom from young children at school.* New Press.

Shieh, E. (2016). After Eric Garner: Invoking the Black radical tradition in practice and in theory #BlackLivesMatter. *Action, Criticism, and Theory for Music Education, 15*(2), 126–145.

Shor, I., & Freire, P. (1987). *A pedagogy for liberation: Dialogues on transforming education.* Greenwood.

Simmons, D. (2019a). *How to be an anti-racist educator*. www.ascd.org

Simmons, D. (2019b). *Why we can't afford white-washed social-emotional learning*. www.ascd.org

Simmons, D. (2021). *Why SEL alone isn't enough*. www.ascd.org

Sleeter, C. (2008). Equity, democracy, and neoliberal assaults on teacher education. *Teaching and Teacher Education, 24*(8), 1947–1957.

Sleeter, C. E. (2017). Critical race theory and the whiteness of teacher education. *Urban Education, 52*(2), 155–169.

Sondel, B., Baggett, H. C., & Dunn, A. H. (2018). "For millions of people, this is real trauma": A pedagogy of political trauma in the wake of the 2016 US presidential election. *Teaching and Teacher Education, 70*, 175–185.

Swalwell, K., & Schweber, S. (2016). Teaching through turmoil: Social studies teachers and local controversial current events. *Theory and Research in Social Education, 44*(3), 283–315.

Tatum, B. D. (2017). *"Why are all the Black kids sitting together in the cafeteria?": And other conversations about race* (20th Anniversary Edition). Basic Books. (Original work published 1997)

Thomas, M. S., Crosby, S., & Vanderhaar, J. (2019). Trauma-informed practices in schools across two decades: An interdisciplinary review of research. *Review of Research in Education, 43*(1), 422–452.

Tiedt, S., & Tiedt, I. (1967). Teaching current events. *The Social Studies, 53*(3), 112–114.

Trauma Responsive Educational Practices Project. (2017). *4 Rs of a trauma responsive educator*. https://www.trepeducator.org/trauma-responsive-educator

Tuck, E. (2009). Suspending damage: A letter to communities. *Harvard Educational Review, 79*(3), 409–428.

Venet, A. S. (2021). *Equity-centered trauma-informed education*. Norton Professional Books.

Warren, C. A., Presberry, C., & Louis, L. (2020). Examining teacher dispositions for evidence of (transformative) social and emotional competencies with Black boys: The case of three urban high school teachers. *Urban Education*. Advance online publication.

Watson, D., Hagopian, J., & Au, W. (2018). *Teaching for Black lives*. Rethinking Schools.

Watts, R. J., Diemer, M. A., & Voight, A. M. (2011). Critical consciousness: Current status and future directions. *New Directions for Child and Adolescent Development, 2011*(134), 43–57.

Watts, R. J., & Hipolito-Delgado, C. P. (2015). Thinking ourselves to liberation? Advancing sociopolitical action in critical consciousness. *Urban Review, 47*(5), 847–867.

Watts, R. J., Williams, N. C., & Jagers, R. J. (2003). Sociopolitical development. *American Journal of Community Psychology, 31*(1–2), 185–194.

WBEZ Chicago. (2018). *16 Shots podcast*. www.wbez.org

Zion, S., Allen, C. D., & Jean, C. (2015). Enacting a critical pedagogy, influencing teachers' sociopolitical development. *Urban Review, 47*(5), 914–933.

Index

About the Author

Dr. Alyssa Hadley Dunn is an Associate Professor of Teacher Education at Michigan State University. A former high school English teacher, Dr. Dunn now focuses her teaching, research, and service on urban education for social and racial justice. She studies how to best prepare and support teachers to work in urban schools and how to teach for justice and equity amid school policies and reforms that negatively impact teachers' working conditions and students' learning conditions. She is also the author of the award-winning *Teaching Without Borders? The Hidden Consequences of International Teachers in U.S. Urban Schools* (Teachers College Press, 2013) and co-author of *Urban Teaching in America: Theory, Research, and Practice in K–12 Classrooms* (SAGE, 2011). A committed public scholar, she has contributed to the Huffington Post and National Public Radio, in addition to many podcasts, blogs, and radio programs, and currently runs a social media group about Teaching on Days After for over 19,000 educators from around the world. Dr. Dunn is the winner of many national and university-wide awards, most recently the Michigan State University Teacher-Scholar Award for exemplary teaching and research and the Critical Educators for Social Justice Revolutionary Mentor Award from the American Educational Research Association. She is also the mom of two young children.

About the Cover Artist

Allyssa Harris is a graphic and visual artist from Detroit, Michigan. She graduated with her Bachelor of Fine Arts in Graphic Design from Michigan State University in 2021. She is set to complete her Masters of Information Science in UX Research and Design from the University of Michigan–Ann Arbor in 2023. Allyssa is committed to exploring the intersection between design, science, and social justice.

Proceeds from this book will be donated to two organizations for educational equity and justice: the Abolitionist Teaching Network and Woke Kindergarten. You can learn more about their work at abolitionistteachingnetwork.org and wokekindergarten.org.